Blackwood's Edinburgh Magazine, Volume 21...

W. Blackwood Ltd. (Edinburgh)

without occasionally casting wistful glances at the more luxurious repast of their neighbour. The soldier and the muleteer had apparently met before; and when the new-comers approached them, they were discussing with great animation the merits of the various players in a ball-match which they had recently witnessed near Tudela. Thence they glided into a discussion concerning ball-players in general; the muleteer, who was a Navarrese, asserting the invincibility of his country at the game of pelota, whilst the corporal, who came from the neighbourhood of Oviedo, was equally confident of the superiority of the Asturians.

Whilst the younger of the travellers was ascertaining from the *patrona* the state of the larder, which, as is usual enough in Spanish inns, was but meagrely provided, his companion sought out the landlord of the venta, whom he found in the chimney-corner, enjoying a supplementary siesta amidst a cloud of wood smoke.

"The Conde de Villabuena," inquired the young man, when he had shaken the drowsy host out of his slumbers—"is he still at his house between this and Tudela?"

The *ventero*, a greasy, ill-conditioned Valencian, rubbed his eyes, muttered a coarse oath, and seemed half disposed, instead of replying, to pick a quarrel with his interrogator; but a glance at the athletic figure and resolute countenance of the latter, dissipated the inclination, and he answered by a surly affirmative.

"And his daughter also?" continued the stranger in a lower tone.

"Doña Rita? To be sure she is, or was yesterday; for I saw her ride by with her father and some other cavaliers. What eyes the little beauty has; and what a foot! It was peeping from under her habit as she passed. Sant' Antonio, what a foot!"

And now thoroughly awakened, the ventero launched out into a panegyric on the lady's beauty, interlarded by appeals to various saints as to the justice of his praise, which was continued, in the manner of a soliloquy, for some time after the stranger had turned his back upon him and descended the stairs.

At the door of the venta the young man encountered his companion, who was issuing forth with a jug of wine in his hand.

"Well, Luis," said the latter, "have you ascertained it? Is she still here, or has our journey been in vain?"

"She is here," was the reply.

"Good. Then I hope you will put aside your melancholy, and eat and drink with better appetite than you have lately done. We have plenty of time; it will not be dark for the next two hours. So let us to supper, such as it is; ham as rancid as an old oil cask, eggs that would have been chickens to-morrow, and wine—but the wine may atone for the rest—it is old Peralta, or the patrona is perjured. I have had the table spread under the tree, in hopes that fresh air may sweeten musty viands, and in order that we may see the ball-play of yonder soldier and muleteer."

The young man who had been addressed by the name of Luis, glanced in the direction of the ball-court, where the two men to whom his companion referred were preparing for a match. The discussion as to the superiority of Navarrese or Asturian ball-players had increased in warmth, until the disputants, each obstinate in his opinion, finding themselves, perhaps, at a loss for verbal arguments, had agreed to refer the matter to a trial of individual skill. The challenge came from the dragoon, who, as soon as he heard it accepted, proceeded to lighten himself for his task. With great alacrity he threw aside his foraging-cap, stripped off his pouch-belt and uniform coat, and unfastened his spurs. The preparations of the muleteer were even more rapidly completed. When he had thrown off his jacket—the back of which was adorned, according to the custom of his class, with flowers and various quaint devices, cut out in cloth of many colours, and sewn upon the brown material of which the garment was composed—he stood in his shirt and trousers of unbleached linen, with light sandals of plaited hemp upon his feet. In this latter respect he had the advantage of the soldier, who, not choosing to play barefooted, was obliged to retain his heavy boots. In apparent activity, too, the advantage was greatly on the side of the

Navarrese, who was spare and sinewy, without an ounce of superfluous flesh about him, but with muscles like iron, and limbs as elastic and springy as whalebone. His very face partook of the hard, wiry character of his person; the cheekbones were slightly prominent, and, although he evidently wanted some years of thirty, two deep furrows or lines, such as are rarely seen on the countenance of so young a man, curved outwards from either nostril to considerably below the mouth, increasing in depth when he talked or smiled, and giving, in conjunction with a quick grey eye, considerable character to his frank, and by no means disagreeable countenance.

The game began with great spirit, and with much appearance of equality between the players, who would both have been deemed first-rate in any ball-court in Europe. The great strength of the dragoon seemed at first to give him the advantage; the tremendous blows he delivered sent the ball against the wall with as much seeming force as if it had been driven out of a cannon, and caused it to rebound to an immense distance, keeping the muleteer continually at the very top of his speed. The match was to be the best two out of three games. The first of the three was won by the muleteer, after the victory had been long and well contested.

"*Bien!*" said the dragoon, as he wiped the perspiration from his face, and took a deep draught out of a jug of wine which the ventero presented to him. "*Bien*—that is one for you; the next may go differently. I only missed the ball through my foot slipping. Curse boots for playing ball in, say I! Hola, Valenciano! have you never a pair of shoes or espadrillas to lend me?"

The landlord, who acted as umpire, and who, as well as his wife and two or three loitering peasants, was taking an intense interest in the game, ran into the house and brought out a pair of sandals. These the soldier tied upon his feet, in lieu of the boots to which he attributed his defeat. Then, with renewed confidence, he took his place opposite the wall, where the muleteer was waiting for him.

But if, as the dragoon said, an accident had lost him the first game, it soon became evident that the superior activity and endurance of his antagonist were equally certain to make him lose the second. The idleness of a garrison life, fat feeding, and soft lying, had disqualified the soldier to compete for any length of time with a man like the Navarrese, accustomed to the severest hardships, whose most luxurious meal was a handful of boiled beans, his softest couch a bundle of straw or the packsaddles of his mules. Constant exposure and unceasing toil had given the muleteer the same insensibility to fatigue attributed to certain savage tribes. Whilst his antagonist, with inflamed features and short-drawn breath, and reeking with perspiration, was toiling after the ball, the Navarrese went through the same, or a greater amount of exertion, without the least appearance of distress. Not a bead of moisture upon his face, nor a pant from his broad, well-opened chest, gave token of the slightest inconvenience from the violent exercise he was going through. On the contrary, as he went on and got warm in the harness, he seemed to play better, to run faster, to catch the ball with greater address, and strike it with more force. Sometimes he would be standing close to the wall, when a mighty blow from the strong arm of the dragoon sent the ball scores of yards in his rear. It seemed impossible that he should arrive soon enough to strike it. But before it had time to rebound, he was behind it, and by a blow of his horny palm, less forcible perhaps, but more dexterously applied than the one his opponent had given, he sent it careering back to the wall with greater swiftness than it had left it. He rarely struck the ball in the air, even when the opportunity offered, but allowed it to rebound—a less dashing, but a surer game than he would perhaps have played, had he not considered the honour of "Navarra la bella" to be at stake, represented in his person. Again, when the ball fell near the wall, he would sometimes swing his arm as though about to strike it a violent blow, and, whilst the dragoon was already beginning to retire in the direction he expected it to take, he would change his apparent intention, and drop it gently just above the line, so that his opponent, although rushing up in desperate haste, could scarcely arrive in time to avoid being, put out. It was by a feint of this description that the second game was decided in favour of the Navarrese.

" *Viva la Navarra !*" shouted the winner, bounding like a startled roebuck three or four feet from the ground, in front of the discomfited soldier.

" *Viva el demonio !*" growled the latter in reply. " Do you think that because you have beaten me to-day, thanks to your herring guts and dog's hide, that you could do the same if I were in training, or had a month's practice ? You would find it very different, Master Paco."

" Viva la Navarra ! " repeated Paco, chucking the small hard ball up into the air, to a height at which it appeared scarcely bigger than a bullet. Then replying to the words of the dragoon ; " At your orders, Señor Velasquez," said he, " I shall pass through Tudela some time next month, and shall be ready to give you your revenge."

And catching the ball as it fell, the Navarrese, whom victory had put into extravagant spirits, began tossing it from one hand to the other, catching it behind his back, and performing various other small feats of address, looking the while at the corporal with a sort of jeering smile, which greatly aggravated the irritation of the latter.

" *Pues,*" said Velasquez at last, after gazing at Paco for the space of a minute with a stern look, which was insufficient, however, to make the other lower his eyes, or alter the expression of his countenance ; " Well, what do you stare at ? Oh ! I forgot— you may well stare. It is the first time that you have seen an Asturian caballero beaten at anything by a cur of a Navarrese."

" Not at all," replied the muleteer coolly ; " your Señoria is mistaken. It is only the first time that I have seen an Asturian *caballero* with a pipeclayed belt over his shoulder, and a corporal's bars upon his arm."

And he broke out into one of those wild shrill laughs of scorn and defiance with which the peasant soldiers of Navarre have so often, during recent Spanish wars, caused the rocks and ravines of their native province to ring again.

" *Hijo de zorra !*" muttered the soldier, enraged beyond endurance by this last taunt ; and drawing back his right arm, he dealt so heavy and unexpected a blow upon the breast of the muleteer that the latter reeled a couple of paces backwards, and then fell headlong and with considerable violence to the ground. The dragoon gazed for an instant at the fallen man, as if expecting him to rise and attack him in turn ; but, seeing that he did not do so, he turned round and walked slowly in the direction of his charger.

He had taken but a few steps when the Navarrese sprang to his feet, and thrust his hand into the red sash which girded his waist, as though seeking a weapon. He found none, and, instantly darting forward, he passed the soldier, and reached his mules a moment sooner than the former did his horse. The next instant a long brown barrel was projected across the packsaddles, and behind it was seen. the blue cap and pale countenance of Paco, who, with glittering eye and face livid from fury, was taking a deadly aim at the soldier, now standing beside the shoulder of his charger. Without a moment's hesitation the Navarrese pulled the trigger. As he did so, the dragoon, suddenly aware of his danger, threw himself on one side, and at the same time his horse, either startled by the movement or tormented by a fly, tossed his head violently up and backwards. The muleteer's bullet, intended for the rider, entered the brain of the steed. There was a convulsive quivering of the animal's whole frame, and then, before the smoke cleared away, the horse fell over so heavily and suddenly that he bore down Velasquez under him. The soldier lay with the whole weight of the expiring animal resting upon his legs and thighs ; and, before he could make an attempt to extricate himself, the Navarrese, with a large dagger-shaped knife gleaming in his hand, sprang across the space that separated him from his antagonist. The fate of the latter would speedily have been decided, had not the innkeeper, his wife, and the two young men, who had been observing with much interest these rapidly occurring incidents, thrown themselves between Paco and the object of his wrath.

" Out of the way !" roared the infuriated muleteer. " He has struck me, and by the Holy Trinity I will have his blood. He has struck *me*, a free Navarrese !" repeated he, striking his own breast with the points of his fingers, one of the expressive and customary gestures of his countrymen.

" Let him be, Señor Don Paco !" yelled the ventero and his wife, greatly alarmed at the prospect of a murder in broad daylight and at their very threshold. " You have done enough already to send you to the galleys. Get on your mules, and ride away before worse comes of it."

" *A los infiernos !*" shouted Paco. " As the horse now is, so shall be the rider." And he gave a long sweep of his arm, making the bright blade of his knife flash in the last red sun-rays like a curved line of burnished gold. The point of the weapon passed within an inch or two of the face of the innkeeper, who started back with a cry of alarm. At the same moment the wrist of the Navarrese was caught in a firm grasp by the elder of the two travellers, and the knife was wrested from his hand. The muleteer turned like a madman upon his new antagonist. The latter had laid aside the hat which shaded his face, and now fixed his eyes upon the angry countenance of the Navarrese.

" Do you not know me, Paco ?" said he, repulsing the first furious onset of the muleteer.

Paco stared at him for a moment with a look of doubt and astonishment.

" Don Luis !" he at last exclaimed.

" The same," replied the stranger. " You have been too hasty, Paco, and we expose ourselves to blame by not detaining you to answer for your attempt on yonder soldier's life, and for the death of his horse. But you had some provocation, and I, for one, am willing to take the risk. Begone, and that immediately."

" I shall do your bidding, Señorito," said Paco, " were it only for old acquaintance sake. But let that cowardly Asturian beware how he meets

me in the mountains. I have missed him once, but will answer for not doing so again."

" And you," retorted the soldier, whom the innkeeper and a peasant had dragged from under the dead horse, and placed upon a bench, where he sat rubbing his legs, which were numbed and bruised by the weight that had fallen upon them— " and you, have a care how you show yourself in Tudela. If there is a stirrup-leather or sword-scabbard in the garrison, I promise you as sound a beating as you ever yet received."

The Navarrese, who had returned to his mules and was busied reloading his gun, snapped his fingers scornfully at this menace. Don Luis walked up to him.

" Listen, Paco," said he, in a low voice, " take my advice, and avoid this neighbourhood for a while. Are you still in the service of Count Villabuena? "

" No, Señor," replied the man, " I have left his Señoria, and the mules are my own. I shall be passing near the count's house to-morrow, if you have anything to send."

" I have nothing," answered Don Luis. " Should you by chance see any of the family, it is unnecessary to mention our meeting."

Paco nodded his head significantly, seated himself sideways on one of his mules, his gun across his knees, and, leading the other by the bridle, trotted off at a brisk pace down a mountain path nearly opposite to the venta. Ten minutes later, the dragoon having regained, in some degree, the use of his legs, resumed his boots, took his saddle and valise on his shoulders, and set out on foot for his garrison.

The sun had set, and the twilight passed away, the night was clear and starlight, but moonless, when Luis and his companion left the venta and resumed their progress northwards. After following the highway for a short league, they took a cross-road on either side of which the richly cultivated plain was sprinkled with farmhouses, and with a few country villas. In spite of the darkness which was increased by the overhanging foliage of the fruit-trees that on either hand bordered the road, Luis moved rapidly and confidently forward, in the manner of one perfectly acquainted with the ground; and presently, leaving the beaten track, he passed through a plantation of young trees, crossed a field, and arrived with his companion at a low hedge surrounding a spacious garden. Jumping over this boundary, the young men penetrated some distance into the enclosure, and soon found themselves within fifty yards of a house, of which the white walls were partially visible, rising out of a thick garland of trees and bushes in which the building was embowered. Several of the windows were lighted up, and the sound of music reached the ears of Luis and his companion.

"This is far enough, Mariano," said the former. "To the right, amongst the trees, you will find an old moss-grown bench, upon which I have often sat in happier days than these. There await my return."

"Let me accompany you further," replied Mariano. "There is no saying what reception the count may give you."

"I shall not see the count," answered Luis; "and if by chance I should, there is nothing to apprehend. But my plan, as I have already explained to you, is only to seek one moment's interview with Rita. I am well acquainted with the arrangements of the house, and you may depend that I shall be seen by no one whom I wish to avoid."

Mariano turned into the shrubbery, and Luis, with rapid, but silent step, advanced towards the villa, favoured in his clandestine approach by the darkness of the night and the trees of the thickly planted garden.

The house was a square edifice, without balconies, and the windows that were lighted up were those of the first floor. On the side on which Luis first approached the building, the windows were closed, but, upon moving noiselessly round to the front, he perceived one which the fineness of the weather, still mild and genial although at the end of September, had induced the occupants of the room to leave open. The sound of laughter and merriment issued from it; but this was presently hushed, and two voices, accompanied by guitars, began to sing a lively *seguidilla*, of which, at the end of each piquant couplet, the list-

eners testified their approbation by a hum of mirthful applause. Before the song was over, Luis had sought and found a means of observing what was passing within doors. Grasping the lower branch of a tree which grew within a few feet of the corner of the house, he swung himself up amongst the foliage. A large bough extended horizontally below the open window, and by climbing along this, he was enabled to look completely into the apartment; whilst, owing to the thickness of the leafage and the dark colour of his dress, there was scarcely a possibility of his being discovered.

The room was occupied by about twenty persons, the majority of whom were visitors, inhabitants of Tudela or of neighbouring country-houses. With four or five exceptions, the party consisted of men, for the most part elderly or middle-aged. One of the ladies and a young officer of the royal guard were the singers, and their performance seemed partially to interrupt the conversation of a group of the seniors who were seated round a card-table at the further end of the apartment. The cards, however, if they had been used at all, had long been thrown aside, and replaced by a discussion carried on in low tones, and with an earnestness of countenance and gesture, which gave to those engaged in it the appearance rather of conspirators than of friends met together for the enjoyment of each other's society. The ladies, and a few of the younger men, did not appear disposed to let the gravity of their elders interfere with their own pleasures. The song and the dance, the pointed epigram and witty repartee, all the varied resources which Spaniards know so well how to bring into play, and which render a Spanish *tertulia* so agreeable, had been in turn resorted to. When the seguidilla—during the continuance of which Luis had gained his post of observation—was brought to a close, there seemed to ensue a sort of break in the amusements of the evening. The younger members of the company, whose conversation had previously been general, separated into groups of two or three persons; and in more than one of those composed of the former number, the flashing eye, coquettish smile, and rapidly significant motions of the fan, bespoke the existence of an animated flirtation.

Two ladies, neither of whom could have seen more than eighteen summers, now left the sofa upon which they had been sitting, and, with arms intertwined, approached the open window. Luis remained motionless as the leaves that surrounded him, and which were undisturbed by a breath of wind. The ladies leaned forward over the window-sill, enjoying the freshness of the night; and one of them, the lively brunette who had taken a part in the seguidilla, plucked some sprays of jasmine which reared their pointed leaves and white blossoms in front of the window, and began to entwine them in the hair of her companion—a pale and somewhat pensive beauty, in whose golden locks and blue eyes the Gothic blood of old Spain was yet to be traced. Presently she was interrupted in this fanciful occupation by a voice within the room calling upon her to sing. She obeyed the summons, and her friend remained alone at the window.

No sooner was this the case than a slight rustling occurred amongst the branches of the tree, and the name of "Rita" was uttered in a cautious whisper. The lady started, and but half suppressed a cry of terror. The next instant the leaves were put aside, and the light from the apartment fell upon the countenance of Luis, who, with uplifted finger, warned the agitated girl to restrain her emotion.

"Santa Virgen!" she exclaimed, leaning far out of the window, and speaking in a hurried whisper, "this is madness, Luis. My father is unchanged in his sentiments, and I dread his anger should he find you here."

"I will instantly depart," replied Luis, "if you promise me an interview. I am about to leave Spain—perhaps for ever; but I cannot go without bidding you farewell. You will not refuse me a meeting which may probably be our last."

"What mean you?" exclaimed the lady. "Why do you leave Spain, and when? But we shall be overheard. To-morrow my father goes to Tudela. Be here at mid-day. Brigida will admit you."

She held out her hand, which Luis pressed to his lips. At that moment the clatter of a horse's hoofs, rapidly approaching, was heard upon the hard ground of the avenue. The lady hastily withdrew her hand and left the window, whilst Luis again concealed himself behind the screen of foliage. Scarcely had he done so, when a horseman dashed up to the house, forced his steed up the three or four broad steps leading to the door, and without dismounting or looking for a bell or other means of announcing his arrival, struck several blows upon the oaken panels with the butt of his heavy riding-whip. Whilst the party above-stairs hurried to the windows, and endeavoured to discern who it was that disturbed them in so unceremonious a manner, a servant opened the small grated wicket in the centre of the door, and inquired the stranger's pleasure.

"Is the Conde de Villabuena at home?" demanded the horseman. "I must see him instantly."

"The name of your Señoria," inquired the domestic.

"It is unnecessary. Say that I have a message to him from friends at Madrid."

The servant disappeared, and in another moment his place was occupied by a grave stern-looking man, between fifty and sixty years of age.

"I am Count Villabuena," said he; "what is your business?"

The stranger bent forward over his horse's mane, so as to bring his face close to the wicket, and uttered three words in a tone audible only to the count, who replied to them by an exclamation of surprise. The door was immediately opened, and Villabuena stood beside the horseman.

"When?" said he.

"Yesterday. I have ridden night and day to bring you the intelligence, and shall now push on to the interior of Navarre. At the same time as myself, others of our friends started, north and south, east and west. Early this morning, Santos Ladron heard it at Valladolid, and Merino in Castile. To-day the news has reached Vittoria; this night they will be at Bilboa and Tolosa. It is from the northern provinces that most is expected; but 'El Rey y la Religion' is a rallying-cry that will rouse all Spaniards worthy of the name. You are prepared for the event, and know what to do. Farewell, and success attend us !"

The stranger set spurs to his horse, and galloped down the avenue at the same rapid pace at which he had arrived. The count re-entered the house ; and, as soon as he had done so, Luis dropped from his tree, and hurried to rejoin Mariano. In another hour they had returned to the venta.

Luis Herrera was the son of a Castilian gentleman, who had suffered much, both in person and property, for his steady adherence to the constitutional cause in Spain. Severely wounded whilst fighting against the Royalists and their French allies in 1823, Don Manuel Herrera with difficulty escaped to England, taking with him his only son, then a boy of eleven years of age. In 1830 he changed his residence to the south of France, and thence, taking advantage of his proximity to the frontier, and wishing his son's education to be completed in Spain, he dispatched Luis to Madrid, with a recommendation to the Conde de Villabuena, who, notwithstanding that his political principles were diametrically opposed to those of Don Manuel, was one of the oldest friends of the latter. The count welcomed Luis kindly, and received him into his house, where for some months he prosecuted his studies in company with the young Villabuenas, and, at the end of that time, went with them to the university of Salamanca. The vacations were passed by the young men either at the count's house at Madrid, or at a country residence near Tudela, north of which, in the central valleys of his native province of Navarre, the Conde de Villabuena owned extensive estates. The count was a widower, and, besides his two sons, had an only daughter, who, at the time of Luis's arrival, was in her sixteenth year, and who added to great personal attractions a share of accomplishment and instruction larger than is usually found even amongst the higher classes of Spanish women. During the first sojourn of Luis at the count's house, he was naturally thrown a great deal into Doña Rita's society, and a reciprocal attachment grew up

between them, which, if it occasionally afforded the young Villabuenas a subject of good-humoured raillery, on the other hand was unobserved or uncared for by the count—a stern silent man, whose thoughts and time were engrossed by political intrigues. When Luis went to Salamanca, his attachment to Rita, instead of becoming weakened or obliterated, appeared to acquire strength from absence; and she, on her part, as each vacation approached, unconsciously looked forward with far more eagerness to the return of Herrera than to that of her brothers.

The autumn of 1832 arrived, and the count and his family, including Luis, were assembled at the villa near Tudela. The attachment existing between Rita and Luis had become evident to all who knew them; and even the count himself seemed occasionally, by a quiet glance and grave smile, to recognize and sanction its existence. Nor was there any very obvious or strong reason for disapproval. The family of Herrera was ancient and honourable ; and, although Don Manuel's estates had been confiscated when he fled the country, he had previously remitted to England a sum that secured him a moderate independence. The state of things in Spain was daily becoming more favourable to the hopes of political exiles. The declining health of Ferdinand had thrown the reins of government almost entirely into the hands of Queen Christina, who, in order to increase the number of her adherents, and ensure her daughter's succession to the throne, favoured the return to Spain of the Liberal party. Although Don Manuel, who was known to be obstinate and violent in his political views, had not yet been included in the amnesties published, it was thought that he speedily would be so ; and then time and importunity, and an adherence to the established order of things, might perhaps procure him the restitution of some part of his confiscated property.

It chanced, that on the fourth day after the arrival of Luis and the Villabuenas from Salamanca, the two latter rode over to the Ebro, below Tudela, for the purpose of bathing. They were not good swimmers, and were moreover unaccustomed to bathe in so rapid and powerful a stream. A peasant, who observed two horses tied to a tree, and some clothes upon the grass by the river side, but who could see nothing of the owners, suspected an accident, and gave the alarm. A search was instituted, and the dead bodies of the unfortunate young men were found upon the sandy shore of an island some distance down the river.

This melancholy event was destined to have an important influence on the position of Luis Herrera in the family of Count Villabuena, and on his future fortunes. Mingled with the natural grief felt by the count at the untimely death of his children, were the pangs of disappointed pride and ambition. He had reckoned upon the gallant and promising young men, thus prematurely snatched away, for the continuance and aggrandizement of his ancient name. Upon his daughter he had hitherto scarcely bestowed a thought. She would marry—honourably of course, richly if possible; but even in this last respect he would not be inflexible; for where his pride of birth did not interfere, Villabuena was not an unkind father. But the death of his sons brought about great changes. The next heir to his title and estates was a distant and unmarried cousin, and to him the count determined to marry his daughter, whose beauty and large fortune in money and unentailed estates, rendered any objection to the match on the part of her kinsman a most improbable occurrence. As a first step towards the accomplishment of this scheme, the count resolved to put an end at once to what he considered the childish attachment existing between Rita and Luis. Within a week after the death of his sons, he had a conversation with young Herrera, in which he informed him of his intentions with regard to his daughter, and pointed out to him the necessity of forgetting her. In vain did Luis declare this to be impossible, and plead the strength which his attachment had acquired by his long permitted intercourse with Rita. The count cared little for such lover-like arguments; he assured Luis that he was mistaken, that time and absence brought oblivion in their train, and

that after a few months, perhaps weeks, of separation, he would wonder at the change in his sentiments, and laugh at the importance he had attached to a mere boyish fancy. It so happened, that on the day preceding the one upon which this conversation took place, a letter had been received from Don Manuel Herrera, announcing his speedy return to Spain, the much-desired permission having at length been obtained. In order to give Luis an opportunity of speedily testing the effects of absence, the count proposed that he should at once set out for the French frontier to meet his father. Under the existing circumstances, he said, it was undesirable that he should remain under the same roof with his daughter longer than could be avoided.

Although bitterly deploring the prospect of an immediate and lasting separation from Rita, Luis had no choice but to adopt the course proposed; nor would his pride have allowed him to remain in the count's house an instant longer than his presence there was acceptable. He feared that the count would prevent his having a last interview with Rita; but this Villabuena did not think it worth while to do, contenting himself with repeating to his daughter the communication he had already made to Luis. When the latter sought his mistress, he found her in tears and great affliction. The blow was so sudden and unexpected, that she could scarcely believe in its reality, and still less could she bring herself to think that the count would persist in his cruel resolution. "He will surely relent," she said, "when he sees how unhappy his decision makes me; but should he not do so, rest assured, Luis, that I will never be forced into this odious marriage. Sooner than submit to it, a convent shall receive me." And once more repeating the vows of constancy which they had so often interchanged, the lovers separated. At daybreak upon the following morning, Luis set out for Bayonne.

The joy experienced by Don Manuel Herrera upon once more treading his native soil, did not so engross him as to prevent his observing the melancholy of his son. In reply to his father's inquiries, Luis informed him of his attachment to Rita, and of the interdict which the count had put upon its continuance. Don Manuel was indignant at what he termed the selfish and unfeeling conduct of Villabuena, who would thus sacrifice his daughter's happiness to his own pride and ambition. He then endeavoured to rouse the pride of Luis, and to convert his regrets into indignation; but, finding himself unsuccessful, he resolved to try the effect of change of scene and constant occupation. He set out with his son for Old Castile, of which he was a native, and undertook various journeys through the province in search of a small estate, such as his means would permit him to purchase, and upon which he might in future reside. This he at last found, a few leagues to the south of Burgos. This purchase completed, there were still many arrangements to make before Don Manuel could settle down and enjoy the peaceful country life, which he had planned for himself, and in making these arrangements he took care to find his son abundant and varied employment. But all his wellmeant efforts were in vain. Luis could not detach his thoughts from one all-engrossing subject; and at last, although Count Villabuena had expressly forbidden any correspondence between his daughter and young Herrera, the latter, after some weeks' absence, unable to resist any longer his desire to hear from Rita, ventured to write to her. The letter was intercepted by the count, and returned unopened, with a few haughty lines expressive of his indignation at the ingratitude of Luis, who was requiting the kindness he had received at his hands by endeavouring to thwart his plans and seduce the affections of his daughter. The terms in which this letter was couched roused the ire of Don Manuel, who in his turn forbade his son to expose himself to a repetition of similar insults by any communication with the count or his daughter. Shortly afterwards Luis returned to Salamanca to complete his studies.

The profession of the law, to which young Herrera was destined, had never had any charms for him. His own inclinations pointed to a military career, which he had on various occasions urged his father to allow him to adopt; but Don Manuel had invariably refused his request, alleging the poor prospect of advancement in time of peace, and in a service in which nearly all promotion was gained by interest and court-favour. Nevertheless, from his earliest youth Luis had devoted his leisure hours to the attainment of accomplishments qualifying him for the trade of war. He was the boldest horseman, most skilful swordsman, and best shot in the University of Salamanca. His superiority in these respects, his decided character, and agreeable manners, had gained him considerable popularity amongst his fellow-students, who frequently expressed their surprise, that one whose vocation was evidently military should abide by the dusty folios and dry intricacies of the law.

More insupportable than ever did his studies now appear to Luis, who nevertheless persevered in them for several months after his father's return to Spain, endeavouring by strenuous application to divert his thoughts from his hopeless attachment. Weary at length of the effort, he determined to abandon a pursuit so uncongenial to his tastes, and to seek a more active course of life, and one for which he felt he was better suited. His plan was to repair to Africa, and endeavour to obtain a commission in one of the foreign corps which the French were raising for their campaign against the Bedouins. Should he fail in this, he would serve as a volunteer, and trust to his courage and merits for procuring him advancement. Previously, however, to the execution of this scheme, he resolved to see Rita once more, ascertain from her own lips whether there was a chance of the count's relenting, and, should there be none, bid her a last farewell. He would then return to his father's house, and obtain Don Manuel's sanction to his project.

Since the unfortunate death of the young Villabuenas, Herrera's chief intimate at the University had been Mariano Torres, a hot-headed, warmhearted Arragonese, entirely devoted to Luis, to whom he looked up as a model of perfection. To this young man Luis had confided his love for Rita, and her father's opposition, and to him he now communicated his new plans. To his infinite surprise, scarcely had he done so when Mariano, instead of expressing regret at his approaching departure, threw his three-cornered student's hat to the ceiling, tore off his gown, and declared his intention of accompanying his friend to Africa, or to any other part of the world to which he chose to betake himself. Luis tried to persuade him to abandon so mad a resolution; but Torres persisted in it, protesting that it would suit his taste much better to fight against Bedouins than to become a bachelor of arts, and that he had always intended to leave the University with his friend, and to accompany him wherever he might go. Trusting that, by the time they should reach Navarre, Mariano's enthusiasm would cool down, and his resolution change, Luis at length yielded, and the two friends left Salamanca together. Travelling by the public conveyances, they reached Valladolid, and subsequently the town of Soria, whence they had still nearly twenty leagues of high-road to Tudela. The path across the mountains being considerably shorter, and in order to diminish the risk of being seen by persons who might inform the count of his arrival, Luis resolved to complete the journey on foot; and after two short days' march, the young men reached the neighbourhood of Count Villabuena's residence.

The church and convent clocks of the right Catholic city of Tudela had not yet chimed out the hour of noon, when Luis, impatient for the interview promised by Rita, entered the count's domain by the same path as on the previous evening. Before he came in sight of the house, he was met at an angle of the shrubbery by Rita herself.

"I was sure you would take this path," said she, with a smile in which melancholy was mingled with the pleasure she felt at seeing her lover; "it was your favourite in days gone by. Our interview must be very brief. My father was to have remained at Tudela till evening, but something has occurred to derange his plans. He sat up the whole night in close conference with some gentlemen. At daybreak two couriers were dispatched, and the count rode away with his friends without having been in bed. He may return at any moment."

Luis drew the arm of his mistress through his own, and they slowly walked down one of the alleys of the garden. Rita had little to tell him favourable to the hopes which he still, in spite of himself, continued to cherish. The appeals which she had ventured to make to her father's affection, and to his regard for her happiness, had been met by severe reproof. Her evident depression and melancholy remained unnoticed, or at least unadverted to, by the count. All that she said only confirmed Luis in his resolution of seeking high distinction or an honourable death in a foreign service. He was deliberating, with eyes fixed upon the ground, on the best manner of breaking his intentions to Rita, when an exclamation of alarm from her lips caused him to look up, and he saw Villabuena crossing on horseback the end of the walk along which they were advancing. The count's head was turned towards them, and he had without doubt seen and recognized them.

Herrera's resolution was instantly taken. He would seek the count's presence, take upon himself the whole blame of his clandestine meeting with Rita, and appease her father's anger by informing him of his proposed self-banishment. Before, however, he had succeeded in calming Rita's fears, he again perceived the count, who had left his horse, and was advancing slowly towards them, with a grave, but not an angry countenance. On his near approach, Luis was about to address him; but by a wave of his hand Villabuena enjoined silence.

"Return to the house, Rita," said he in a calm voice: "and you, Señor de Herrera, remain here; I would speak a few words with you."

Tremblingly and with one last lingering look at Luis, Rita withdrew.

"We will walk, sir, if you please," said the count; and the two men walked for some distance side by side and in silence; Villabuena apparently plunged in reflection, Luis wondering at his forbearance, and impatient for its explanation.

"You are surprised," said the count at last, "after all that has passed, that I show so little resentment at your uninvited presence here, and at Rita's infringement of my positive commands."

Luis would have spoken, but Villabuena resumed.

"You will be still more astonished to learn, that there is a possibility of your attachment receiving my sanction."

Herrera started, and his face was lighted up with sudden rapture.

"You will of course have heard," continued the count, "of the important intelligence received here last night, and with which this morning all the country is ringing. I allude to the death of Ferdinand VII."

"I had not heard of it," replied Luis, much surprised; for, although the desperate state of the king's health was well known, his malady had lasted so long that men had almost left off expecting his death.

"I know I can depend upon your honour, Luis," said the count; "and I am therefore about to speak to you with a confidence which I should repose in few so young and inexperienced."

Luis bowed.

"Although," resumed Villabuena, "His Majesty Charles the Fifth is at this moment absent from Spain, his faithful subjects will not allow that absence to be prejudicial to him. They intend to vindicate his just rights, and to overturn the contemptible faction which, headed by an intriguing woman, supports the unfounded claims of a sickly infant. In anticipation of Ferdinand's death, all necessary measures have been taken ; and, before three days elapse, you will see a flame lighted up through the land, which will speedily consume and destroy the enemies of Spain, and of her rightful monarch. Navarre and Biscay, Valentia and Arragon, Catalonia and Castile, will rise almost to a man in defence of their king ; the other provinces must follow their example, or be compelled to submission. Although confident of success, it yet behoves us

to neglect no means of securing it ; nor are we so blinded as to think that the faction which at present holds the reins of government will resign them without a struggle. Avoiding overconfidence, therefore, which so often leads to failure, each man must put his shoulder to the wheel, and contribute his best efforts to the one great end, regardless of private sacrifices. What I have to propose to you is this. Time was when our universities were the strongholds of loyalty and religion ; but that time is unfortunately past, and the baneful doctrines of republicanism and equality have found their way even into those nurseries of our priesthood and statesmen. We are well informed that at Salamanca especially, many of the students, even of the better class, incline to the self-styled Liberal party. You, Luis, are ready of speech, bold and prompt in action, and, moreover, you are known to have great influence amongst your fellow-students. Return, then, to Salamanca, and exert that influence to bring back into the right path those who have been led astray. Urge the just claims of Charles V., hold out the prospect of military glory and distinction, and of the gratitude of an admiring country. Let your efforts be chiefly directed to gain over young men of wealthy and influential families, and to induce them to take up arms for the king. Form them into a squadron, of which you shall have the command, and the private soldiers of which shall rank as officers in the army, and subsequently be transferred to other corps to act as such. Appoint a place of rendezvous ; and, when your men are assembled there, march them to join the nearest division of the Royalist army. I guarantee to you a captain's commission ; and as soon as the king, with whom I have some influence, arrives in Spain, I will strongly recommend you to his favour. Our campaign, however brief, must afford opportunities of distinction to brave men who seek them. With your energy, and with the natural military talents which I am persuaded you possess, high rank, honours, and riches may speedily be yours. And when Charles V., firmly seated on the throne of Spain, points you out to me as one of those to whom he owes his crown, and as a man whom he delights to honour, I will no longer refuse to you my daughter's hand."

However distant the perspective of happiness thus offered to his view, and although the avenue leading to it was beset with dangers and uncertainties, it promised to realize the ardent hopes which Luis Herrera had once ventured to indulge. Sanguine and confident, he would at once have caught at the count's proposal, but for one consideration that flashed across his mind. He was himself wedded to no political creed, and had as yet scarcely bestowed a thought upon the different parties into which his countrymen were split. But his father, who had so strenuously adhered to the Liberal side, who had poured out his blood with Mina, fought side by side with Riego, sacrificed his property, and endured a long and wearisome exile for conscience and his opinions' sake—what would be his feelings if he saw his only son range himself beneath the banner of absoluteism? The struggle in the mind of Luis, between love on the one hand and filial duty and affection on the other, was too severe and too equally balanced to be instantly decided. He remained silent, and the count, mistaking the cause of his hesitation, resumed.

"You are surprised," said he, "to find me so willing to abandon my dearest projects for the sake of a remote advantage to the king's cause. But remember that I promise nothing—all is contingent on your own conduct and success. And although you may have thought me unfeeling and severe, I shall gladly, if possible, indulge the inclinations of my only surviving child."

It required all Herrera's firmness and sense of duty to prevent him from yielding to the temptation held out, and pledging himself at once to the cause of Charles V.

"You will not expect me, Señor Conde," said he, "to give an immediate answer to a proposal of such importance. I feel sincerely grateful to you, but must crave a short delay for consideration."

"Let that delay be as brief as possible," said Villabuena. "In the present circumstances, the value of assistance would be doubled by its promptness. When love and loyalty are both in one scale," added he, with a slight smile, "methinks a decision were easy."

They had now approached the gate of the garden, and Luis, desirous of finding himself alone, to arrange his thoughts and reflect on his future conduct, took his leave. The count held out his hand with some of his former cordiality.

"You will write to me from Salamanca!" said he.

Herrera bowed his head, and then, fearful lest his assent should be misconstrued, he replied—

"From Salamanca, or from elsewhere, you shall certainly hear from me, Señor Conde, and that with all speed."

The count nodded and turned towards the house, whilst Luis retook the road to the venta.

He found Mariano impatiently waiting his return, and eager to learn the result of his interview with Rita. Upon being informed of the proposal that had been made to Luis, Torres, seeing in it only a means of happiness for his friend, strongly urged him to accept it. To this, however, Luis could not make up his mind; and finally, after some deliberation, he resolved to proceed to Old Castile, and endeavour to obtain his father's consent to his joining the party of Don Carlos. Should he succeed in this, of which he could not help entertaining a doubt, he would no longer hesitate, but at once inform the count of his decision, and hasten to Salamanca to put his instructions into execution. Without further delay the two friends set out for Tarazona, where they trusted to find some means of speedy conveyance to the residence of Don Manuel.

———

In the kingdom of Old Castile, and more especially in its mountainous portions and the districts adjacent to the Ebro, an extraordinary bustle and agitation were observable during the first days of October, 1833. There was great furbishing of rusty muskets, an eager search for cartridges, much dusting of old uniforms that had long served but as hiding-places for moths, and which were now donned by men, many of whom seemed but ill at ease in their military equipments. For ten years Spain had been tranquil, if not happy ; but now, as if even this short period of repose were too long for the restless spirit of her sons, a new pretext for discord had been found, and an ominous stir, the fore-runner of civil strife, was perceptible through the land. Whilst Santos Ladron, an officer of merit, who had served through the whole of the war against Napoleon, raised his standard of Charles V. in Navarre, various partisans did the same in the country south of the Ebron. In the north-eastern corner of Castile, known as the Rioja, Basilio Garcia, agent for the Pope's bulls in the province of Soria—a man destitute of military knowledge, and remarkable only for his repulsive exterior and cold-blood-ed ferocity — collected and headed a small body of insurgents ; whilst, in other districts of the same province, several battalions of the old Royalist volunteers—a loose, ill-disciplined mi-litia, as motley and unsoldierlike in appearance as they were unsteady and inefficient in the field—ranged themselves under the order of a gen-eral-officer named Cuevillas, and of the veteran Merino. To these soon joined themselves various individuals of the half-soldier half-bandit class, so numerous in Spain—men who had served in former wars, and asked no better than again to enact the scenes of bloodshed and pillage which were their element. The popularity and acknowledged skill of Merino as a guerilla-leader, secured to him the services of many of these daring and desperate ruffians, who flocked joy-ously to the banner of the soldier-priest, under whose orders some of them had already fought.

Through a tract of champaign country in the province of Burgos, a column of these newly-assembled troops was seen marching early upon the third morning after the inerview between Luis Herrera and Count Vil-labuena. It consisted of a battalion of the Realista militia, for the most part middle-aged citizens, who, al-though they had felt themselves bound to obey the call to arms, seemed but indifferently pleased at having left their families and occupations. Their equipment was various : few had a complete uniform, although most of them displayed some part of one ; but all had belts and cartridge-box, mus-ket and bayonet. Although they had as yet gone but a short distance, many of them appeared footsore aad weary ; and it was pretty evident that, in the event of a campaign, their ranks would be thinned nearly as much by the fatigues of the march as by the fire of the enemy. In front and rear of the battalion marched a squadron of cavalry, of a far more soldierly aspect than the foot-soldiers, al-though even amongst them but little uniformity of costume was found. The bronzed and bearded physiog-nomy, athletic form and upright car-riage, which bespeak the veteran soldier, were not wanting in their ranks ; their horses were active and hardy, their arms clean and service-able.

At the head of the column, a few paces in advance, rode a small group of officers, the chief amongst whom was only to be distinguished by the deference shown to him by his companions. Insignia of rank he had none, nor any indication of his military profession, excepting the heavy sabre that dangled against the flank of his powerful black charger. His dress was entirely civilian, con-sisting of a long surtout something the worse for wear, and a round hat. Heavy spurs upon his heels, and an ample cloak, now strapped across his holsters, completed the equipment of the cura Merino, in whose hard and rigid features, and wiry person, scarce-ly a sign of decay or infirmity was visible after more than sixty years of life, a large portion of which had been passed amidst the fatigues and hardships of incessant campaigning.

As if infected by the sombre and taciturn character of their leader, the party of officers had been riding for some time in silence, when they came in sight of a house situated at a short distance from the road, and of a su-perior description to the *caserias* and peasants' cottages which they had hitherto passed. It was a building of moderate size, with an appearance of greater comfort and neatness about it than is usually found in Spanish houses. Stables adjoined it, and, at some distance in its rear, a range of barns and outhouses served to store the crops produced by the extensive tract of well-cultivated land in the centre of which the dwelling was situated. The front of the house was partially masked from the road by an orchard, and behind it a similar growth of fruit-trees seemed intended to intercept the keen blasts from a line of mountains which rose, grey and gloomy, at the distance of a few miles.

"Who lives yonder?" abruptly inquired Merino, pointing to the house, which he had been gazing at for some time from under his bushy eyebrows. The officer to whom the question was addressed referred to another of the party, a native of that part of the country.

"Señor de Herrera," was the answer. "We have been riding for some minutes through his property. He purchased the estate about a year ago, on his return from France."

"What had he been doing in France?"

"Living there, which he could not have done here unless he had been bullet-proof, or had a neck harder than the iron collar of the garrote."

"Herrera!" repeated the cura musingly—"I know the name, but there are many who bear it. There was a Manuel Herrera who sat in the Cortes in the days of the constitutionalists, and afterwards commanded a battalion of their rabble. You do not mean him?"

"The same, general," replied the officer, addressing Merino by the rank which he held in the Spanish army since the war of Independence. A most unpriestly ejaculation escaped the lips of the cura.

"Manuel Herrera," he repeated; "the dog, the *negro,** the friend of

the scoundrel Riego! I will hang him up at his own door!"

All the old hatreds and bitter party animosities of Merino seemed wakened into new life by the name of one of his former opponents. His eyes flashed, his lips quivered with rage, and he half turned his horse, as if about to proceed to Herrera's house and put his threat into execution. The impulse, however, was checked almost as soon as felt.

"Another time will do," said he, with a grim smile. "Let us once get Charles V. at Madrid, and we will make short work of the Señor Herrera and of all who resemble him." And the cura continued his march, silent as before.

He had proceeded but a short half mile when the officer commanding the cavalry rode up beside him.

"We have no forage, general," said he—"not a blade of straw, or a grain in our corn-sacks. Shall I send on an orderly, that we may find it ready on reaching the halting-place?"

"No!" replied Merino. "Send a party to that house on the left of the road which we passed ten minutes ago. Let them press all the carts they find there, load them with corn, and bring them after us."

The officer fell back to his squadron, and the next minute a subaltern and twenty men detached themselves from the column, and, at a brisk trot, began retracting their steps along the road. Upon arriving in sight of the house to which they were proceeding, they leaped their horses over a narrow ditch dividing the road from the fields, and struck across the latter in a straight line, compelled, however, by the heaviness of the ground to slacken their pace to a walk. They had not got over more than half the distance which they had to traverse, when they heard the clang of a bell, continuously rang; and this was followed by the appearance of two men, who issued from the stables and outbuildings, and hurried to the house. Scarcely had they entered when the

---

* *Negro*, or black, was the term commonly applied to the Liberals by their antagonists.

shutters of the lower windows were pushed to, and the heavy door closed and barred. The soldiers were now within a hundred yards of the dwelling.

"Hallo!" cried the officer contemptuously, "they will not stand a siege, will they? The old don is a black-hearted rebel, I know; but he will hardly be fool enough to resist us."

The trooper was mistaken. The courage of Don Manuel Herrera was of that obstinate and uncalculating character which would have induced him to defend his house, single-handed, against a much larger force than that now brought against it. When he had learned, three days previously, that risings were taking place in his own neighbourhood in the name of Charles V., he had attached very little importance to the intelligence. An old soldier himself, he entertained the most unmitigated contempt for the Realista volunteers, whom he looked upon as a set of tailors, whose muskets would rather encumber them than injure anybody else; and who, on the first appearance of regular troops, would infallibly throw down their arms, and betake themselves to their homes. As to the parties of insurgent guerillas which he was informed were beginning to show themselves at various points of the vicinity, he considered them as mere bandits, availing themselves of the stir and excitement in the country to exercise their nefarious profession; and, should any such parties attempt to molest him, he was fully determined to resist their attacks. In this resolution he now persevered, although he rightly conjectured that the horsemen approaching his house were either the rearguard or a detachment of the disorderly-looking column of which he had a short time previously observed the passage.

"Hola! Don Manolo!" shouted the officer, as he halted his party in front of the house; "what scurvy hospitality is this? What are you fastening doors and ringing alarm-bells for, as if there were more thieves than honest men in the land? We come to pay you a friendly visit, and, instead of welcome and the wine-skin,

you shut the door in our faces. Devilish unfriendly, that, Don Manolito!"

The speaker, who, like many of Merino's followers was an inhabitant of the neighbouring country, knew Don Manuel well by name and reputation, and was also known to him as a deserter from the Constitutionalists in 1823, and as one of the most desperate smugglers and outlaws in the province.

"What do you want with me, Pedro Rufin?" demanded Don Manuel, who now showed himself at one of the upper windows; "and what is the meaning of this assemblage of armed men?"

"The meaning is," replied Rufin, "that I have been detached from the division of his Excellency General Merino, to demand from you a certain quantity of maize or barley, or both, for the service of his Majesty King Charles V."

"I know no such persons," retorted Don Manuel, "as General Merino or King Charles V. But I know you well, Rufin, and the advice I give you is to begone, yourself and your companions. We shall have troops here to-day or to-morrow, and you will find the country too hot to hold you."

The officer laughed.

"Troops are here already," he said; "you may have seen our column march by not half an hour ago. But we have no time to lose. Once more, Señor Herrera, open the door, and that quickly."

"My door does not open at your bidding," replied Don Manuel. "I give you two minutes to draw off your followers, and, if you are not gone by that time, you shall be fired upon."

"Morral," said the officer to one of his men, "your horse is a kicker, I believe. Try the strength of the door."

The soldier left the ranks, and turning his rawboned, vicious-looking chestnut horse with its tail to the house-door, he pressed his knuckles sharply upon the animal's loins, just behind the saddle. The horse lashed out furiously, each kick of his iron-shod heels making the door crack and rattle, and striking out white splinters from the dark surface of the oak of which it was composed. At the first kick Don Manuel left the window. The soldiers stood looking on, laughing till they rolled in their saddles at this novel species of sledge-hammer. Owing, however, to the great solidity of the door, and the numerous fastenings with which it was provided on the other side, the kicks of the horse, although several times repeated, failed to burst it open; and at last the animal, as if wearied, by the resistance it met with, relaxed the vigour of its applications.

"Famous horse that of yours, Morral!" said the officer; "as good as a locksmith or a six-pounder. Try it again, my boy. You have made some ugly marks already. Another round of kicks, and the way is open."

"And if another blow is struck upon my door," said Don Manuel, suddenly reappearing at the window, to the soldier, "your horse will go home with an empty saddle."

"Silence! you old rebel," shouted Rufin, drawing a pistol from his holster. "And you, Morral, never fear. At it again, my man."

The soldier again applied his knuckles to his horse's back, and the animal gave a tremendous kick. At the same instant a puff of smoke issued from the window at which Don Manuel had stationed himself, the report of a musket was heard, and the unlucky Morral, shot through the body, fell headlong to the ground.

"Damnation!" roared the officer, firing his pistol at the window whence the shot had proceeded; and immediately his men, without waiting for orders, commenced an irregular fire of carbines and pistols against the house. It was replied to with effect from three of the windows. A man fell mortally wounded, and two of the horses were hit. Rufin, alarmed at the loss the party had experienced, drew his men back under shelter of some trees, till he could decide on what was best to be done. It seemed at first by no means improbable that the Carlists would have to beat a retreat, or at any rate wait the arrival of infantry, which it was not improbable Merino might have sent to their assistance when the sound of the firing reached his ears. The lower windows of the house were protected by strong iron bars; and, although the defenders were so few in number, their muskets, and the shelter behind which they fought, gave them a great advantage over the assailants, whose carbines would not carry far, and who had no cover from the fire of their opponents. At last a plan was devised which offered some chance of success. The party dismounted; and whilst four men, making a circuit, and concealing themselves as much as possible behind trees and hedges, endeavoured to get in rear of the building, the others, with the exception of two or three who remained with the horses, advanced towards the front of the house, firing as rapidly as they could, in order, by the smoke and by attracting the attention of the besieged, to cover the manœuvre of their comrades. The stratagem was completely successful. Whilst Don Manuel and his servants were answering the fire of their assailants with some effect, the four men got round the house, climbed over a wall, found a ladder in an out-building, and applied it to one of the back-windows, which they burst open. A shout of triumph, and the report of their pistols, informed their companions of their entrance, and the next moment one of them threw open the front door, and the guerillas rushed tumultuously into the house.

It was about two hours after these occurrences, that Luis Herrera and Mariano Torres arrived at Don Manuel's residence. They had been delayed upon the road by the disturbed state of the country, which rendered it difficult to procure conveyances, and had at last been compelled to hire a couple of indifferent horses, upon which, accompanied by a muleteer, they had made but slow progress across the mountainous district they had to traverse. The news of the Carlist insurrection had inspired Luis with some alarm on account of his father, whom he knew to be in the highest degree obnoxious to many of that party. At the same time he had not yet heard of the perpetration of any acts of violence, and was far from anticipating the spectacle which met his eyes when he at last came in view of the Casa Herrera. With an exclamation of horror he forced his horse up a bank bordering the road, and, followed by Mariano, galloped towards the house.

Of the dwelling, so lately a model of rural ease and comfort, the four walls alone were now standing. The roof had fallen in, and the tongues of flame which licked and flickered round the apertures where windows had been, showed that the devouring element was busy completing its work. The adjoining stables, owing to their slighter construction, and to the combustibles they contained, had been still more rapidly consumed. Of them, a heap of smoking ashes and a few charred beams and blackened bricks were all that remained. The paling of the tastefully distributed garden was broken down in several places, the parterres and melon-beds were trampled and destroyed by the hoofs of the Carlist horses, which had seemingly been turned in there to feed, or perhaps been ridden through it in utter wantonness by their brutal owners. The ground in front of the house was strewed with broken furniture, and with articles of wearing apparel, the latter of which appeared to have belonged to the Carlists, and to have been exchanged by them for others of a better description found in the house. Empty bottles, fragments of food, and a couple of wine-skins, of which the greater part of the contents had been poured out upon the ground, lay scattered about near the carcase of a horse and three human corpses, two of the latter being those of Carlists, and the third that of one of the defenders of the house. A few peasants stood by, looking on in open-mouthed stupefaction; and above the whole scene of desolation, a thick cloud of black smoke floated like a funereal pall.

In an agony of suspense Luis inquired for his father. The peasant to whom he addressed the question, pointed to the buildings in rear of the house, which the Carlists, weary perhaps of the work of destruction, had left uninjured.

"Don Manuel is there," said he, "if he still lives."

The latter part of the sentence was drowned in the noise of the horse's feet, as Luis spurred furiously towards the buildings indicated, which consisted of barns, and of a small dwelling-house inhabited by his father's steward. On entering the latter, his worst fears were realized.

Upon a bed in a room on the ground floor, Don Manuel Herrera was lying, apparently insensible. His face was overspread with an ashy paleness, his eyes were closed, his lips blue and pinched. He was partially undressed, and his linen, and the bed upon which he lay, were stained with blood. A priest stood beside him, a crucifix in one hand and a cordial in the other; whilst an elderly peasant woman held a linen cloth to a wound in the breast of the expiring man. In an adjacent room were heard the sobbings and lamentations of women and children. With a heart swollen almost to bursting, Luis approached the bed.

"Father!" he exclaimed as he took Don Manuel's hand, which hung powerless over the side of the couch— "Father, is it thus I find you!"

The voice of his son seemed to rouse the sufferer from the swoon or lethargy in which he lay. He opened his eyes, a faint smile of recognition and affection came over his features, and his feeble fingers strove to press those of Luis. The priest made a sign to the woman, and, whilst she gently raised Don Manuel's head, he held the cordial to his lips. The effect of the draught was instantaneous and reviving.

"This is a sad welcome for you, Luis," said Don Manuel. "Your home destroyed, and your father dying. God be thanked for sending you now, and no sooner! I can die happy since you are here to close my eyes."

He paused, exhausted by the exertion of speaking. A slight red foam stood upon his lips, which the priest wiped away, and another draught of the cordial enabled him to proceed.

"My son," said he, "my minutes are numbered. Mark my last words, and attend to them as you value my blessing, and your own repose. I foresee that this country is on the eve of a long and bloody struggle. How it may end, and whether it is to be the last that shall rend unhappy Spain, who can tell? But your course is plain before you. By the memory of your sainted mother, and the love you bear to me, be stanch to the cause I have ever defended. You are young, and strong, and brave ; your arm and your heart's best blood are due to the cause of Spanish freedom. My son, swear that you will defend it !"

No selfish thought of his own happiness, which would be marred by the oath he was required to take, nor any but the one absorbing idea of smoothing his dying father's pillow by a prompt and willing compliance with his wishes, crossed the mind of Luis as he took the crucifix from the hand of the priest, and, kneeling by the bedside, swore on the sacred emblem to obey Don Manuel's injunctions both in letter and spirit, and to resist to his latest breath the traitors who would enslave his country. His father listened to the fervent vow with a well-pleased smile. By a last effort he raised himself in his bed, and laid his hand upon the head of his kneeling son.

"May God and his saints prosper thee, Luis," said he, "as thou observest this oath !"

He sank back, his features convulsed by the pain which the movement occasioned him.

"Mother of God !" exclaimed the woman, who was still holding the bandage to the wound. The bleeding, which had nearly ceased, had recommenced with redoubled violence, and a crimson stream was flowing over the bed. The death-rattle was in Don Manuel's throat, but his eyes were still fixed upon his son, and he seemed to make an effort to extend his arms towards him. With feelings of unutterable agony, Luis bent forward and kissed his father's cheek. It was that of a corpse.

For the space of a minute did the bereaved son gaze at the rigid features before him, as if unable to comprehend that one so dear was gone from him for ever. At last the sad truth forced itself upon his mind ; he bowed his face upon the pillow of his murdered parent, and his overcharged feelings found relief in a passion of tears. The priest and the woman left the apartment. Mariano Torres remained standing behind his friend, and after a time made an effort to lead him from the room. But Luis motioned him away. His grief was of those that know not human consolation.

It was evening when Mariano, who had been watching near the chamber of death, without venturing to intrude upon his friend's sorrow, saw the door open and Luis come forth. Torres started at seeing him, so great was the change that had taken place in his aspect. His cheeks were pale and his eyes inflamed with weeping, but the expression of his countenance was no longer sorrowful ; it was stern even to fierceness, and his look was that of an avenger rather than a mourner. Taking Mariano's arm, he led him out of the house, and, entering the stable, began to saddle his horse with his own hands. Torres followed his example in silence, and then both mounted and rode off in the direction of the high road. Upon reaching it, Mariano first ventured to address a question to his friend.

"What are your plans, Luis ?" said he. "Whither do we now proceed ?"

"To provide for my father's funeral," was the reply.

"And afterwards ?" said his friend, with some hesitation

"To revenge his death !" hoarsely shouted Herrera, as he spurred his horse to its utmost speed along the rough road that led to the nearest village.

HUMBOLDT.

WE hear much, and much that is true, of the ephemeral character of a large part of our literature; but to no branch of it are the observations more truly applicable, than to the greater number of travels which now issue from the British press. It may safely be affirmed that our writers of travels, both male and female, have of late years arrived at a pitch of weakness, trifling, and emptiness, which is unparalleled .in the previous history of literature in this or perhaps any other country. When we see two post octavos of travels newly done up by the binder, we are prepared for a series of useless remarks, weak attempts at jokes, disquisitions on dishes, complaints of inns, stale anecdotes and vain flourishes, which almost make us blush for our country, and the cause of intelligence over the world. The Russian Emperor, who unquestionably has the power of licensing or prohibiting any of his subjects to travel at his own pleasure, is said to concede the liberty only to the men of intelligence and ability in his dominions; the fools are all obliged to remain at home. Hence the high reputation which the Muscovites enjoy abroad, and the frequent disappointment which is felt by travellers of other nations, when they visit their own country. It is evident, from the character of the books of travels which every spring issue from the London press, with a few honourable exceptions, that no such restraining power exists in the British dominions. We have no individuals or particular works in view in these observations. We speak of things in general. If any one doubts their truth, let him inquire how many of the numberless travels which annually issue from the British press are ever sought after, or heard of, five years after their publication.

Our annual supply of ephemeral travels is far inferior in point of merit to the annual supply of novels. This is the more remarkable, because travels, if written in the right spirit, and by persons of capacity and taste, are among the most delightful, and withal instructive, species of composition of which literature can boast. They are so, because by their very nature they take the reader, as well as the writer, out of the sphere of everyday observation and commonplace remark. This is an immense advantage: so great indeed, that if made use of with tolerable capacity, it should give works of this sort a decided superiority in point of interest and utility over all others, excepting History and the higher species of Romance. Commonplace is the bane of literature, especially in an old and civilized state; monotony—the thing to be principally dreaded. The very air is filled with ordinary ideas. General education, universal reading, unhappily make matters worse; they tend only to multiply the echoes of the original report—a new one has scarce any chance of being heard amidst the ceaseless reverberation of the old. The more ancient a nation is, the more liable is it to be overwhelmed by this dreadful evil. The Byzantine empire, during a thousand years of civilisation and opulence, did not produce one work of original thought; five hundred years after the light of Athenian genius had been extinguished, the schools of Greece were still pursuing the beaten paths, and teaching the doctrines of Plato and Aristotle. It is the peculiar and prodigious advantage of travelling, that it counteracts this woful and degrading tendency, and by directing men's thoughts, as well as their steps, into foreign lands, has a tendency to induce into their ideas a portion of the variety and freshness which characterize the works of nature. Every person knows how great an advantage this proves in society. All must have felt what a relief it is to escape from the eternal round of local concerns or country politics, of parish grievances or neighbouring railroads, with which in every-day life we are beset, to the conversation of a person of intelligence who has visited foreign lands, and can give to the inquisitive at home a portion of the new ideas, images, and recollections with which his mind is stored. How, then, has it happened, that the same acquaintance with foreign and distant countries, which is universally felt to be such an advantage in conversation, is attended with such opposite effects in literature; and that, while our travellers are often the most agreeable men in company, they are beyond all question the dullest in composition?

Much of this extraordinary and woful deficiency, we are persuaded, is owing to the limited range of objects to which the education of the young of the higher classes is so exclusively directed in Oxford and Cambridge. Greek and Latin, Aristotle's logic and classical versification, quadratic equations, conic sections, the differential calculus, are very good things, and we are well aware that it is by excellence in them that the highest honours in these seminaries of learning can alone be attained. They are essential to the fame of a Parr or a Porson, a Herschel or a Whewell. But a very different species of mental training is required for advantageous travelling. Men will soon find that neither Greek prose nor Latin prose, Greek verse nor Latin verse, will avail them when they come to traverse the present states of the world. The most thorough master of the higher mathematics will find his knowledge of scarce any avail in Italy or Egypt, the Alps or the Andes. These acquisitions are doubtless among the greatest triumphs of the human understanding, and they are calculated to raise a few, perhaps one in a hundred, to distinction in classical or scientific pursuits: but upon the minds of the remaining ninety-nine, they produce no sort of impression. Nature simply rejects them; they are not the food which she requires. They do not do much mischief to such persons in themselves; but they are of incalculable detriment by the time and the industry which they absorb to no available purpose. Ten years of youth —the most valuable and important period of life—are wasted in studies which, to nineteen-twentieths of the persons engaged in them, are of no

use whatever in future years. Thus our young men, of the highest rank and best connexions, are sent out into the world without any ideas or information which can enable them to visit foreign countries with advantage. Need we wonder that, when they come to write and publish their travels, they produce such a woful brood of ephemeral bantlings?*

The reaction against this enormous evil in a different class of society, has produced another set of errors in education—of an opposite description, but perhaps still more fatal to the formation of the mental character, which is essential to the useful or elevating observation of foreign countries. The commercial and middle classes of society, educated at the London university, or any of the numerous academies which have sprung up in all parts of the country, have gone into the other extreme. Struck with the uselessness, to the great bulk of students, of the classical minutiæ required at one of the universities, and the mathematical depth deemed indispensable at the other, they have turned education into an entirely different channel. Nothing was deemed worthy of serious attention, except what led to some practical object in life. Education was considered by their founders as merely a step to making money. Science became a trade—a mere handmaid to art. Mammon was all in all. Their instruction was entirely utilitarian. Mechanics and Medicine, Hydraulics and Chemistry, Pneumatics and Hydrostatics, Anatomy and Physiology, constituted the grand staples of their education. What they taught was adapted only for professional students. One would suppose, from examining their course of study, that all men were to be either doctors or surgeons, apothecaries or druggists, mechanics, shipwrights, or civil-engineers. No doubt we must have such persons—no doubt it is indispensable that places of instruction should exist in which they can learn their various and highly important avocations; but is that the

---

* We lately heard of a young man who had gone through the examination at Cambridge with distinction, inquiring, "whether the Greek church *were Christians?*" What sort of a traveller would he make in the East or Russia?

school in which the enlarged mind is to be formed, the varied information acquired, the appreciation of the grand and the beautiful imbibed, which are essential to an accomplished and really useful writer of travels? Sulphuric acid and Optics, Anatomy and Mechanics, will do many things; but they will never make an observer of Nature, a friend of Man, a fit commentator on the world of God.

Persons of really cultivated minds and enlarged views will probably find it difficult to determine which of these opposite systems of education is the best calculated to attain what seems the grand object of modern instruction, the cramping and limiting the human mind. But without entering upon this much-disputed point—upon which much is to be said on both sides, and in which each party will perhaps be found to be in the right when they assail their opponents, and in the wrong when they defend themselves—it is more material to our present purpose to observe, that both are equally fatal to the acquisition of the varied information, and the imbibing of the refined and elegant taste, which are essential to an accomplished writer of travels. Only think what mental qualifications are required to form such a character? An eye for the Sublime and the Beautiful, the power of graphically describing natural scenery, a vivid perception of the peculiarities of national manners, habits, and institutions, will at once be acknowledged to be the first requisites. But, in addition to this, how much is necessary to make a work which shall really stand the test of time, in the delineation of the present countries of the world, and the existing state of their inhabitants? How many branches of knowledge are called for, how many sources of information required, how many enthusiastic pursuits necessary, to enable the traveller worthily to discharge his mission? Eyes and no Eyes are nowhere more conspicuous in human affairs; and, unhappily, eyes are never given but to the mind which has already seen and learned much.

An acquaintance with the history of the country and the leading characters in its annals, is indispensable to enable the traveller to appreciate the historical associations connected with the scenes; a certain degree of familiarity with its principal authors, to render him alive to that noblest of interests —that arising from the recollection of Genius and intellectual Achievement. Without an acquaintance with political economy and the science of government, he will be unable to give any useful account of the social state of the country, or furnish the most valuable of all information—that relating to the institutions, the welfare, and the happiness of man. Statistics form almost an indispensable part of every book of travels which professes to communicate information; but mere statistics are little better than unmeaning figures, if the generalizing and philosophical mind is wanting, which, from previous acquaintance with the subjects on which they bear, and the conclusions which it is of importance to deduce from them, knows what is to be selected and what laid aside from the mass. Science, to the highest class of travellers, is an addition of the utmost moment; as it alone can render their observations of use to that most exalted of all objects, an extension of the boundaries of knowledge, and an enlarged acquaintance with the laws of nature. The soul of a poet is indispensable to form the most interesting species of travels—a mind, and still more a heart, capable of appreciating the grand and the beautiful in Art and in Nature. The eye of a painter and the hand of a draughtsman are equally important to enable him to observe with accuracy the really interesting features of external things, and convey, by faithful and graphic description, a correct impression of what he has seen, to the mind of the reader. Such are the qualifications necessary for a really great traveller. It may be too much to hope to find these ever united in one individual; but the combination of the majority of them is indispensable to distinction or lasting fame in this branch of literature.

Compare these necessary and indispensable qualifications for a great traveller, with those which really belong to our young men who are sent forth from our universities or academies into the world, and take upon themselves to communicate what they have seen to others. Does the youth come from Oxford? His head is full of Homer and Virgil, Horace and Æschylus: he could tell you all the amours of Mars and Venus, of Jupiter and Leda; he could rival Orpheus or Pindar in the melody of his Greek verses, and Cicero or Livy in the correctness of his Latin prose; but as, unfortunately, he has to write neither about gods nor goddesses, but mere mortals, and neither in Greek verse nor Latin verse, but good English prose, he is utterly at a loss alike for thought and expression. He neither knows what to communicate, nor is he master of the language in which it is to be conveyed. Hence his recorded travels dwindle away into a mere scrap-book of classical quotations—a transcript of immaterial Latin inscriptions, destitute of either energy, information, or eloquence. Does he come from Cambridge? He could solve cubic equations as well as Cardan, is a more perfect master of logarithms than Napier, could explain the laws of physical astronomy better than Newton, and rival La Grange in the management of the differential calculus. But as, unluckily, the world which he visits, and in which we live, is neither a geometric world nor an algebraic world, a world of conic sections or fluxions; but a world of plains and mountains, of lakes and rivers, of men and women, flesh and blood—he finds his knowledge of little or no avail. He takes scarce any interest in the sublunary or contemptible objects which engross the herd of ordinary mortals, associates only with the learned and the recluse in a few universities, and of course comes back without having a word to utter, or a sentence to write, which can interest the bulk of readers. Does he come from the London University, or any of the provincial academies? He is thinking only of railroads or mechanics, of chemistry or canals, of medicine or surgery. He could descant without end on sulphuric acid or decrepitating salts, on capacity for caloric or galvanic batteries, on steam-engines and hydraulic machines, on the discoveries of Davy or the conclusions of Berzelius, of the systems of Hutton or Werner, of Liebig or Cuvier. But although an acquaintance with these different branches of practical knowledge is an indispensable preliminary to a traveller in foreign countries making himself acquainted with the improvements they have respectively made in the useful or practical arts, they will never qualify for the composition of a great or lasting book of travels. They would make an admirable course of instruction for the overseer of a manufactory, of a canal or railway company, of an hospital or an infirmary, who was to visit foreign countries in order to pick up the latest improvements in practical mechanics, chemistry, or medicine; but have we really become a race of shopkeepers or doctors, and is Science sunk to be the mere handmaid of Art?

We despair, therefore, as long as the present system of education prevails in England (and Scotland of course follows in the wake of its great neighbour), of seeing any traveller arise of lasting celebrity, or book of travels written which shall attain to durable fame. The native vigour and courage, indeed, of the Anglo-Saxon race, is perpetually impelling numbers of energetic young men into the most distant parts of the earth, and immense is the addition which they are annually making in the sum-total of *geographical* knowledge. We have only to look at one of our recent maps as compared to those which were published fifty years ago, to see how much we owe to the courage and enterprise of Parry and Franklin, of Park and Horneman, of Burckhardt and Lander. But giving all due credit—and none give it more sincerely than we do—to the vigour and courage of these very eminent men, it is impossible not to feel that, however well fitted they were to explore unknown or desert regions, and carry the torch of civilisation into the wilderness of nature, they had not the mental training, or varied information, or powers of composition, necessary to form a great *writer of travels.* Clarke and Bishop Heber are most favourable specimens of English travellers, and do honour to the great universities of which they were such distinguished ornaments; but they did not possess the varied accomplishments and information of the continental travellers. Their education, and very eminence in their peculiar and exclusive lines, precluded it. What is wanting in that character above everything, is an acquaintance with, and interest in, a *great many and different branches of knowledge*, joined to considerable power of composition, and unconquerable energy of mind; and that is precisely what our present system of education in England renders it almost impossible for any one to acquire. The system pursued in the Scottish universities, undoubtedly, is more likely to form men capable of rising to eminence in this department; and, the names of Park and Bruce show what travellers they are capable of sending forth. But the attractions of rank, connexion, and fashion, joined to the advantage of speaking correct English, are fast drawing a greater proportion of the youth of the higher ranks in Scotland to the English universities; and the education pursued at home, therefore, is daily running more and more into merely utilitarian and professional channels. That system is by no means the one calculated to form an accomplished and interesting writer of travels.

In this deficiency of materials for the formation of a great body of male travellers, the ladies have kindly stepped in to supply the deficiency; and numerous works have issued from the press, from the pens of the most accomplished and distinguished of our aristocratic beauties. But alas! there is no royal road to literature, any more than geometry. Almack's and the exclusives, the opera and ducal houses, the lordlings and the guards, form an admirable school for manners, and are an indispensable preliminary to success at courts and coronations, in ball-rooms and palaces. But the world is not made up of courts or palaces, of kings or princes, of dukes or marquesses. Men have something more to think of than the reception which the great world of one country gives to the great world of another— of the balls to which they are invited, or the fêtes which they grace by their charms—or the privations to

which elegant females, nursed in the lap of luxury, are exposed in roughing it amidst the snows of the North or the deserts of the South. We are grateful to the lady travellers for the brilliant and interesting pictures they have given us of capitals and manners,* of costume and dress, and of many eminent men and women, whom their rank and sex gave them peculiar opportunities of portraying. But we can scarcely congratulate the country upon having found in them a substitute for learned and accomplished travellers of the other sex; or formed a set-off, on the part of Great Britain, to the Humboldts, the Chateaubriands, and Lamartines of continental Europe.

It is impossible to contemplate the works of these great men without arriving at the conclusion, that it is in the varied and discursive education of the Continent, that a foundation has been laid for the extraordinary eminence which its travellers have attained. It is the vast number of subjects with which the young men are in some degree made acquainted at the German universities, which has rendered them so capable in after life of travelling with advantage in any quarter of the globe, and writing their travels with effect. This advantage is in a peculiar manner conspicuous in HUMBOLDT, whose mind, naturally ardent and capacious, had been surprisingly enlarged and extended by early and various study in the most celebrated German universities. He acquired, in consequence, so extraordinary a command of almost every department of physical and political science, that there is hardly any branch of it in which facts of importance may not be found in his travels. He combined, in a degree perhaps never before equalled in one individual, the most opposite and generally deemed irreconcilable mental qualities. To an ardent poetical temperament, and an eye alive to the most vivid impressions of external things, he united a power of eloquence rarely given to the most gifted orators, and the habit of close and

* Lady Londonderry's description of Moscow is the best in the English language.

accurate reasoning, which belongs to the intellectual powers adapted for the highest branches of the exact sciences. An able mathematician, a profound natural philosopher, an exact observer of nature, he was at the same time a learned statistician, an indefatigable social observer, an unwearied philanthropist, and the most powerful describer of nature that perhaps ever undertook to portray her great and glorious features. It is this extraordinary combination of qualities that renders his works so surprising and valuable. The intellectual and imaginative powers rarely coexist in remarkable vigour in the same individual; but when they do, they produce the utmost triumphs of the human mind. Leonardo da Vinci, Johnson, Burke, and Humboldt, do not resemble single men, how great soever, but rather clusters of separate persons, each supremely eminent in his peculiar sphere.

Frederick Henry Alexander, Baron of Humboldt, brother of the celebrated Prussian statesman of the same name, was born at Berlin on the 14th September, 1769, the same year with Napoleon, Wellington, Goethe, Marshal Ney, and many other illustrious men. He received an excellent and extensive education at the university of Gottingen, and at an academy at Frankfort on the Oder. His first step into the business of life was as a clerk in the mercantile house of Buch, at Hamburg, where he soon made himself master of accounts and bookkeeping, and acquired that perfect command of arithmetic, and habit of bringing everything, where it is possible, to the test of figures, by which his political and scientific writings are so pre-eminently distinguished. But his disposition was too strongly bent on scientific and physical pursuits, to admit of his remaining long in the comparatively obscure and uninviting paths of commerce. His thirst for travelling was from his earliest years unbounded, and it ere long received ample gratification. His first considerable journey was with two naturalists of distinction, Messrs. Fontu and Genns, with whom he travelled in Germany, Holland, and England, in the course of which his attention

was chiefly directed to mineralogical pursuits. The fruit of his observations appeared in a work, the first he ever published, which was printed at Brunswick in 1790, when he was only twenty-one years of age, entitled *Observations sur les Basaltes du Rhin.*

To extend his information, already very considerable, on mineralogical science, Humboldt in 1791 repaired to Freyburg, to profit by the instructions of the celebrated Werner; and, when there, he devoted himself, with the characteristic ardour of his disposition, to make himself master of geology and botany, and prosecuted in an especial manner the study of the fossil remains of plants in the rocks around that place. In 1792, he published at Berlin a learned treatise, entitled *Specimen Floræ Friebergensis Subterraneæ;* which procured for him such celebrity, that he was soon after appointed director-general of the mines in the principalities of Anspach and Bayreuth, in Franconia. His ardent and philanthropic disposition there exerted itself for several years in promoting, to the utmost of his power, various establishments of public utility; among others, the public school of Streben, from which has already issued many distinguished scholars. Charmed by the recent and brilliant discoveries of M. Galvani in electricity, he next entered with ardour into that new branch of science; and, not content with studying it in the abstract, he made a great variety of curious experiments on the effects of galvanism on his own person, and published the result in two octavos, at Berlin, in 1796, enriched by the notes of the celebrated naturalist Blümenbach. This work was translated into French by J. F. Jadelot, and published at Paris in 1799. Meanwhile Humboldt, consumed with an insatiable desire for travelling, resumed his wanderings, and roamed over Switzerland and Italy, after which he returned to Paris in 1797, and formed an intimacy with a congenial spirit, M. Aimé Bonpland, who afterwards became the companion of his South American travels. At this time he formed the design of joining the expedition of Captain Baudin, who was destined to circumnavigate the globe; but the continuance of hostilities prevented him from carrying that design into effect. Baffled in that project, upon which his heart was much set, Humboldt went to Marseilles with the intention of embarking on board a Swedish frigate for Algiers, from whence he hoped to join Napoleon's expedition to Egypt, and cross from the banks of the Nile to the Persian Gulf and the vast regions of the East. This was the turning point of his destiny. The Swedish frigate never arrived; the English cruisers rendered it impossible to cross the Mediterranean, except in a neutral vessel; and after waiting with impatience for about two months, he set out for Madrid, in the hope of finding means in the Peninsula of passing into Africa from the opposite shores of Andalusia.

Upon his arrival in the Spanish capital, the German philosopher was received with all the distinction which his scientific reputation deserved; and he obtained from the government the extraordinary and unlooked-for boon of a formal leave to travel over the whole South American colonies of the monarchy. This immediately determined Humboldt. He entered with ardour into the new prospects thus opened to him; wrote to his friend Aimé Bonpland to propose that he should join him in the contemplated expedition—an offer which was gladly accepted; and soon the visions of Arabia and the Himalaya were supplanted by those of the Pampas of Buenos Ayres and the Cordilleras of Peru. The two friends embarked at Corunna on board a Spanish vessel, and after a prosperous voyage, reached Cumana, in the New World, in July, 1799. From that city they made their first expedition in Spanish America, during which they travelled over Spanish Guiana, New Andalusia, and the Missions of the Caribbees, from whence they returned to Cumana in 1800. There they embarked for the Havannah; and the whole of the summer of that year was spent in traversing that great and interesting island, on which he collected much important and valuable information. In September, 1801, he set out for Quito, where he arrived in January of the succeeding year, and

was received with the most flattering distinction. Having reposed for some months from their fatigues, Humboldt and Bonpland proceeded, in the first instance, to survey the country which had been devastated in 1797 by the dreadful earthquake, so frequent in those regions, and which swallowed up in a minute forty thousand persons. Then he set out, in June, 1802, to visit the volcano of Tungaragno and the summit of Chimborazo. They ascended to the height of 19,500 feet on the latter mountain; but were prevented from reaching the top by impassable ravines. Perched on one of the summits, however, of this giant of mountains, amidst ice and snow, far above the abode of any living creature except the condor, they made a great variety of most interesting observations, which have proved of essential service to the cause of science. They were 3485 feet above the most elevated point which the learned Condamine, who had hitherto ascended highest, reached in 1745, but were still 2140 feet below the loftiest summit of the mountain. They determined, by a series of strict trigonometrical observations, the height of the chief peaks of that celebrated ridge—

" Where Andes, giant of the western star,
Looks from his throne of clouds o'er half the world."

Having returned, after this fatiguing and dangerous mountain expedition, to Lima, Humboldt remained several months enjoying the hospitality of its kind-hearted inhabitants, whose warm feelings and excellent qualities excited in him the warmest admiration. In the neighbouring harbour of Callao, he was fortunate enough to see the passage of the planet Mercury over the disk of the sun, of which transit he made very important observations; and from thence passed into the province of New Spain, where he remained an entire year, sedulously engaged in agricultural, political, and statistical, as well as physical inquiries, the fruits of which added much to the value of his published travels. In April, 1803, he proceeded to Mexico, where he was so fortunate as to discover the only specimen known to exist of the tree called

Cheirostomon Platanoïdès, of the highest antiquity and gigantic dimensions. During the remainder of that year, he made several excursions over the mountains and valleys of Mexico, inferior to none in the world in interest and beauty; and in autumn, 1804, embarked for the Havannah, from whence he passed into Philadelphia, and traversed a considerable part of the United States. At length, in 1805, he returned to Europe, and arrived safe at Paris in November of that year, bringing with him, in addition to the observations he had made, and recollections with which his mind was fraught, the most extensive and varied collection of specimens of plants and minerals that ever was brought from the New World. His herbarium consisted of four thousand different plants, many of them of extreme rarity even in South America, and great part of which were previously unknown in Europe. His mineralogical collection was of equal extent and value. But by far the most important additions he has made to the cause of science, consist in the vast series of observations he has made in the New World, which have set at rest a great many disputed points in geography, mineralogy, and zoology, concerning that interesting, and, in a great degree, unknown part of the world, and extended in a proportional degree the boundaries of knowledge regarding it. Nor have his labours been less important in collecting the most valuable statistical information regarding the Spanish provinces of those vast regions, especially the condition of the Indian, negro, and mulatto race which exist within them, and the amount of the precious metals annually raised from their mines; subjects of vast importance to Great Britain, and especially its colonial and commercial interests, but which have hitherto been in an unaccountable manner neglected, even by those whose interests and fortunes were entirely wound up in the changes connected with these vital subjects.

The remainder of Baron Humboldt's life has been chiefly devoted to the various and important publications, in which he has embodied the fruit of his vast and extensive researches in the New-World. In many of these he has been assisted by M. Aimé Bon-

pland, who, his companion in literary labour as in the dangers and fatigues of travelling, has, with the generosity of a really great mind, been cóntent to diminish, perhaps destroy, his prospect of individual celebrity, by associating himself with the labours of his illustrious friend. Pursued even in mature years by the desire of fame, the thirst for still greater achievements, which belongs to minds of the heroic cast, whether in war or science, he conceived, at a subsequent period, the design of visiting the upper provinces of India and the Himalaya range. After having ascended higher than man had yet done on the elevated ridges of the New World, he was consumed with a thirst to surmount the still more lofty summits of the Old, which have remained in solitary and unapproachable grandeur since the waves of the Deluge first receded from their sides. But the East India Company, within whose dominions, or at least beneath whose influence, the highest ridges of the Himalaya are situated, gave no countenance to the design, and even, it is said, refused liberty to the immortal Naturalist to visit their extensive territories. Whatever opinion we may form on the liberality or wisdom of this resolution, considered with reference to the interests, physical, moral, and political, of British India, it is not to be regretted, for the cause of science and literature over the world, that the great traveller has been prevented from setting out late in life to a fresh region of discovery. It has left the remainder of his life, and his yet undiminished powers, to illustrate and explain what he has already seen. To do that, was enough for the ordinary span of human life.

Humboldt's works relating to the New World are very numerous. I. He first published, in 1805, at Paris, in four volumes quarto, the *Personal Narrative* of his travels from 1799 to 1804. Of this splendid and interesting work, several editions have since been published in French, in twelve volumes octavo. It is upon it that his fame with the generality of readers mainly rests. II. *Vues des Cordilleras et Monumens des Peuples Indigènes de l'Amerique* — two volumes folio: Paris, 1811. This magnificent work, the cost of which is now

£130, contains by far the finest views of the Andes in existence. Its great price renders it very scarce, and not more than a few copies are to be met with in Great Britain; but a cheap edition, without the great plates, was published at Paris in 1817. III. *Recueil d'Observations Astronomiques et de Mésures exécutées dans le Nouveau Continent:* two volumes quarto. This learned work contains the result of Humboldt's astronomical and trigonometrical observations on the lunar distances, the eclipses of the satellites of Jupiter, the transit of Mercury, and upwards of five hundred elevated points in the New World, taken from barometrical observations, with all the requisite allowances and calculations carefully made. IV. *Essai sur la Geographie des Plantes, ou Tableau Physique des Regions Equinoxiales:* in quarto, with a great map. V. *Plantes Equinoxiales recueillies au Mexique, dans l'Ile de Cuba, dans les Provinces de Caraccas,* &c.: two volumes folio. A splendid and very costly work. VI. *Monographie des Mélastomes:* two volumes folio. A most curious and interesting work on a most interesting subject. VII. *Nova Genera et Species Plantarum:* three volumes folio. Containing an account of the botanical treasures collected by him in the New World, and brought home in his magnificent herbarium. VIII. *Recueil des Observations de Zoologie et d'Anatomie comparée faites dans un Voyage aux Tropiques:* two volumes quarto. IX. *Essai Politique sur la Nouvelle Espagne.* 1811: two volumes quarto. Of this admirable work a subsequent edition has been published in 1822, in four volumes octavo. It contains an astonishing collection of important statistical facts, arranged and digested with the utmost ability, and interspersed with political and philosophical reflections on the state of the human race, and the relation of society in the New World. X. *Ansichden der Natur.* Tubingen, 1808: in octavo. It is remarkable that this is the only one of the learned author's works on Spanish America which originally appeared in his own language; but it was soon translated into French under the title of *Tableaux de la Nature.* Paris:

1808. It contains a series of descriptions of the different styles of scenery and remarkable objects in the vast regions he had visited, portrayed with all the vigour and accuracy for which the author is distinguished. XI. *De Distributione Geographicá Plantarum secundum Cœli Temperiem et Altitudinem Montium, Prolegomena.* In octavo. Paris; 1817. The title of this work explains its object and its importance, in describing a portion of the globe consisting of such lofty and successive ridges and table-lands as rise from the level of the sea to the summits of the Cordilleras of Mexico and Peru. XII. *Sur l'Elevation des Montagnes de l'Inde.* Octavo. Paris: 1818. A work prepared when the author was contemplating a journey to the Himalaya and mountains of Thibet. XIII. *Carte du Fleuve Orenoque.* Presented to the Academy of Sciences in 1817. M. Humboldt has there demonstrated the singular fact of the junction of the great rivers Orinoco and of the Amazon by the intermediate waters of the Rio Negro; a fact which the sagacity of D'Anville had long ago led him to suspect, but which the travels of the indefatigable German have established beyond a doubt. XIV. *Examen Critique de l'Histoire de la Geographie du Nouveau Continent, et du Progrès de l'Astronomie Nautique aux 15me et 16me siècles.* Paris: 1837. XV. "*Cosmos:*" in German—a "Scheme of a Physical Description of the Universe." This last work embraces a much wider sphere of learning and speculation than any of the preceding, and is more characteristic of the vast erudition and ardent genius of the author.

From the brief account which has now been given of the published works of this indefatigable traveller and author, the reader will be able to appreciate the extent and variety of his scientific and political attainments. We shall now present him under a different aspect, as an eloquent and almost unrivalled describer of nature. It need hardly be said that it is on these splendid pictures, more even than the numerous and valuable additions he has made to the treasures of science, that his reputation with the world in general is founded.

The rapids of the Orinoco—one of the

most striking scenes in America—are thus described by our author :*—

" When we arrived at the top of the Cliff of Marimi, the first object which caught our eye was a sheet of foam, above a mile in length and half a mile in breadth. Enormous masses of black rock, of an iron hue, started up here and there out of its snowy surface. Some resembled huge basaltic cliffs resting on each other ; many, castles in ruins, with detached towers and forta-lices, guarding their approach from a distance. Their sombre colour formed a contrast with the dazzling whiteness of the foam. Every rock, every island, was covered with flourishing trees, the foliage of which is often united above the foaming gulf by creepers hanging in festoons from their opposite branches. The base of the rocks and islands, as far as the eye can reach, is lost in the volumes of white smoke, which boil above the surface of the river ; but above these snowy clouds, noble palms, from eighty to a hundred feet high, rise aloft, stretching their summits of dazzling green towards the clear azure of heaven. With the changes of the day these rocks and palm-trees are alternately illuminated by the brightest sunshine, or projected in deep shadow on the surrounding surge. Never does a breath of wind agitate the foliage, never a cloud obscure the vault of heaven. A dazzling light is ever shed through the air, over the earth enamel-led with the loveliest flowers, over the foaming stream stretching as far as the eye can reach ; the spray, glittering in the sunbeams, forms a thousand rain-bows, ever changing, yet ever bright, beneath whose arches, islands of flowers, rivalling the very hues of heaven, flourish in perpetual bloom. There is nothing austere or sombre, as in northern climates, even in this scene of elemental strife ; tranquillity and repose seem to sleep on the very verge of the abyss of waters. Neither time, nor the sight of the Cordilleras, nor a long abode in the charming valleys of Mexico, have been able to efface from my recollec-tion the impression made by these cata-racts. When I read the description of

similar scenes in the East, my mind sees again in clear vision the sea of foam, the islands of flowers, the palm-trees sur-mounting the snowy vapours. Such recollections, like the memory of the sublimest works of poetry and the arts, leave an impression which is never to be effaced, and which, through the whole of life, is associated with every sentiment of the grand and the beauti-ful."—(Vol. vii., 171, 172.)

Such is a specimen of the descrip-tive powers of the great German natural philosopher, geographer, bo-tanist, and traveller. When our senior wranglers from Cambridge, our high-honoured men from Oxford, or lady travellers from London, pre-duce a parallel to it, we shall hope that England is about to compete with the continental nations in the race of illustrious travellers—but not till then.

As a contrast to this, we cannot resist the pleasure of laying before our readers the following striking descrip-tion of a night on the Orinoco, in the placid part of its course, amidst the vast forests of the tropical regions :—

" The night was calm and serene, and a beautiful moon shed a radiance over the scene. The crocodiles lay ex-tended on the sand ; placed in such a manner that they could watch our fire, from which they never turned aside their eyes. Its dazzling evidently at-tracted them, as it does fish, crabs, and the other inhabitants of the waters. The Indians pointed out to us in the sand the recent marks of the feet of three tigers, a mother and two young, which had crossed the open space be-tween the forest and the water. Find-ing no tree upon the shore, we sank the end of our oars into the sand, in order to form poles for our tents. Every-thing remained quiet till eleven at night, when suddenly there arose, in the neigh-bouring forest, a noise so frightful that it became impossible to shut our eyes. Amidst the voice of so many savage animals, which all roared or cried at once, our Indians could only distinguish the howling of the jaguar, the yell of

---

* We have translated all the passages ourselves. A very good translation of Humboldt's *Personal Narrative* was published many years ago, by Miss H. Williams ; but we could not resist the pleasure of trying to transfer to English such noble specimens of descriptive eloquence.

the tiger, the roar of the cougar, or American lion, and the screams of some birds of prey. When the jaguars approached near to the edge of the forest, our dogs, which to that moment had never ceased to bark, suddenly housed; and, crouching, sought refuge under the shelter of our hammocks. Sometimes, after an interval of silence, the growl of the tiger was heard from the top of the trees, followed immediately by the cries of the monkey tenants of their branches, which fled the danger by which they were menaced.

"I have painted, feature by feature, these nocturnal scenes on the Orinoco, because, having but lately embarked on it, we were as yet unaccustomed to their wildness. They were repeated for months together, every night that the forest approached the edge of the river. Despite the evident danger by which one is surrounded, the security which the Indian feels comes to communicate itself to your mind; you become persuaded with him, that all the tigers fear the light of fire, and will not attack a man when lying in his hammock. In truth, the instances of attacks on persons in hammocks are extremely rare; and during a long residence in South America, I can only call to mind one instance of a Llanero, who was found torn in pieces in his hammock opposite the island of Uhagua.

"When one asks the Indians what is the cause of this tremendous noise, which at a certain hour of the night the animals of the forest make, they answer gaily, 'They are saluting the full moon.' I suspect the cause in general is some quarrel or combat which has arisen in the interior of the forest. The jaguars, for example, pursue the pecaris and tapirs, which, having no means of defence but their numbers, fly in dense bodies, and press, in all the agony of terror, through the thickets which lie in their way. Terrified at this strife, and the crashing of boughs or rustling of thickets which they hear beneath them, the monkeys on the highest branches set up discordant cries of terror on every side. The din soon wakens the parrots and other birds which fill the woods, they instantly scream in the most violent way, and ere long the whole forest is in an uproar. We soon found that it is not so much during a full moon, as on the approach of a whirlwind or a storm, that this frightful concert arises among the wild beasts. 'May heaven give us a peace-

able night and rest, like other mortals !' was the exclamation of the monk who had accompanied us from the Rio Negro, as he lay down to repose in our bivouac. It is a singular circumstance to be reduced to such a petition in the midst of the solitude of the woods. In the hotels of Spain, the traveller fears the sound of the guitar from the neighbouring apartment: in the bivouacs of the Orinoco, which are spread on the open sand, or under the shade of a single tree, what you have to dread is, the infernal cries which issue from the adjoining forest."—(Vol. vi., 222-3).

One of the most remarkable of the many remarkable features of Nature in South America, is the prodigious plains which, under the name of Llanos and Pampas, stretch from the shores of the Atlantic to the foot of the Andes, over a space from fifteen hundred to two thousand miles in breadth. Humboldt traversed them more than once in their full extent, and has given the following striking description of their remarkable peculiarities.

"In many geographical works, the savannahs of South America are termed *prairies*. That word, however, seems not properly applicable to plains of pasturage, often exclusively dry, though covered with grass four or five feet high. The Llanos and Pampas of South America are true *steppes*: they present a rich covering of verdure during the rainy season; but in the months of drought, the earth assumes the appearance of a desert. The turf is then reduced to powder, the earth gapes in huge cracks; the crocodiles and great serpents lie in a dormant state in the dried mud, till the return of rains, and the rise of the waters in the great rivers, which flood the vast expanse of level surface, awaken them from their long slumber. These appearances are often exhibited over an arid surface of fifty or sixty leagues square—everywhere, in short, where the savannah is not traversed by any of the great rivers. On the borders, on the other hand, of the streams, and around the lakes, which in the dry season retain a little brackish water, the traveller meets from time to time, even in the most extreme drought, groves of Mauritia, a species of palm, the leaves of which, spreading out like a fan, preserve amidst the surrounding sterility a brilliant verdure.

"The steppes of Asia are all out of the region of the tropics, and form in general the summit of very elevated plateaux. America also presents, on the reverse of the mountains of Mexico, of Peru, and of Quito, steppes of considerable extent. But the greatest steppes, the Llanos of Cumana, of Caraccas, and of Meta, all belong to the equinoctial zone, and are very little elevated above the level of the ocean. It is this which gives them their peculiar characters. They do not contain, like the steppes of Southern Asia, and the deserts of Persia, those lakes without issue, or rivers which lose themselves in the sand or in subterraneous filtrations. The Llanos of South America incline towards the east and the south; their waters are tributary to the Orinoco, the Amazon, or the Rio de la Plata.

"What most strongly characterizes the savannahs or steppes of South America, is the entire absence of hills, or inequalities of any kind. The soil, for hundreds of miles together, is perfectly flat, without even a hillock. For this reason, the Castilian conquerors, who penetrated first from Coro to the banks of the Apuré, named the regions to which they came, neither deserts, nor savannahs, nor meadows, but *plains—los Llanos.* Over an extent of thirty leagues square, you will often not meet with an eminence a foot high. The resemblance to the sea which these immense plains bear, strikes the imagination the more forcibly in those places, often as extensive as half of France, where the surface is absolutely destitute of palms, or any species of trees, and where the distance is so great from the mountains, or the forests on the shores of the Orinoco, as to render neither visible. The uniform appearance which the Llanos exhibit, the extreme rarity of any habitations, the fatigues of a journey under a burning sun, and in an atmosphere perpetually cloudy with dust, the prospect of a round girdle of an horizon, which appears constantly to recede before the traveller, the isolated stems of the palm-trees, all precisely of the same form, and which he despairs to reach, because he confounds them with other seemingly identical trunks which appear in the distant parts of the horizon: all these causes combine to make these steppes appear even more vast than they really are.

Yet are their actual dimensions so prodigious, that it is hard to outstrip

them, even by the wildest flights of the imagination. The colonists, who inhabit the slopes of the mountains which form their extreme boundary on the west and north, see the steppes stretch away to the south and east, as far as the eye can reach, an interminable ocean of verdure. Well may they deem it boundless! They know that from the Delta of the Orinoco, crossing the province of Vannos, and from thence by the shores of the Meta, the Guaviare, and the Caguan, you may advance in the plains, at first from east to west, then from north-east to south-east, three hundred and eighty leagues—a distance as great as from Tombuctoo to the northern coast of Africa. They know, by the report of travellers, that the Pampas of Buenos Ayres—which are also Llanos, destitute of trees, covered with rich grass, filled with cattle and wild horses—are equally extensive. They imagine, according to the greater part of maps, that this huge continent has but one chain of mountains, the Andes, which forms its western boundary; and they form a vague idea of the boundless sea of verdure, stretching the whole way from the foot of this gigantic wall of rock, from the Orinoco and the Apuré, to the Rio de la Plata and the Straits of Magellan. Imagination itself can hardly form an idea of the extent of these plains. The Llanos, from the Caqueta to the Apuré, and from thence to the Delta of the Orinoco, contain 17,000 square marine leagues —a space nearly equal to the area of France; that which stretches to the north and south is of nearly double the extent, or considerably larger than the surface of Germany; and the Pampas of Buenos Ayres, which extend from thence towards Cape Horn, are of such extent, that while one end is shaded by the palm-trees of the tropics, the other, equally flat, is charged with the snows of the antarctic circle."—(Vol. vi., 52, 67.)

These prodigious plains have been overspread with the horses and cattle of the Old World, which, originally introduced by the Spanish settlers, have strayed from the enclosures of their masters, and multiplied without end in the vast savannahs which nature had spread out for their reception.

"It is impossible," says Humboldt, "to form an exact enumeration of the cattle in the Pampas, or even to give an approximation to it, so immensely have they augmented during the three centuries which have elapsed since they were first introduced ; but some idea of their number may be formed from the following facts in regard to such portions of these vast herds as are capable of being counted. It is calculated that in the plains from the mouths of the Orinoco to the lake Maracaybo, there are 1,200,000 head of cattle, 180,000 horses, and 90,000 mules, which belong to individual proprietors. In the Pampas of Buenos Ayres there are 12,000,000 cows and 3,000,000 horses belonging to private persons, besides the far greater multitude which are wild, and wander altogether beyond the reach of man. Considerable revenues are realized from the sale of the skins of these animals, for they are so common that the carcases are of scarcely any value. They are at the pains only to look after the young of their herds, which are marked once a-year with the initial letter of the owner. Fourteen or fifteen thousand are marked by the greater proprietors every year, of which five or six thousand are annually sold."—(Vol. vi., 97.)

The enormous number of beasts of prey which multiply with this vast accumulation of animals to be devoured, as well those introduced by man as those furnished by the hand of nature, renders the life of many of the inhabitants of these regions little else than a constant struggle with wild animals. Many hairbreadth escapes and heroic adventures are recounted by the natives, which would pass for fabulous if not stated on such unquestionable authority as that of M. Humboldt, and supported by the concurring testimony of other travellers. The number of alligators, in particular, on the Orinoco, the Rio Apuré, and their tributary streams, is prodigious ; and contests with them constitute a large portion of the legendary tales of the Indian and European settlers in the forest.

" The numerous wild animals," says Humboldt, " which inhabit the forests on the shores of the Orinoco, have made apertures for themselves in the wall of vegetation and foliage by which the woods are bounded, out of which they come forth to drink in the river. Tigers, tapirs, jaguars, boars, besides numberless lesser quadrupeds, issue out of these dark arches in the green wilderness, and cross the strip of sand which generally lies between it and the edge of the water, formed by the large space which is annually devastated and covered with shingle or mud, during the rise of the water in the rainy season. These singular scenes have always possessed a great attraction for me The pleasure experienced was not merely that of a naturalist in the objects of his study ; it belongs to all men who have been educated in the habits of civilisation. You find yourself in contact with a new world, with savage and unconquered Nature. Sometimes it is the jaguar, the beautiful panther of America, which issues from its dark retreat ; at others the hosco, with its dark plumes and curved head, which traverses the *sauso*, as the band of yellow sand is called. Animals of the most various kinds and opposite descriptions succeed each other without intermission. 'Es como en el Paraiso' (It is as in Paradise), said our pilot, an old Indian of the Missions. In truth, everything here recalls that primitive world of which the traditions of all nations have preserved the recollection, the innocence, and happiness ; but on observing the habits of the animals towards each other, it is evident that the age of gold has ceased to them as well as to the human race ; they mutually fear and avoid each other ; and in the lonely American forests, as elsewhere, long experience has taught all living beings that gentleness is rarely united to force."

" When the sands on the river side are of considerable breadth, the sauso often stretches to a considerable distance from the water's edge. It is on this intermediate space that you see the crocodiles, often to the number of eight or ten, stretched on the sand. Motionless, their huge jaws opened at right angles, they lie without giving any of those marks of affection which are observable in other animals which live in society. The troop separate when they leave the coast ; they are probably composed of several females and one male. The former are much more numerous than the latter, from the number of males which are killed in fighting during the time of their amours. These monstrous reptiles have multiplied to such a degree, that there was hardly an instant during our voyage along the whole course of the river that we had not five or six in view. We measured one dead which was lying on the sand ; it was sixteen feet nine inches long. Soon after, Mr. Bonpland found a dead male on the shore, measuring twenty-two feet three inches. Under every zone—in America as in Egypt—this animal attains the same dimensions. The Indians told us, that at San Fernando scarce a year passes without two or three grown up persons, usually women, who are drawing from the river, being devoured by these carnivorous lizards.

" They related to us an interesting story of a young daughter of Urituen, who, by extraordinary intrepidity and presence of mind, succeeded in extricating herself from the very jaws of a crocodile. When she felt herself seized by the voracious animal in the water, she felt for its eyes, and thrust her fingers into them with such violence that she forced the animal to let go, but not before he had torn off the lower part of her left arm. The Indian girl, notwithstanding the enormous quantity of blood which she lost, succeeded in swimming to shore with the hand which was left, and escaped without further injury. In those desert regions, where man is constantly in strife with animated or inanimate nature, they daily speak of similar or corresponding means by which it is possible to escape from a tiger, a great boa, or a crocodile. Every one prepares himself against a danger which may any day befall him, ' I knew,' said the young girl calmly, when praised for her presence of mind, ' that the crocodile lets go his hold when you plunge your fingers in his eyes.' Long after my return to Europe, I learned that the negroes in the interior of Africa make use of the same method to escape from the alligators in the Niger. Who does not recollect with warm interest, that Isaaco the guide, in his last journey of the unfortunate Mungo Park, was seized twice near Boulinkombro, and that he escaped from the throat of the monster solely by thrusting his fingers into his two eyes?* The African Isaaco and the young American girl owed their safety to the same presence of mind, and the same combination of ideas."—(Vol. vi., 203—205.)

If there is any one fact more than another demonstrated by the concurring testimony of travellers, historians, and statistical observers, in all ages and quarters of the world, it is, that the possession of *property in land*

is the first step in social improvement, and the only effectual humanizer of Savage Man. Rousseau's famous paradox, " The first Man who enclosed a field, and called it mine, is the author of all the social ills which followed," is not only false but decidedly the reverse of the truth. He was the first and greatest benefactor of his species. Subsequent ills have arisen, not from following but forgetting his example; and preferring to the simplicity of country life the seductions and vices of urban society. Humboldt adds his important testimony to the noble army of witnesses in all ages, and from all parts of the world, on this all important subject.

" The Guamos are a race of Indians whom it is extremely difficult to fix down to the soil. Like other wandering savages, they are distinguished by their dirt, revengeful spirit, and fondness for wandering. The greater part of them live by fishing and the chase, in the plains often flooded by the Apuré, the Meta, and the Guaviare. The nature of those regions, their vast extent, and entire want of any limit or distinguishing mark, seems to invite their inhabitants to a wandering life. On entering, again, the mountains which adjoin the cataracts of the Orinoco, you find among the Piroas, the Macos, and the Macquiritares, milder manners, a love of agriculture, and remarkable cleanliness in the interior of their cabins. On the ridges of mountains, amidst impenetrable forests, man is forced to fix himself, to clear and cultivate a corner of the earth. That culture demands little care, and is richly rewarded: while the life of a hunter is painful and difficult. The Guamos of the Mission of Santa Barbara are kind and hospitable; whenever we entered their cottages, they offered us dried fish and water."—(Vol. vi., 219.)

No spectacle in nature can exceed, few equal, the sublimity and magnificence of the scenery presented by the vast chain of mountains which, under the name of Cordilleras, Andes, and Rocky Mountains, traverses the whole continent of America, both north and south, in the neighbourhood of the

---

* Park's *Last Mission to Africa*, 1815, p. 89.

Pacific Ocean. Of this prodigious pile of rocks and precipices, Humboldt, in another of his works, has given the following admirable account :—

"The immense chain of the Andes, traversing its whole extent near the Pacific Ocean, has stamped a character upon South American nature which belongs to no other country. The peculiarity which distinguishes the regions which belong to this immense chain, are the successive plateaux, like so many huge natural terraces, which rise one above another, before arriving at the great central chain, where the highest summits are to be found. Such is the elevation of some of these plains that they often exceed eight and nine, and sometimes reach that of twelve thousand feet above the level of the sea. The lowest of these plateaux is higher than the summit of the Pass of the Great St. Bernard, the highest inhabited ground in Europe, which is 7545 feet above the level of the sea. But such is the benignity of the climate, that at these prodigious elevations, which even in the south of Europe are above the line of perpetual snow, are to be found cities and towns, corn-fields and orchards, and all the symptoms of rural felicity. The town of Quito itself, the capital of a province of the same name, is situated on a plateau, or elevated valley, in the centre of the Andes, nearly 9000 feet above the level of the sea. Yet there are found concentrated a numerous population, and it contains cities with thirty, forty, and even fifty thousand inhabitants. After living some months on this elevated ground, you experience an extraordinary illusion. Finding yourself surrounded with pasture and corn-fields, flocks and herds, smiling orchards and golden harvests, the sheep and the lama, the fruits of Europe and those of America, you forget that you are as it were suspended between heaven and earth, and elevated to a height exceeding that by which the European traveller makes his way from France into Italy, and double that of Ben Nevis, the highest mountain in Great Britain.

"The different gradations of vegetation, as might be expected in a country where the earth rises from the torrid zone by a few steep ascents to the regions of eternal congelation, exhibit one of the most remarkable features in this land of wonders. From the borders of the sea to the height of two thousand feet, are to be seen the magnificent palm-tree, the musa, the heleconia, the balms of Tolu, the large flowering jasmin, the date-tree, and all the productions of tropical climates. On the arid and burning shores of the ocean, flourish, in addition to these, the cotton-tree, the magnolias, the cactus, the sugar cane, and all the luscious fruits which ripen under the genial sun, and amidst the balmy breezes of the West India Islands. One only of these tropical children of nature, the *Carosylou Andicola*, is met with far in advance of the rest of its tribe, tossed by the winds at the height of seven and eight thousand feet above the sea, on the middle ridges of the Cordillera range. In this lower region, as nature exhibits the riches, so she has spread the pestilence, of tropical climates. The humidity of the atmosphere, and the damp heats which are nourished amidst its intricate thickets, produce violent fevers, which often prove extremely destructive, especially to European constitutions. But if the patient survives the first attack, the remedy is at hand; a journey to the temperate climate of the elevated plateau soon restores health; and the sufferer is as much revived by the gales of the Andes, as the Indian valetudinarian is by a return to Europe.

"Above the region of the palms commences the temperate zone. It is there that vegetation appears in its most delightful form, luxuriant without being rank, majestic yet not impervious; it combines all that nature has given of the grand, with all that the poets have figured of the beautiful. The bark-tree, which she has provided as the only effectual febrifuge in the deadly heats of the inferior region; the cyprus and melastoma, with their superb violet blossoms; gigantic fuchsias of every possible variety, and evergreen trees of lofty stature, covered with flowers, adorn that delightful zone. The turf is enamelled by never-fading flowers; mosses of dazzling beauty, fed by the frequent rains attracted by the mountains, cover the rocks; and the trembling branches of the mimosa, and others of the sensitive tribe, hang in graceful pendants over every declivity. Almost all the flowering shrubs which adorn our conservatories, are to be found there in primeval beauty, and what to Europeans appears a gigantic scale; magnificent arums of many different kinds spread their ample snowy petals above the surrounding thickets; and innumerable creepers, adorned by splendid blossoms, mount even to the summit of the highest trees, and diffuse a perennial fragrance around.

"The oaks and trees of Europe are not found in those parts of the Andes which lie in the torrid zone, till you arrive at the height of five thousand feet above the sea. It is there you first begin to see the leaves fall in winter, and bud in spring, as in European climates: below that level the foliage is perpetual. Nowhere are the trees so large as in this region: not unfrequently they are found of the height of a hundred and eighty or two hundred feet; their stems are from eight to fifteen feet across at their base, and sometimes rise a hundred feet without a single cross branch. When so great an elevation as the plains of Quito, however, which is nine thousand five hundred and fifteen above the sea, is reached, they become less considerable, and not larger than those usually found in the forests of Europe. If the traveller ascends 2000 feet higher, to an elevation of eleven or twelve thousand feet, trees almost entirely disappear; but the frequent humidity nourishes a thick covering of arbutus and other evergreens, shrubs three or four feet high, covered with flowers generally of a bright yellow, which form a striking contrast to the dark evergreen foliage with which they are surrounded. Still higher, at the height of thirteen thousand feet, near the summit of the lower ranges of the Cordilleras, almost constant rains overspread the earth with a verdant and slippery coating of moss; amidst which a few stunted specimens of the melastoma still exhibit their purple blossoms. A broad zone succeeds, covered entirely with Alpine plants, which, as in the mountains of Switzerland, nestle in the crevices of rocks, or push their flowers, generally of yellow or dark blue, through the now frequent snow. Higher still, grass alone is to be met with, mixed with the grey moss which conducts the wearied traveller to the region of perpetual snow, which in those warm latitudes is general only at an elevation of fifteen thousand feet. Above that level no animated being is found, except the huge condor, the largest bird that exists, which there, amidst ice and clouds, has fixed its gloomy abode."—(*Tableau de la Nature dans les Regions Equatoriales*, 59, 140–144.)

In the rhythm of prose these are the colours of poetry; but it is of poetry chastened and directed by the observation of reality, and possessing the inimitable charm of being drawn from real life, and sharing the freshness and variety which characterize the works of nature, and distinguish them from the brightest conceptions of human fancy. As we have set out in this article with placing Humboldt at the head of modern travellers, and much above any that Great Britain has produced, and assigned as the main reason of this superiority the exclusive and limited range of objects on which the attention of our youth is fixed at our great universities, we shall, in justice to Oxford and Cambridge, present the reader with a specimen of the finest passages, from Clarke and Bishop Heber, that he may judge for himself on their merit, great as it often is, when compared with that of the ardent and yet learned German.

Clarke, on leaving Greece, gives the following brilliant summary of the leading features of that classic land :—

"The last moments of this day were employed in taking one more view of the superb scenery exhibited by the mountains Olympus and Ossa. They appeared upon this occasion in more than usual splendour; like one of those imaginary Alpine regions suggested by viewing a boundary of clouds when they terminate the horizon in a still evening, and are gathered into heaps, with many a towering top shining in fleecy whiteness. The great Olympian chain forms a line which is exactly opposite to Salonica; and even the chasm between Olympus and Ossa, constituting the defile of Tempe, is here visible. Directing the eye towards that chain, there is comprehended in one view the whole of Pieria and Bottiæa; and with the vivid impressions which remain after leaving the country, memory easily recalled to one mental picture the whole of Greece. Every reader may not duly comprehend what is meant by this: but every traveller who has beheld the scenes to which allusion is made, will readily admit its truth; he will be aware that, whenever his thoughts were directed to that country, the whole of it recurred to his imagination, as if he were actually indulged with a view of it.

"In such an imaginary flight he enters, for example, the defile of Tempe; and as the gorge opens to the south, he beholds

all the Larissian plain. This conducts
him to the fields of Pharsalia, whence
he ascends the mountains south of Phar-
salus; then, crossing the bleak and still
more elevated region extending from
these mountains towards Lamia, he
views Mount Pindus far before him, and
descending into the plain of the Sper-
chius, passes the straits of Thermopylæ.
Afterwards, ascending Mount Œna, he
beholds opposite to him the snowy point
of Lycorea, with the rest of Parnassus,
and the villages and towns lying at its
base: the whole plain of Elataia lying
at his feet, with the course of the Ce-
phissus to the sea   Passing to the summit of Parnassus, he looks down upon
all the other mountains, plains, islands,
and gulfs of Greece; but especially sur-
veys the broad bosom of Cithæron, Heli-
con, and Hymettus. Thence, roaming
into the depths and over all the heights
of Eubœa and Peloponnesus, he has
their inmost recesses again submitted to
his contemplation. Next, resting upon
Hymettus, he examines, even in the
minutest detail, the whole of Attica, to
the Sunian promontory; for he sees it
all—and all the shores of Argos, Sicyon,
Corinth, Megara, Eleusis, and Athens.
Thus, although not in all the freshness
of its living colours, yet in all its grandeur, doth GREECE actually present itself to the mind's eye—and may the impression never be obliterated! In the
eve of bidding it farewell for ever, as
the hope of visiting this delightful country constituted the earliest and warmest
wish of his youth, the author found it
to be some alleviation of his regret excited by a consciousness of never returning, that he could thus summon to his
recollection the scenes over which he
had passed."—(*Clarke's Travels*, Vol.
vii., pp. 476–478.)

So far Clarke—the accomplished
and famed traveller of Cambridge.
We now give a favourable specimen
of Bishop Heber—his companion in
traversing Russia—the celebrated author, in early life at Oxford, of *Pales-
tine*, the amiable and upright Bishop of
Calcutta, whose life, if ever that could
be said of mortal, was literally spent
in doing good. This accomplished and
excellent prelate thus describes the
first view of the Himalaya range and
the summits of Nundidevi, the highest
mountain in the world, nearly 5000 feet
above the loftiest peak of Chimborazo.

"After coasting the lake for a mile,
we ascended for thirteen more by a most
steep and rugged road over the neck of
Mount Gaughur, through a succession
of glens, forests, and views of the most
sublime and beautiful description. I
never saw such prospects before, and
had formed no adequate idea of such.
My attention was completely strained,
and my eyes filled with tears; everything around was so wild and magnificent that man appeared as nothing, and
I felt myself as if climbing the steps of
the altar of the great temple of God.
The trees, as we advanced, were in a
large proportion fir and cedar; but many
were ilex, and to my surprise I still saw,
even in these wild Alpine tracts, many
venerable Peepul trees, on which the
white monkeys were playing their gam-
bols. Tigers used to be very common
and mischievous; but since the English
have begun to frequent the country,
they have become very scarce. There
are many wolves and bears, and some
chamois, two of which passed near us.
After wending up

" A wild romantic chasm, that slanted
    Down the steep hill athwart a cedar
      cover—
A savage place, as holy and enchanted
As e'er beneath the waning moon was
      haunted
    By woman's wailing for her demon
      lover,"

we arrived at the gorge of the Pass,
in an indent between the two principal
summits of Mount Gaughur, near 8600
feet above the sea. And now the snowy
mountains, which had been so long
eclipsed, opened upon us in full magnificence. To describe a view of this kind
is only lost labour: and I found it nearly as impossible to make a sketch of it.
Nundidevi was immediately opposite,
Kedar Nath was not visible, but Marvo
was visible as a distant peak. The eastern mountains, for whom I could procure no name, rose into great consequence, and were very glorious objects
as we wound down the hill on the other
side. The guides could only tell us they
were a great way off, and on the borders
of the Chinese empire. Nundidevi, the
highest peak in the world, is 25,689 feet
above the sea, 4000 higher than Chimborazo. Bhadinath and Kedernath,
which are merely summits of it, are
22,300 feet high. They are all in the
British dominions."—(*Heber's India,*
Vol. ii., pp. 193-194, 209.)

On comparing the descriptions of

the most interesting objects in Europe and Asia—Greece and the Himalaya range — by these two distinguished British travellers, with the pictures given by Humboldt of the Andes, the falls of the Orinoco, the forests of the same river, and the expanse of the Pampas in South America, every one must admit the great superiority of the German's powers of painting Nature. Neither Clarke nor Heber appear to attempt it. They tell you, indeed, that certain scenes were grand and beautiful, certain rocks wild, certain glens steep; but they make no attempt to portray their features, or convey to the reader's mind the pictures which they tell you are for ever engraven on their own. This is a very great defect, so great indeed that it will probably prevent their works, how valuable soever as books of authority or reference, from ever acquiring lasting fame. It is a total mistake to say that it is in vain to attempt describing such scenes; that is the same mistake as was formerly committed by pacific academical historians, who said it was useless to attempt painting a battle, for they were all like each other. How like they really are to each other, has been shown by Colonel Napier, and many other modern historians. We question if even the sight of the rapids of the Orinoco would make so vivid an impression on the imagination, as Humboldt's inimitable description; or a journey over the Pampas or the Andes, convey a clearer or more distinct idea of their opposite features than what has been derived from his brilliant pencil. It is the same with all the other scenes in nature. Description, if done by a masterly hand, can, to an intelligent mind, convey as vivid an idea as reality. What is wanting is the enthusiasm which warms at the perception of the sublime and the beautiful, the poetic mind which seizes as by inspiration its characteristic features, and the pictorial eye which discerns the appearances they exhibit, and by referring to images known to all, succeeds in causing them to be generally felt by the readers.

With all Humboldt's great and transcendent merits, he is a child of Adam, and therefore not without his faults. The principal of these is the want of arrangement. His travels are put together without any proper method; there is a great want of indexes and tables of contents; it is scarcely possible, except by looking over the whole, to find any passage you want. This is a fault which, in a person of his accurate and scientific mind, is very surprising, and the more inexcusable that it could so easily be remedied by mechanical industry, or the aid of compilers and index-makers. But akin to this, is another fault of a more irremediable kind, as it originates in the varied excellence of the author, and the vast store of information on many different subjects which he brings to bear on the subject of his travels. He has so many topics of which he is master himself, that he forgets with how few, comparatively, his readers are familiar; he sees so many objects of inquiry—physical, moral, and political—in the countries which he visits, that he becomes insensible to the fact, that though each probably possesses a certain degree of interest to each reader, yet it is scarcely possible to find one to whom, as to himself, they are *all alike* the object of eager solicitude and anxious investigation. Hence, notwithstanding his attempt to detach his personal narrative from the learned works which contain the result of his scientific researches, he has by no means succeeded in effecting their separation. The ordinary reader, who has been fascinated by his glowing description of tropical scenery, or his graphic picture of savage manners, is, a few pages on, chilled by disquisitions on the height of the barometer, the disk of the sun, or the electricity of the atmosphere; while the scientific student, who turns to his works for information on his favourite objects of study, deems them strangely interspersed with rhapsodies on glowing sunsets, silent forests, and sounding cataracts. It is scarcely possible to find a reader to whom all these objects are equally interesting; and therefore it is scarcely to be expected that his travels, unrivalled as their genius and learning are, will ever be the object of general popularity.

In truth, here, as in all the other branches of human thought, it will be found that the rules of composition are the same, and that a certain *unity of design* is essential to general success or durable fame. If an author has many different and opposite subjects of interest in his head, which is not unfrequently the case with persons of the higher order of intellect, and he can descant on all with equal facility, or investigate all with equal eagerness, he will do well to recollect that the minds of his readers are not likely to be equally discursive, and that he is apt to destroy the influence, or mar the effect of each, if he blends them together; separation of works is the one thing needful there. A mathematical proposition, a passage of poetry, a page of history, are all admirable things in their way, and each may be part of a work destined to durable celebrity; but what should we say to a composition which should present us, page about, with a theorem of Euclid, a scene from Shakspeare, and a section from Gibbon? Unity of effect, identity of train of thought, similarity of ideas, are as necessary in a book of travels as in an epic poem, a tragedy, or a painting. There is no such thing as one set of rules for the fine arts, and another for works of thought or reflection. The *Iliad* is constructed on the same principles as the *Principia* of Newton, or the history of Thucydides.

What makes ordinary books of travels so uninteresting, and, in general, so shortlived, is the want of any idea of composition, or unity of effect, in the minds of their authors. Men and women seem to think that there is nothing more to do to make a book of travels, than to give a transcript of their journals, in which everything is put down of *whatever* importance, provided only it really occurred. Scenes and adventures, broken wheels and rugged rocks, cataracts and omelets, lakes and damp beds, thunderstorms and waiters, are huddled together, without any other thread of connection than the accidental and fortuitous one of their having successively come under the notice of the traveller. What should we say to any other work composed on the same principle? What if Milton, after the speech of Satan in *Paradise Lost*, were to treat us to an account of his last dinner; or Shakspeare, after the scene of the bones in Juliet, were to tell us of the damp sheets in which he slept last night; or Gibbon, after working up the enthusiasm of his readers by the account of the storming of Constantinople by the Crusaders, was to favour us with a digression on the insolence of the postilions in Roumelia? All the world would see the folly of this: and yet this is precisely what is constantly done by travellers, and tolerated by the public, because it is founded on nature. Founded on nature! Is everything that is actually true, or real, fit to be recorded, or worthy of being recounted? Sketches from nature are admirable things, and are the only foundation for correct and lasting pictures; but no man would think of interposing a gallery of paintings with chalk drawings or studies of trees. Correctness, fidelity, truth, are the only secure bases of eminence in all the arts of imitation; but the light of genius, the skilful arrangement, the principles of composition, the selection of topics, are as necessary in the writer of travels, as in the landscape painter, the historian, or the epic poet.

HAKEM THE SLAVE.

A Tale extracted from the History of Poland.

Chapter I.

ALBERT GLINSKI, the powerful, ostentatious, and intriguing Duke of Lithuania, was passing, distinguished by his glancing plume and gorgeous mantle, through one of the more retired streets of the city of Cracow, at this time (A.D. 1530) the capital of Poland, when a domestic wearing the livery of the palace deferentially accosted him.

"Her Majesty," he said, "commands me to deliver these tablets into your hands ; you dropped them in the palace."

"I dropped no tablets," replied the duke ; but instantly added, "Yes, they are mine—Give them me."

He took from the hands of the domestic certain tablets of ivory, which folded into a case of gold exquisitely wrought by one of the most skilful artists of Italy, and dismissed the bearer with a liberal gratuity for his services.

"Ha! my excellent Bona! youthful bride of our too aged monarch Sigismund!" said the duke to himself when he was left alone. "Each day some new device. What have we in these tablets? Here, in the corner of each leaf, I see a solitary figure finely pencilled in, which to any other eye than mine would mean nothing, but which tells me that at eight o'clock this evening you will receive your favoured duke. So, so! But, charming Bona! it is not love—loveable as you are—it is not love—it is ambition gives its zest, and must bring the recompense to this perilous intrigue. The Duke of Lithuania is no hot-brained youth to be entangled and destroyed by a woman's smiles. To have a month's *happiness*, as men phrase it, and then the midnight dagger of a jealous monarch—I seek no such adventures. It is the crown of Poland—yes, the crown—that you must help me to, fair lady."

As he stood reflecting on his ambitious schemes, his rival in the state, Count Laski, minister and chancellor of the king, passed by him on his way to the palace. The duke, assuming a frank and cordial manner, called to him. Laski paused. "What would the Duke of Lithuania?" he asked in his usual calm and reserved manner.

"Peace!" replied the duke—"amicable terms. Political opponents it seems we are destined to be. The world gives us out as the selected champions of two hostile factions. You affect the commons, I side with the nobility. Be it so. But there exists, between us, I hope, a mutual respect ; and it would be my greatest boast if, in spite of this political antagonism, I might reckon Count Laski amongst my personal friends."

A derisive smile played upon the countenance of the chancellor as he replied—"Such friendship, my lord, as is consistent with perpetual strife —open and concealed—shall, if it please you, subsist between us. Pardon me, but we prate a silly jargon when we talk of private friendship and public hostility."

"At all events," rejoined the duke, "political rivalry does not exclude the practice of the courtesies of life. It has been reported to me that you admire the marble statue of a nymph which an Italian sculptor has lately wrought for me. I, on my part, have envied you the possession of a certain Arab slave, a living statue, a moving bronze, that you have amongst your retainers. Let us, like Homeric heroes, make an exchange. Give me your statue-man, your swart Apollo, and accept from me what many have been pleased to call the living statue."

Glinski had a secret motive for the acquisition of this slave : his known fidelity, his surprising address and power, had protected the life of the minister against more than one scheme of assassination.

"The exchange," replied Laski, "is too much in my favour. Your Italian marble would purchase a hundred slaves. It would be a present in disguise ; and you know my rule—

even from his Majesty himself I never *receive*."

"Yes, we know your tyrannous munificence; but this," said the duke with a smile, "shall be pure barter."

"What say you, then," said the count, "to these golden tablets which you hold in your hand? Give me leave to look at them. They might suit my pedantic way of life. But," added he, as he examined their delicate workmanship, "come you honestly by this toy, my lord? What fair frailty have you cheated of this knack, that never, I will be sworn, was a man's marketing?"

"1 am glad to hear so grave a gentleman indulge so pleasant a view," said the duke.

As Count Laski was handling the tables, he touched, whether by accident or design, a spring that had not been observed by him to whom the present had been sent. The outer case flew back, and disclosed a miniature of the queen!

"I have been indiscreet," said the count, and immediately folded up and returned the tablets. "This is perilous ware to deal in, Duke of Lithuania. Have you aught else in the way of honest barter to propose?"

"What you may infer," said the duke, reddening with anger, and grievously embarrassed at his discovery— "What you may infer from this silly bauble I shall not be at the pains to inquire. I addressed you, my lord, in courteous and amicable terms; you have ill responded to them; our conversation had better close here."

"As you will," said the chancellor, bowing; and he continued his way towards the palace, with the same deliberate step with which he was proceeding when accosted by the duke.

"He is master of our secret," muttered the duke. "He or I"—

CHAPTER II.

In an apartment of the palace fitted up with every luxury her native Italy could supply, sat Bona, the young and beautiful queen of Poland. She is known to have transplanted into that northern clime, not only the arts and civilisation of her own genial soil, but also the intrigue and voluptuousness, and the still darker crimes for which it was celebrated. Daughter of the crafty Sforza, Duke of Milan, educated in a city and at a court where pleasure reigned predominant, married out of policy to a monarch many years older than her own father, it was almost to be expected that she should seek, in the society of some gay cavalier, a compensation for this banishment to a northern country, and a sexagenarian spouse. Nor had she hesitated long in her choice. Albert Glinski, Duke of Lithuania, who, though he was the father of a son ripening into manhood, was still in the vigour of life, and surpassed all his younger rivals in grace of manner and charm of conversation, had soon fixed her regard, and won whatever of affection or love the luxurious princess had to bestow.

She now sat waiting his arrival. Punctually at the hour of eight he entered. If any observer could have watched the duke as he traversed the corridor which led to the queen's apartment, he would have had great difficulty in believing that it was a favoured lover that was passing before him; so serious a brow did he wear, and so deep an air of abstraction was there on his countenance. No sooner, however, did he enter that apartment, than, by a sudden effort, his countenance lit up; his manner grew free and unrestrained, and he assumed that mingled tone of gaiety and pathos so effective with the fair sex. Never had the queen felt more entirely convinced of the merits of her cavalier; never had she more thoroughly approved of the choice she had made.

When this favourable disposition was at its height, the duke, adopting gradually a more serious tone of conversation, said—

"Has it never occurred to you, charming Bona, that the most exalted of your sex share with the humblest this one privilege—love alone must be the motive which brings a suitor to their feet. That passion must be genuine, must be fever high, which makes a subject quite forget his queen in the lovely woman before him, and tempts him to dare the vengeance of a Monarch, as well as of a husband."

"True, there is danger—perhaps to both of us," she replied, "but it daunts us not."

"No;—but it is at hand."

"What mean you, Glinski?"

"We are betrayed."

"How?—by whom?"

"How, or by whom, it matters little; but that subtle demon, Count Laski, knows that which in his hands is a warrant for our destruction."

"What is to be done? We will bribe him. All my jewels, all my hoards shall go to purchase his silence.'

"Bribe Laski! bribe the north wind! bribe destiny itself, whose nature it is to distribute good and ill, but to feel neither. No, but I would have a dagger in his throat before the night were passed, but that his short light slumbers are guarded by a slave of singular power, whom the villains fear to attack. I had meant to beg or buy of him this same fierce automaton, but something broke off the treaty."

"We will poison the mind of the king against him: he shall be dismissed from all his offices."

"That poison is too slow. Besides, if he once communicate his suspicions to the king—which at this very moment he may be doing—see you not, that it is no longer the minister, but the jealous monarch that we have to guard against. Hear me, Bona, one of two fates must now be mine. Death —or thy hand, and with it the crown of Poland. Do not start. There is for *me* no middle station. You may be safe. A few tears, a few smiles, and the old king will lapse into his dotage."

"You speak in riddles, Glinski; I comprehend nothing of all this."

"Yet it is clear enough. Thus it stands: the Duke of Lithuania loved the wife of Sigismund, king of Poland. Love!—I call to witness all the saints in heaven!—love alone prompted his daring suit. But now that fortune has first favoured and then betrayed him, where think you does his safety lie? Where, but in the bold enterprises of ambition? His only place of refuge is a throne. He who has won a queen must protect her with a sceptre. You must be mine—my very queen—you must extend your hand and raise me to the royalty of

Poland, or see my blood flow ignominiously upon the scaffold."

"I extend my hand!" exclaimed the agitated queen, "how can a feeble woman give or take away the crown of Poland?"

"Him who wears the crown—she can take away."

"Murder the king!" shrieked Bona.

"Or sentence me," replied the duke.

It was no affected horror that the queen here displayed. Though at a subsequent period of her life, if history speaks true, her imagination had grown familiar with deeds of this very nature, and she had become skilful in the art of poisoning, she was at this time young, and unpractised in crime, and received its first suggestions with the horror which it naturally inspires. She had sought for pleasure only in the society of Glinski; it was a cruel disappointment, it was a frightful surprise, to find herself thrust suddenly, with unsandaled feet, on the thorny path of ambition. She sank back on the couch where they had both been sitting, and, hiding her face in both her hands, remained in that position while the duke continued to unfold his schemes at greater length.

He represented to her that the possession of the duchy of Lithuania, the inhabitants of which were distinguished by their bravery and their turbulence, would enable him—should the king opportunely die—to seize upon the vacant throne of Poland;— that he had numerous and powerful friends among the nobility;—that he had already drawn together his Lithuanians, under pretence of protecting the frontier from the incursion of predatory bands;—that he intended immediately to place himself at their head, and march towards Cracow. Now, if at this moment the throne should suddenly become vacant, what power on earth could prevent him from ascending it, and claiming the hand of his then veritable queen? And then he expatiated on the happiness they should enjoy, when they should live in fearless union,

"Like gods together, careless of mankind."

"What is this," exclaimed Bona, suddenly starting up—"what is this you would tempt me to? You dare not even *name* the horrid deed you would have me *commit.* Avaunt! you are a devil, Albert Glinski!—you would drag me to perdition." Then, falling in tears upon his neck, she implored him not to tempt her further. "Oh, Albert! Albert!" she cried, "I beseech you, plunge me not into this pit of guilt. You *can!* I feel you can. Have mercy! I implore you, I charge you on your soul, convert me not into this demon. Spare me this crime!"

"Is it I alone," said the duke, who strove the while by his caresses to soothe and pacify her—"Is it I alone who have brought down upon us this distressful alternative? Neither of us, while love decoyed us on step by step, dreamed of the terrible necessity towards which it was hourly conducting us. But here we *are*—half-way up, and the precipice below. We must rush still upwards. There is safety only on the summit. Pause, and we fall. Oh, did you think that you, a queen, could play as securely as some burgher's wife the pleasant comedy of an amorous intrigue? No, no; you must queen it even in crime. High station and bold deed become each other. We are committed, Bona. It is choice of life or death. His death or *ours.* For—scarcely dare I breathe the thought—the sudden revenge of your monarch husband, whose jealousy, at least, age has not tamed, *may* execute its purpose before his dotage has had time to return."

"Where do you lead me? What shall I become?" cried the bewildered queen. "I have loved thee, Albert, but I hate not him."

"I ask thee not to *hate*"——

"They married me to Sigismund out of state policy. You I have chosen for the partner of my heart, and I will protect you to the uttermost. Let things rest there—'tis well enough."

"We will consult further of our plans, sweet Bona," said the duke, and, circling her with his arm, he led the weeping queen into an adjoining room. The victory, he felt, was his.

Chapter III.

The scene changes to an apartment of a very different style. We enter the house of the chancellor; but it is not the chancellor himself who is first presented to our view. In an antique Gothic chamber, in the decoration and structure of which the most costly material had been studiously united with the severest simplicity of taste, sat Maria, the only daughter and child of Count Laski. She sat at her embroidery. The embroidery, however, had fallen upon her lap: she leaned back, resigned to her meditations, in a massive arm-chair covered with purple velvet, which it is impossible not to think must have felt something like pride and pleasure as her slight and lovely form sank into it. It was a long reverie.

In an angle of this lofty room, at some distance, but not out of the range of clear vision, stood, motionless as a statue, the slave Hakem. His arms were folded on his breast, his eye rested, without, as it seemed, a power to withdraw it, on the beautiful figure of the young girl before him. It was one of those long intense looks which show that the person on whom it is fixed is still more the object of meditation than of vision—where it is the soul that looks. Hakem gazed like a devotee upon the sacred image of his saint.

Maria, quite unconscious of this gaze, pursued her meditations. Her eye caught the hour-glass that stood on a small table beside her. "Sand after sand," said she, musing to herself—"Sand after sand, thought after thought. The same sand ever trickling there; the same thought ever coursing through my mind. Oh, love! love! They say it enlarges the heart; I think it contracts it to a single point."

"Hakem," she said, after a pause, and turning towards the slave, "you are true to my father, will you be true also to me?"

"To her father!" he murmured to himself, "as if"——And then, checking himself and speaking aloud, he answered—"The Christians are not so true to your sweet namesake, the Holy Virgin, whom they adore, as I will be to you."

"A simple promise will suffice," said Maria. "You have, Hakem— let me say it without offence—a style of language—Eastern I suppose— hyperbolical—which either I must learn to pardon, or you must labour to reform. It does not suit our northern clime."

"I am mute. Yet, lady, you have sometimes chid me for my long silence."

"And is it for your *much* speaking that I chide you now?" said the maiden, with a smile. "You will stand half the day like a statue there; and, when spoken to, answer with a gesture only—so that many have thought you really dumb. Much speaking is certainly not thy fault."

"I understand. The slave speaks as one who felt the indescribable charm of thy presence. It is a presumption worthy of death. Shall I inflict the punishment?"

"Is this amendment of thy fault, good Hakem, or repetition of it?"

"I await your commands. What service can Hakem render?"

But Maria relapsed again into silence. She seemed to hesitate in making the communication she had designed. Meantime, the arrival of her father was announced, and the slave left the apartment.

Never man felt more tender love for his daughter than did the proud, high-minded minister for this his beautiful Maria. His demeanour towards her, from childhood upwards, had been one of unalterable, uninterrupted fondness. He knew no other mood, no other tone, in which he could have addressed her. Did the grave chancellor, then—some one, who in his way, also, is very grave, may ask—did he, by constant fondness, *spoil* his child? No. It is the fondness which is *not* constant that spoils. It is the half-love of weak and irritable natures, who are themselves children amongst their children, who can themselves be petulant, selfish, and capricious—it is this that mars a temper. But calm and unalterable love—oh, believe it not that such ever spoilt a child! Maria grew up under the eye of affection, and the ever-open hand of paternal love; and she herself seemed to have learned no other impulses but those of affection and generosity.

Alas for fathers! when the child grows into the budding woman, and by her soft, intelligent companionship fills the house with gladness, and the heart with inappreciable content, then comes the gay, permitted spoiler— comes the lover with his suit—his honourable suit—and robs them of their treasure. The world feels only with the lover—with the youth, and the fair maiden that he wins. For the bereaved parent, not a thought! No one heeds the sigh that breaks from him, as, amidst festivities and mirth, and congratulatory acclamations, he sees his daughter, with all her prized affections, borne off from him, in triumph, for ever.

There was, on this occasion, in the manner of Laski towards his child, an evident sadness. It was not that the political horizon was darkening; he had never permitted *that* to throw its gloom over his companionship with his daughter. It was because he had grounds to believe that the events which threatened the tranquillity of Poland threatened also the peace of his daughter, whose affections he had divined were no longer exclusively his own.

She, observing his emotion, and attributing it to some untoward event in the political world, could not refrain from expressing the wish that he would quit the harassing affairs of state, and live wholly in his home.

"I would long since have done so," he replied, "if personal happiness had been the sole aim of my existence. But I have a taskwork to accomplish —one, I think, which God, by fitting me thereto, has pointed out as mine. Else it is indeed here, with thee beside me, that I find all that can bear the name of happiness. The rest of life is but sternest duty—strife, hostility, contempt. But away with this gloomy talk—what gossip is there stirring in your idle world, Maria?"

"Pray, is there war forward?"

"I hope not. Why do you ask?"

"A maid of mine, who in the city gathers news as busily as bees, in the open fields, their honey"——

"Your simile, I fear, would scarce hold good, as to the *honey*."

"No, in faith; and there is no honey in the news she brings. She tells me that a camp is forming in the frontiers between Poland and Lithuania, and that Augustus Glinski is sent there to command the troops. Is this true?"

"It is; and she might have added that the duke himself secretly left the city last night, to place himself at their head."

"Is it a dangerous service?"

"The service on which the duke has entered, and into which he misleads his son, *is* dangerous. You tremble, Maria. It was no maiden, nor the tattle of the town, that brought you this. When did you last see or hear from him—from Augustus Glinski?"

"Believe me," said Maria, while a crimson blush suddenly spread over her countenance, "if I have concealed anything from you, it was not from craft, nor subtlety, nor fear, but from"——

"From a mere delicacy, a simple bashfulness," said the father, coming to her assistance. "I know it well. Had you a mother living, I would bid you confide these sentiments of your heart to her, and to her only; but, having no other parent, make me your confidant. Trust me, you shall not find a woman's heart more open to your griefs, your fears, your joys, than mine shall be. Make me your sole confidant—you love this young Augustus?"

"When I was at my aunt's we met each other often—but to you, my father, I have ever referred him as our final arbiter. I need not say that the known political rivalry between his father and yourself has made him backward in addressing you."

"All men speak well of Augustus Glinski. I blame you not, my child; I only tremble for you. The duke, his father, is a restless, bold, ambitious man, who will lead him—honourable as he is, but too young to judge, or to resist his parent—into treasonable enterprises. Both father and son—if they will play the rebel, and bring down war on Poland—I stand prepared to meet. The sword of justice shall sweep them from the earth. But if thy heart, my child, is doomed to bleed in this encounter, the wound will not be more, yours than mine. There shall be no secrets between us. I will protect thee all I can; and if I cannot prevent thy sorrows, I will at least share them."

A low tap was here heard at the door, and a page made his appearance. On seeing the minister, the stripling was about to retire. Maria, however, called him in, and bade him deliver his message. "You come," she said to the youth, who still hesitated to speak—"you come from the younger Glinski: speak openly—what is it he has commissioned you to say?"

"This, my lady," answered the page, "that he has ridden in all haste from the camp—that he must quit the city again before nightfall, and craves an audience if only for one minute."

Maria looked towards her father, and thus referred the answer to him.

Count Laski was silent.

"Will you not," said his daughter, "tell this messenger, whether his master may come here or not?"

"My child, he *cannot!* he is at this moment under my arrest. Return, sir page," and he motioned him from the room—"but return to the fortress of —— ; you will find your master there a prisoner, under charge of high treason."

"Oh, spare him! spare him!" cried Maria, as she sank back almost senseless with terror and alarm.

"My child! my child!" exclaimed the minister in heart-breaking anguish, as he bent over his weeping daughter.

CHAPTER IV.

After having in some measure soothed the terrors of his daughter, the chancellor called to him his trusty Hakem. He briefly explained to him that the Duke of Lithuania was at that moment in open rebellion against his majesty, and placed in his hands a warrant for his execution. "The law cannot reach him through its usual servants," he said; "it is a bold enterprise I propose to you—to decapitate a general at the head of his troops."

If this was a measure which hardly another minister than Laski would have contemplated, it was one also which he would have hardly found another than Hakem to undertake and accomplish. The bravery of this man was all but miraculous, and was only rescued from madness by the extreme skill and address by which it was supported. In battle, he rushed on danger as a bold and delighted swimmer plunges in the waves, which to him are as innocuous as the breeze that is freshening them. Yet, when the excitement was passed, he relapsed into a state of apparent apathy. He had been taken captive in one of those engagements, at this time not unfrequent, between the Poles and the Turks, with the latter of whom he had served as a soldier of fortune. To say that he was taken prisoner, is hardly correct; for he was found lying half dead on the field of battle, and was brought home by the Poles, by some caprice of compassion, with their own sick and dying. Neither was it constraint that held him beneath the roof of Laski, or in the nominal condition of a slave, for at all times escape would have been easy to him. It was either attachment to those who lived beneath that roof, or an equal indifference to everything without or beyond it, that retained him there.

To propose to Hakem some bold and perilous enterprise, was to offer him one of the few pleasures to which he was open. He accepted, therefore, of the strange commission now entrusted to him without hesitation; stipulating, only, that he might take from the stables of the king a horse which was much celebrated for its amazing power and fleetness.

Mounted upon this incomparable steed, he pursued his way to the camp of the Duke of Lithuania. On his journey he had made trial of its speed, and yet had husbanded its strength. Arrived at the plain where the insurgent army was encamped, he there lay in ambush for some time, till he saw where the duke, passing his troops in review, rode somewhat in advance of what in the language of modern warfare we should call his staff. Hakem set spurs to his horse, and rushed upon him with the velocity of lightning, his drawn cimeter flashing in the sun, and his loud cry of defiance calling the duke to his defence. Thus challenged, he put his lance in rest to meet his furious assailant. But the thrust of the lance was avoided, and the next moment the head of the duke was seen to roll upon the field. The Arab wheeled round, and, without quitting his steed, picked up the severed head, placed it on his saddle-bows, and darted off fleeter than the wind. A cry of horror and a shout of pursuit arose from the whole army, who were spectators of this scene. Every horse was in motion. But where the contest is one of speed, of what avail are numbers? In the whole camp there was not a steed which could compete with that on which the solitary fugitive was mounted, and was already seen scouring the plain at a distance. As he fled, a paper was observed to fall from his hands, which the wind bore amongst his innumerable pursuers; it was the judicial warrant that had been thus strangely executed.

Meanwhile, at the palace, the royal mind of Sigismund was not a little disquieted and alarmed by this sudden rebellion of the powerful Duke of Lithuania. That alarm would not have been diminished had he been aware that this open rebellion was to be aided by a secret domestic treason, which, in his own palace, was lying in ambush for his life. The queen, whilst watching her opportunity to perform her part in this criminal enterprise, affected to throw all the blame of this formidable rebellion on the unpopularity of the minister Laski, whose measures, indeed, the duke proclaimed as the main motive of his conduct.

Matters were in this condition when Count Laski, attended by his slave, entered the royal apartment. There were present, beside the queen, several of the nobility—all prepared, by the insinuations and address of the queen, to give but a cold greeting to the minister.

"In good time," said the queen, "Count Laski makes his appearance. We wish to know how you will extricate his Majesty from the peril in which your unpopular counsels have thrust him. With what forces will you meet the Duke of Lithuania? Now, when there is need of the brave chivalry of Poland to defend the king from rebellion, we find the nobility alienated from the crown by your unwise, and arrogant, and plebeian policy. But let us hear what is the excellent advice, what is the good intelligence, that you now bring us?"

"The Duke of Lithuania, madam," said the chancellor, slightly raising his voice, but preserving the same calm dignity as if he had been presiding in a high court of justice—"the Duke of Lithuania is in open, manifest rebellion; and rebellion is, in the laws of all nations, punished by death."

"Punished!" said the queen scoffingly: "are you speaking of some trembling caitiff who holds up his naked hand at your bar of justice? Punished! you must conquer him."

"Your Majesty will be pleased to hear," continued the chancellor with a look full of significance, "that Albert Glinski, Duke of Lithuania, whose treason was open and proclaimed, has been by the royal warrant sentenced"——

Count Laski paused.

"Sentenced!" exclaimed Bona, and repeated her scornful laugh, which this time but ill concealed a certain vague terror that was rising in her mind. "Is our chancellor mad, or does he sport with us? This rebel, whom you talk of sentencing—of condemning, we presume, to the block—stands at the head of a greater army than his Majesty can at this moment assemble."

"And the sentence," pursued the minister, "has been executed!"

As he pronounced these words, the slave Hakem advanced, and drawing aside his robe, which had hitherto concealed it, he held up by the hair the severed head of the Duke of Lithuania.

There ran a thrill of horror through the assembly. But, the next moment, a loud hysterical shriek drew the attention of all parties to the queen: she had fallen insensible at the feet of the king. The council was abruptly dismissed.

CHAPTER V.

Thus far the cause of the chancellor had prospered. Poland had been preserved from the horrors of a civil war. The king's life had also been saved, and a great crime prevented; the career of assassination and of poisoning, into which the queen afterwards entered, was at all events postponed. As a public man, the minister was fully triumphant. But the minister was a father; at this side he was vulnerable; and fortune dealt her blow with cruel and unexpected severity.

We have seen with what stern fidelity to his ministerial duty, and at how great a peril to his daughter's happiness, the chancellor had arrested Augustus Glinski. The rebellion quelled, the author of it punished and decapitated, there seemed no just motive for holding longer in imprisonment a youth who could not be accused of having any guilty participation in the crime of his father. He accordingly proposed his release. But the anger of the king against the late duke, who to his political offence had added that of personal ingratitude (for it was Sigismund himself who had bestowed on him the powerful duchy of Lithuania), was still unappeased, and he

insisted upon including the son in the guilt and punishment of his parent. The representations of the minister were here unavailing; he would listen to nothing but the dictates of his own vindictive feelings.

Count Laski detailed the manner of his arrest, and explained the singular interest he felt in the pardon and liberation of this youth; adding, that if Augustus Glinski died upon the scaffold, he feared the life of his daughter. But even this was unavailing. The old monarch thought he was displaying a great acuteness when he detected, as he imagined, in this plea of a daughter's happiness, a scheme of selfish aggrandizement. "Ha! ha!" said he, "so the wind sits in that quarter. A good match—duchess of Lithuania! I would rather you asked for the dukedom yourself, and married your daughter to another."

It was in vain that the minister again repeated his simple and true statement; it was in vain that he limited his request to the life of the younger Glinski, consenting to the forfeiture of his title and estates; Sigismund was resolved this time not to be *overreached* by his subtle minister. The language of entreaty was new to Laski; he had tried it, and had failed. It was new to Laski to endure tamely the misconstruction of his motives, or the least impeachment of his veracity. He had no other resource, no other response, left than the resignation of his ministerial office. But the obstinacy and anger of the king were proof against this also. The danger which threatened his reign had been dispelled. He could afford to be self-willed. He would not be controlled. In short, Count Laski left the royal presence— a discarded minister.

In a monarchy uncontrolled and unaided by representative assemblies, the power which is secured perhaps to one of the weakest of men or women, perhaps to a child, has often struck the observer of human affairs as a strange anomaly. But the insecure and precarious foundation of the power of the great minister in such a monarchy, is scarcely less curious to contemplate. The sagacious counsellor, the long-experienced governor, who has for years wielded the powers of the state, may be reduced to obscurity and impotence by a word—a word of puerile passion, kindled perhaps by a silly intrigue. A great ruler is displaced at the caprice of a dotard. When Count Laski entered the presence of the king, he was in reality the governor of Poland; Europe acknowledged him amongst the controllers and directors of human affairs; his country expected many signal improvements at his hands; the individual happiness of thousands depended upon him; but this power which had devised great schemes, and which was the rock of support to so many, could itself be shaken and overthrown in a moment, by the splenetic humour of an angry old man.

Who shall describe the grief and despair of Maria when she heard of the cruel resolution which the king had taken, of the dreadful fate which threatened Augustus Glinski? As she sat this time in her Gothic chamber, and in her accustomed chair, what a mortal paleness had settled upon her countenance! Her eye glared out, and was fixed on the vacant wall, as if a spirit had arisen before her, and arrested her regard. There *was* a spirit there. It was the form of the young Augustus, whom she saw withering and wasting in his dungeon; a dungeon which would deliver him up only to the scaffold. After the events which had occurred all idea of a union with Augustus, presuming that his life should be spared, had been resigned. How could he, on whom the maxims of that age especially imposed the duty of revenging his parent, ally himself to her? How could he choose for his second father the very man who had deprived him of his first and natural parent? If she could but hear that he had broken loose from imprisonment, that he was but safe— this was all that she felt entitled to wish or to pray for. It need hardly be added that it was additional bitterness to reflect, that but for his unhappy attachment to herself, his arrest and captivity would never have taken place.

Again, in the same angle of the apartment, the Arab slave might have been seen standing, silent and motionless as before, regarding with deep interest and commiseration the beautiful daughter of Laski. The secret which she was about, on one occasion, to betray to Hakem, had now betrayed itself to his own observation. She loved—she loved the son of him whom he had assassinated, or executed. There was a profound sadness on the features of the slave.

The silence of the room was suddenly broken by Maria, who, turning to the slave, exclaimed in a tone of anguish—"Hakem, you must save him! you must save him!" This was said in mere desperation, certainly not with any distinct hope that it was in the power of Hakem to obey. When, therefore, she heard his voice reply, in a calm but saddened tone, "I will!" she was almost as much surprised as if she had not addressed herself to him. She rose to be assured that it was he who spoke; to bid him repeat his consolatory promise; to question him on his means of fulfilling it: but Hakem was no longer there; he had suddenly quitted the apartment. It seemed as if some voice in the air had sported with her grief.

CHAPTER VI.

But it was no voice that mocked at her grief. Hakem proceeded that very day to the palace, and sought an interview with the queen. The guard or sentinel to whom he addressed himself, laughed at his request. "Give her majesty this paper," said the slave, "and refuse to deliver it at your peril."

The paper was forwarded to the queen — Hakem was immediately ushered into her presence.

"You promise here," she said, pointing to the missive she had received, "to revenge the death of the Duke of Lithuania. I presume some private motive of revenge against the minister and your master, prompts your conduct, and you seek from me an additional recompense for an act which you have already resolved on, but which you think will be grateful to me. Is it not so?"

"Your majesty is penetrating."

"And this recompense, what is it?"

"That which will cost you nothing, though you alone can accomplish it—the release and pardon of Augustus Glinski. Obtain this from the king—which to you will be easy —and with my own hand I will assassinate the assassin (for such you will doubtless deem him) of the Duke of Lithuania."

"I will not ask what are your motives in all this, nor how you have divined my wishes, but revenge the death of the Duke of Lithuania, and far more than the liberation of the young Augustus shall be your reward."

"I ask, and will accept no other. But his rescue must *first* be obtained."

The queen had no objection to urge against this condition; although she had hitherto, for reasons which may be easily surmised, avoided any appearance of interest in the fate of Augustus. She acquiesced, therefore, in Hakem's demand; surprised indeed that she should have obtained the gratification of her revenge at so slight a cost.

What the influence and the reasonings of the minister could not effect, was very speedily brought about by the blandishments of the queen. Augustus Glinski was pardoned, and restored to a portion of his father's wealth and dignities.

The warrant for the release of the prisoner was conveyed to the hand of Hakem, together with a message that he was now expected to perform his part of the engagement.

Hakem, bearing this warrant, and accompanied by one of the officers of justice, proceeded to the prison of Augustus, and having liberated him, carried him forthwith to the house of the chancellor; the young man, who as yet hardly apprehended that he was master of his own movements, permitting himself without remonstrance to be led by his new conductor.

The chancellor and his daughter sat together in the same apartment to which we have already twice introduced the reader. Had his daughter been happy, what a release for Laski had been his enfranchisement from public office! "Banishment from court!" he exclaimed to one who would have condoled with him — "make way there for a liberated prisoner!" But the grief of his daughter, who strove in vain to check her flowing tears, entirely pre-occupied his mind. These tears he never chid; her sadness he never rebuked; he shared it, and by renewed kindness strove to alleviate it. They sat in silence together, when Hakem, entering, made his obeisance, and presented Augustus to the astonished Maria.

"I have saved him!" was all he said.

The joy of Maria was extreme. It was soon, however, followed by a painful embarrassment. Amongst all parties there was a sad conflict of feeling. Augustus would have given worlds to have thrown himself at the feet of Maria; but if the memory of what had occurred had not been sufficient, there stood her father in person before him—the author of his own father's death.

Hakem broke the silence. "Beautiful being!" he said, kneeling on one knee before Maria, "whom I have in secret worshipped, whom alone to worship I have lingered here in the guise and office of a slave—you bade me save *him*—and I have! Is there anything further for thy happiness which the Arab can accomplish?"

"No, Hakem, and I feel already overburdened with gratitude for this service you have rendered me—*how* rendered I cannot as yet divine. There is no other service now I think that any one can render me." As she spoke, her eye had already turned to the spot where Augustus, hesitating to approach or to retreat, was still standing.

"No other service! But, by the living God, there is!" cried Hakem, starting to his feet. His countenance flushed with sudden excitement; his eye kindled with some generous sentiment. "Hear me, gentle sir," he said, addressing himself to Augustus. "Nature calls for vengeance—is it not so? Christian and Mahometan, we all resemble in this. Blood cries for blood. But the hand that slew your father—it was mine. I am the first and direct object of your resentment. Let now one victim suffice. Is the Arab too ignoble a victim? That

Arab is the preserver of your life, at what cost you may one day learn. Let this enhance the value of the sacrifice. Over my blood let peace be made between you." Turning once more, and bowing with deep emotion before Maria, he then, with a movement quick as thought, plunged a poniard in his bosom, and fell to the ground. "Go, tell the queen," he said to the officer of justice, who had stood a mute spectator of this scene—"tell her what you have witnessed; and add, that my promise has been fulfilled. And you, Augustus Glinski—will not this suffice? The assassin of the duke lies here before you. Oh, take her by the hand!" Then, looking his last towards Maria, he murmured—"And I, too—loved!" and closed his eyes in death.

The prayer of Hakem was granted. It was impossible to demand another sacrifice — impossible not to accept this as full atonement to the spirit of revenge. Over the body of Hakem, whom all lamented and admired, peace was made.

The generous object of the slave was fully accomplished. His death procured the long happiness of Maria.

THE LAY OF STARKATHER.

[THE following lines are founded on the account given by Saxo-Grammaticus (Lib. VIII.) of the guilt, penitence, and death of Starkàther, a fabulous Scandinavian hero, famous throughout the North for his bodily strength and warlike achievements, as well as for his poetical genius, of which traces are still to be found in the metrical traditions and phraseology of his country. According to the old legend, the existence of Starkàther was prolonged for three lifetimes, in each of which he was doomed to commit some act of infamy; but this fiction has not here been followed out. Oehlenschläger's drama, bearing the name of this hero, has many beauties; but deviates widely from Saxo's story of his death.]

IT was an aged man went forth with slow and tottering tread,
The frosts of many a Northland Yule lay thick upon his head;
A staff was in his outstretched hand, to lead him on his way,
And vainly rolled his faded eyes to find the light of day.

Yet in that ancient form was seen the pride of other years,
In ruined majesty and might the HERO there appears.
The awful brow, the ample breast, a shelter from the foe,
And there the massive weight of arm that dealt the deadly blow.

He stopped a passing stranger's steps, and thus his purpose told,—
"See here the twin swords by my side, and see this purse of gold;

Thy weapon choose to cope with One who should no longer live,
And by an easy slaughter earn the guerdon I would give.

" A hundred winters o'er my soul have shed their gathering gloom,
And still I seek, but seek in vain, an honourable tomb ;
With friendly enmity consent to quench this lingering breath,
And give, to crown a warrior's life, one boon—a warrior's death.

" Of matchless might and fearless soul, with powers of song sublime,
I spread afar my name and fame in every Gothic clime ;
Those godlike gifts were treasured long from blot and blemish clear,
But one dark act of fraudful guilt bedimmed my bright career.

" When Olo sat, the people's choice, in Sealand's kingly seat,
And trampled liegemen and the laws beneath his tyrant feet,
His nobles placed this glittering hoard within my yielding hand,
And bade me rid them of a rule that wide enslaved the land.

" I watched my royal victim well, I tracked his every path,
And found him with a faithless guard within the secret bath ;
Yet rather had I faced an host fast rushing to the fight,
Than the eye of that unarmed man, there gleaming bold and bright.

" The fear of my defenceless foe awhile unnerved my arm,
But thoughts of glory or of gain dispelled the better charm ;
The water reddened with his blood, I left the lifeless corse,
To meet myself a living death,—a lifetime of remorse.

" In every feud, in every fray, on every field of strife,
I since have fondly sought release from such a loathed life ;
The foremost, who suborned my crime, have perished at my feet ;
But none had heart or hand to strike the blow I longed to meet.

" Even as I am, I seek the fight, and offer as the prize
The untasted bait that bribed my soul, nor thou the boon despise ;
Else, like some worn-out beast of prey, Starkàther soon must lie,
Nor gain the bliss that Odin gives to men who nobly die."

" I know thee now," the stranger said, " I hear thy hated name,
I take thy gold, I take thy life, a forfeit to my claim ;
My father fell beneath thy hand, his image haunts me still—
But the hour of his revenge is come, and he shall drink his fill."

He seized a sword ; its sweeping edge soon laid the Hero low,
But not before his sinking arm was felt upon his foe :
" Thanks, youthful friend !" the Hero said ; " now Odin's hall is won,
Its rays already greet my soul, its raptures are begun."

MOZART.*

THE true position of the creative musical power in the scale of human genius is difficult to determine; and will be differently estimated by different minds. That it is a heavenly gift of a high order, admits of no doubt; that it exercises over men's minds a mighty, and, under due safeguards, a beneficent influence, is equally indisputable; and that its existence implies, and is closely connected with, the possession of other superior faculties, moral and intellectual, must also, we think, be clear upon reflection, though this last proposition is not so likely to be readily conceded. Yet the place which the great COMPOSER is generally allowed to occupy, in relation to the PAINTER or the POET, does not correspond either to the qualities or to the effects displayed in his art. Many would think it a disparagement to connect the names of Milton or Virgil, Raphael or Michael Angelo, with those of the greatest musical masters; and it may seem not easy to say whether this feeling is the result of injustice or accident, on the one hand; or, on the other, is founded on some deep and solid truth in the laws and elements of our nature.

The mighty magic that lies in the highest manifestations of musical composition, must command the wonder and reverence of all who understand, or even observe, its operation. The power of giving birth to innumerable forms of exquisite melody, delighting the ear and stirring every emotion of the soul, agitating us with fear or horror, animating us with ardour and enthusiasm, filling us with joy, melting us with grief, now lulling us to repose amidst the luxurious calm of earthly contentment, now borrowing wings more ethereal than the lark's, and wafting us to the gate of heaven, where its notes seem to blend undistinguishably with the songs of superior beings — this is a faculty that bears no unequivocal mark of a divine descent, and that nothing but prejudice or pride can deem of trivial or inferior rank. But when to this is added a mastery over the mysterious combinations of harmony, a spirit that can make subservient to its one object immense masses of dissimilar, and sometimes discordant, sounds; and, like the leader of a battle, can ride on the whirlwind and direct the storm, till it subdue the whole soul, taking captive all our feelings, corporeal and mental, and moulding them to its will—a power of this nature seems to equal in dignity the highest faculties of genius in any of its forms, as it undoubtedly surpasses all the others in the overwhelming and instantaneous efficacy of its agency while thus working its wonders. Fame is the triumph of the artist in the exhibition-room, dim and distant the echo which the poet receives of the public praise, compared with the unequivocal and irrepressible bursts of admiration which entrance the great composer in the crowded theatre, or even with that silent incense which is breathed in the stifled emotions of his audience in some more sacred place. The nearest approach to any such enthusiastic tribute, is that which sometimes awaits the successful tragic poet at the representation of his dramas; but, besides the lion's share of applause which the actor is apt to appropriate, what dramatic writer, in our own experience or history, has been greeted with such homage as that paid to Handel, when the king and people of England stood up in trembling awe to hear his *Hallelujah* chorus ?—that which hailed Mozart from the enraptured theatres of Prague when listening to his greatest operas ?—that which fanned into new fire the dying embers of Haydn's spirit, when the *Creation* was performed at Vienna, to delight his declining days, before an audience of 1500 of the Austrian nobility and gentry ?

The ancient poets felt the force of those emotions which musical sound produces, and shadowed out under its name the great principles of human harmony and social order. Societies were founded, cities built, and countries cultivated by Orpheus and Amphion, and men of analogous fame,

---

* *The Life of Mozart, including his Correspondence.* By EDWARD HOLMES, Author of "A Ramble among the Musicians of Germany." London: Chapman and Hall. 1845.

who wielded at will this mythic power, and made all the susceptibilities of nature "sequacious of the lyre."

In one respect the fame of the composer is less diffusible than that of the poet. He requires various mechanical means and appliances for his full success. His works must be performed in order to be felt. He cannot be read, like the poet, in the closet, or in the cottage, or on the street-stall, where the threadbare student steals from day to day, as he lingers at the spot, new draughts of delicious refreshment. Few can sit down and peruse a musical composition even for its melody; and very few, indeed, can gather from the silent notes the full effect of its splendid combinations. Yet even here the great master has analogous compensations. The idle amateur, the boarding-school girl, the street minstrel, and the barrel-organ, reflect his more palpable beauties; and, subjecting them to the severe test of incessant reiteration, make us wonder that "custom cannot stale" the infinite variety that is shut up even in his simplest creations.

But the creative musician has an immeasurable advantage over both the painter and the poet in the absence of all local limitation to his popularity. Here, indeed, the painter is the least favoured by the nature of his art. The immediate presence of the prophet could only be felt at Mecca; the perfection of painting can only be seen at Rome. The poet has a wider range, and can be prized and appreciated wherever the language is known in which he writes. But the musician is still more highly privileged. He speaks with a tongue intelligible alike to every nation and class; he expresses himself in a universal character, which Bishop Wilkins would have died to possess; he needs no translation; he can suffer nothing by change of place; his works are equally and at once capable of being enjoyed at London and Naples, Paris and Prague, Vienna and St. Petersburg. If the enjoyment received from his powers is not everywhere equally great, it is not from the want of a medium to make them understood, but from a difference in the minds to which they are presented.

The creative art of the musician is not one of mere talent, or of a certain sensual refinement and dexterity. It involves deep systematic study, closely akin to that of the severer sciences. It has a sequence and logic of its own, and excellence in it is unattainable without good sense and strong intellect. It involves great moral and pathetic sensibility, and a ready sympathy with all the joys and sorrows of mankind. And finally, the highest branch of it is beyond the reach of any but those who are lifted up by strong feelings of reverence and devotion. Handel was a man of sincere piety, who avowed it to be the object of his compositions not merely to please men, but "to make them better."

"The character of Handel," says Mr. Hogarth, in his excellent *Musical History*, "in all its great features, was exalted and amiable. Throughout his life he had a deep sense of religion. He used to express the great delight he felt in setting to music the most sublime passages of Holy Writ; and the habitual study of the Scriptures had constant influence on his sentiments and conduct. For the last two or three years of his life, he regularly attended divine service in his parish church of St. George's, Hanover Square, where his looks and gestures indicated the fervour of his devotion. In his life he was pure and blameless."—(Vol. i., 209.)

"Haydn," in like manner (we quote from the same biographer), "was a stranger to every evil and malignant passion; and, indeed, was not much under the influence of passion of any sort. But his disposition was cheerful and gentle, and his heart was brimful of kindly affections. He was friendly and benevolent, open and candid in the expression of his sentiments, always ready to acknowledge and aid the claims of talent in his own art, and, in all his actions, distinguished by the most spotless integrity. Such is the account of him given by all those who knew him best; and they add, as the most remarkable feature of his character, that strong and deeply-rooted sense of religion, which is the only solid foundation of moral excellence. Haydn's piety was not a mere feeling, capable, as is often the case with worldly men, of being excited for the moment by circumstances, and dying away when the external influence is removed; it was an active principle, which guided the whole tenor of his life and conduct. His sacred music was exalted by the existence, in his mind, of those devout sentiments which it is the object of sacred music to express. 'When I was engaged in composing *The Creation,*' he used to say, 'I felt myself so penetrated with religious feeling, that before I sat down to write, I earnestly prayed to God that he would enable me to praise him worthily.'"—(Vol. i., 304.)

Similar feelings of strong piety, as well as of generous benevolence, animated and inspired the great and amiable man whose character is more immediately the subject of this article. It would be difficult, indeed, to think of an oratorio or requiem written by a scoffer or a sceptic.

With such exalted requisites, so intense a power,. and so extensive a range of influence, it is strange that the composer should not have taken the rank and relative dignity to which he seems entitled in the province of the arts. But honour and fame are chiefly dispensed by poets and literary men; and it is impossible not to feel that, generally speaking, the musician is treated by men of letters as an alien from their own lineage. Music may be praised in vague and evasive terms; but the individual composer is not deemed deserving of mention. All the great masters of the pencil have been cordially commended in immortal verse; but of the great composers' names scarce a notice is to be found.

It is not wonderful that the poet should prize above all others his own form of art. Poetry, as the mouthpiece of practical wisdom, as the clearest interpreter of all instruction, must ever hold an undisputed pre-eminence. Painting, too, as nearest akin to poetry in the objects it presents and the effects it produces, may be allowed .at least to contest the palm for the second rank. But that music in the person of her most inspired sons, should have been sternly excluded from a participation in the honours awarded to her sister arts, seems an injustice which can be defended on no pleadable grounds. The explanation of it seems to be, that most of our great poets—and this has certainly been the case in England—have had no love or knowledge, and no true appreciation, of high musical composition. Milton alone seems to have been an exception; and, we cannot doubt, that if he had lived in the same age with Handel, he would have given utterance to his admiration in strains worthy of them both. The rest of our *vates sacri*, on whom immortality is proverbially said to depend, seem, generally speaking, to have been ignorance itself in this department. Several of them, indeed, have written odes for St. Cecilia's day, but this does not prove that they had a taste for more than rhythm. Pope had the tact to call Handel a giant, and speaks cleverly of his " hundred hands " as sure to be fatal to the reign of Dulness.

> " Strong in new arms, lo! giant Handel stands,
> Like bold Briareus, with his hundred hands,
> To stir, to rouse, to shake the soul he comes,
> And Jove's own thunders follow Mars's drums.
> Arrest him, goddess! or you sleep no more."

But no reference is made to the exquisite beauty of his compositions. The loudness is all that seems to be praised, and we suspect, that in private Pope was inclined to laugh with Swift in his disparaging comparison between Tweedledum and Tweedledee. Wordsworth has written on the " Power of Sound;" but the small part of it that touches on the musical art, does not impress us with the idea of his knowing or caring much about it, though in this, as in other things, he has the sense and philosophy to sacrifice a cock to Esculapius, and to

bow down to what others worship, even where he does not himself feel the influence of a warm devotion. Collins and Moore, and perhaps a few others whom we have overlooked, ought to be excluded from this condemnation; but they have not been led to speak of individual musicians, or have not had courage to leave the beaten track.

Thus neglected by those who would have been its most faithful depositaries and most effective champions, the fame of the musical composer has been left to the guardianship of the few sound and enlightened judges who thoroughly comprehend him, to the humble but honest admiration of professional performers, to the practice and imitation of effeminate amateurs, to the cant of criticism of the worthies on the free list, and to the instinctive applause of the popular voice. Even with these humbler hands to build up his monument, the great master of music has a perpetual possession within the hearts of men, that the poet and the painter may well envy. Every chord in the human frame that answers to his strains, every tear that rises at the bidding of his cadences, every sob that struggles for an outlet at his touches of despairing tenderness, or at the thunders of his massive harmony, is a tribute to his power and his memory, enough to console his spirit if it can still be conscious of them, or to have rewarded his living labours in their progress by a bright anticipation of their effects. If nobles, and even nations, do not contend for the possession of his works, or offer a ransom for their purchase, such as is daily given for the masterpieces of the painter's power, it is the pride of his genius that his compositions cannot be appropriated or possessed. An oratorio of Handel, or an opera of Mozart, cannot become property like a picture of Raphael or Guido. They belong to mankind at large, open to all, and enjoyable by all who have the faculty to perceive, and delight in, their beauties; and in every theatre and public place, in every church and in every chamber throughout Christendom, a portion of their divine and various influence, suited to the scene and occasion, is always within reach, to make men gentler and better, happier and holier, than they would otherwise be without such manifestations of their Maker's wondrous gifts.

Nowhere can the views we have above suggested be better illustrated, than in the fate and character of the singular man who, if not the first, was yet only second to one other, among those on whom music has shed her fullest inspiration.

It is not our intention to follow minutely the events of Mozart's life. They are generally well known; and to those who wish to have a clear, complete, and judicious view of them, we can safely recommend the book noticed at the outset of this article.

Mozart was born at Salzburg in 1756, and died at Vienna in 1791, in his thirty-sixth year. But into that short space were compressed as many proofs and compositions of genius, as much joy and sorrow, as much triumph and humiliation, as would have crowded a much longer lifetime. His early indications of genius are well known, and were indeed wonderful, even as compared with those of other great composers—for Handel, Haydn, and Beethoven, all gave proofs of their musical powers in boyhood—though none of them as children showed that full maturity of mind which distinguished Mozart, and which only a few of those who witnessed it could fully appreciate. Mozart's organization was obviously of the finest and tenderest texture; but he had also many advantages in his nurture, and, among others, the inestimable blessing of a happy home, where harmony reigned in the hearts, as well as upon the lips and fingers of the inmates. His father was a man of sense and education, as well as of musical talent, and in all respects did his duty to his son throughout life, amidst many difficulties and disappointments, resulting partly from his own dependent situation at Salzburg, and partly from an over-estimate of the worldly prosperity which his son's genius should have commanded. His mother seems also to have been an excellent person; and from the remarkable letters which Mozart wrote from Paris to prepare his father for her death, after the event had happened, she appears to have been the object of the tenderest affection to her family. Mozart uniformly discharged towards his parents all the offices of pious devotion; and he was always affectionately attached to his sister, who was a few years older than himself, and whose early and distinguished skill as a performer must have been useful in assisting her brother's tastes. In 1829 the Novello family saw this lady at Salzburg, a widow and in narrow circumstances.

"We found Madame Sonnenberg, lodged in a small but clean room, bed-ridden and quite blind. Hers is a complete decay of nature; suffering no pain, she lies like one awaiting the stroke of death, and will probably expire in her sleep. . . . Her voice was scarcely above a whisper, so that I was forced to lean my face close to hers to catch the sound. In the sitting-room still remained the old clavichord, on which the brother and sister had frequently played duets together; and on its desk were some pieces of his composition, which were the last things his sister had played over previous to her illness."

With becoming delicacy, the fruits of an English subscription were presented to her on her name-day, as a remembrance from some friends of her brother.

The bane of Mozart's fortunes was the patronage on which he was dependent. His father had got into the trammels of the Archbishop of Salzburg—a sordid, arrogant, and ignorant man, who saw Mozart's value in the eyes of others, though he could not himself estimate it, and would neither pay him nor part with him. When in his twentieth year, and already a great composer and an efficient performer, Mozart was in the receipt, from this princely prelate, for the liberal use of his musical talents, of a salary equal in amount to about £1. 1s. English, per annum.

" Among a multitude of compositions that he wrote for the archbishop's concerts, in 1775, are five concertos for the violin, which he probably performed himself. His gentle disposition made him easily comply with any proposal to augment pleasure, however out of his usual course. During the following year, 1776, he seems to have made his last great effort to awaken the archbishop to some sense of his desert, and a due generosity of acknowledgment, by producing masses, litanies, serenades, divertimentos for instruments, clavier concertos, &c., too numerous for detail. But in vain; and what aggravated the injury of this monstrous appropriation of labour was, that the father, whose household economy was now somewhat pinched, on applying for permission to remedy these circumstances by a tour, was refused. From that hour Wolfgang threw by his pen in disgust—at least as far as it concerned voluntary labour."

It was now resolved that Mozart should leave Salzburg with his mother,

and try his fortune in the world. He was everywhere admired; but the wonder of his childhood had passed away, and empty praise was all that he could, for the most part, earn. After lingering, in the sickness of hope deferred, at several of the German courts, his destination was at last fixed for Paris. His chance of success as a courtier was probably diminished by the blunt though kindly frankness of his opinions, and by his inability to stoop to unworthy means of rising. He had also many rivals to encounter, particularly those of the more slender school of Italian melody; and few of the public had knowledge or independence enough to forsake the inferior favourites that were then in vogue.

In approaching Paris, Mozart became alarmed at the prospect of his being there compelled to resort to the drudgery of tuition for his support. " I am a composer," he said, " and the son of a kapell-meister, and I cannot consent to bury in teaching the talent for composition which God has so richly bestowed upon me." His father, more experienced in the world, and more prudential in his ideas, endeavoured to modify his alarm, and urge him to perseverance in any honourable course of employment. The father's letter at this time to his son, to apprise him of the true position of the family, and preserve him against the dangers in his path, is honourable to both, and worthy of perusal.

" This being in all probability the last letter that you will receive from me at Mannheim, I address it to you alone. How deeply the wider separation which is about to take place between us affects me, you may partly conceive, though not feel it in the same degree with which it oppresses my heart. If you reflect seriously on what I have undergone with you two children in your tender years, you will not accuse me of timidity, but, on the contrary, do me the justice to own that I am, and ever have been, a man with the heart to venture everything, though indeed I always employed the greatest circumspection and precaution. Against accidents it is impossible to provide, for God only sees into futurity. Up to this time we cannot be said to have been either successful or unsuccessful; but,

God be thanked, we have steered between the two. Everything has been attempted for your success, and through you for our own. We have at least endeavoured to settle you in some appointment on a secure footing; though fate has hitherto decreed that we should fail in our object. This last step of ours, however, makes my spirit sink within me. You may see as clearly as the sun at noonday, that, through it, the future condition of your aged parents, and of your affectionately attached sister, entirely depends upon you. From the time of your birth, and indeed earlier, ever since my marriage, I have found it a hard task to support a wife, and, by degrees, a family of seven children, two relatives by marriage, and the mother, on a certain income of twenty-five florins a month; out of this to pay for maintenance and the expenses of child-bed, deaths, and sicknesses; which expenses, when you reflect upon them, will convince you that I not only never devoted a kreutzer to my own private pleasure, but that I could never, in spite of all my contrivances and care, have managed to live free from debt without the especial favour of God; and yet I never was in debt till now. I devoted all my time to you two, in the hope and indeed reliance upon your care in return; that you would procure for me a peaceful old age, in which I might render account to God for the education of my children, and, without any other concern than the salvation of my soul, quietly await death. But Providence has so ordered, that I must now afresh commence the ungrateful task of lesson-giving, and in a place, too, where this dreary labour is so ill paid, that it will not support one from one end of the year to the other; and yet it is to be thought a matter of rejoicing if, after talking oneself into a consumption, something or other is got by it.

"I am far, my dear Wolfgang, from having the least mistrust in you—on the contrary, on your filial love I place all confidence and every hope. Everything now depends upon fortunate circumstances, and the exercise of that sound understanding which you certainly possess, if you will listen to it: the former are uncontrollable—but that you will always take counsel of your understanding I hope and pray.

"You are now a young man of twenty-two years of age; here is none of that seriousness of years which may dissuade a youth, let his condition be what it may—an adventurer, a libertine, a deceiver—be he old or young, from courting your acquaintance, and drawing you into his society and his plans. One may fall into this danger unawares, and then not know how to recede. Of the other sex I can hardly speak to you, for there the greatest reserve and prudence are necessary, Nature herself being our enemy; but whoever does not employ all his prudence and reserve in his intercourse, will with difficulty extricate himself from the labyrinth—*a misfortune that usually ends in death.* How blindly, through inconsiderate jests, flattery, and play, one may fall into errors at which the returning reason is ashamed, you may perhaps have already a little experienced, and it is not my intention to reproach you. I am persuaded that you do not only consider me as your father, but as your truest and most faithful friend, and that you know and see that our happiness or unhappiness—nay, more, my long life or speedy death is, under God, so to speak, in your hands. If I know you aright, I have nothing but pleasure to expect in you, which thought must console me in your absence for the paternal pleasure of seeing, hearing, and embracing you. Lead the life of a good Catholic Christian; love and fear God; pray to him with devotion and sincerity, and let your conduct be such, that should I never see you more, the hour of my death may be free from apprehension. From my heart I bless you."

His reception at Paris was comparatively cold. The Parisians were scarcely done with the "faction fight" in which the rivalry of Gluck and Piccini had involved them; but none of the partisans were inclined to be enthusiastic about the new-comer. His only great admirer, and his best friend, seems to have been his acute and accomplished countryman Grimm, who prophesied that monarchs would dispute for the possession of Mozart. The prediction was fulfilled, but not in sufficient time to benefit the unhappy subject of their competition.

"Baron Grimm and myself often vent our indignation at the state of music here, that is to say, between ourselves; but in public it is always, '*bravo! bravissimo!*' and clapping till the fingers burn. What most displeases me is, that the French gentlemen have only so far improved their taste as to be able to *endure* good things; but as for any perception that their music is bad— Heaven help them !—and the singing— *oimè!*"

Again he writes—

"You advise me to visit a great deal, in order to make new acquaintances, or to revive the old ones. That is, however, impossible. The distance is too great, and the ways too miry to go on foot; the muddy state of Paris being indescribable; and to take a coach, one may soon drive away four or five livres, and all in vain, for the people merely pay you compliments, and then it is over. They ask me to come on this or that day—I play, and then they say, '*O c'est un prodige, c'est inconcevable, c'est étonnant;*' and then '*à Dieu.*'"

"All this, however," Mr. Holmes observes, "might have been endured, so far as mere superciliousness and *hauteur* to the professional musician were involved, if these people had possessed any real feeling or love for music; but, it was their total want of all taste, their utter viciousness, that rendered them hateful to Mozart. He was ready to make any sacrifice for his family, but longed to escape from the artificial and heartless Parisians.

"Were I in a place," he writes, "where people had ears to hear, hearts to feel, and some small degree of perception and taste, I should laugh heartily over all these things—but really, as it regards music, I am living among mere brute beasts. How can it be otherwise? It is the same in all their passions, and, indeed, in every transaction of life; no place in the world is like Paris. Do not think that I exaggerate when I speak thus of the state of music here—ask any one except a native Frenchman, and if he be fit to answer the question, he will tell you the same. I must endure out of love to you —but I shall thank God Almighty if I leave this place with my healthful natural taste. It is my constant prayer that I may be enabled to establish myself that I may do honour to the German nation, and make fame and money, and so be the means of helping you out of your present narrow circumstances, and of our all living together once more, cheerfully and happily."

Take the following vivid sketch of his task in teaching composition to a young lady :—

"Among these pupils one is daughter of the Duc de Guines, with whom I am in high favour, and I give her two hours' instruction in composition daily, for which I am very liberally paid. He plays the flute incomparably, and she magnificently on the harp. She possesses much talent and cleverness, and, in particular, a very remarkable memory, which enables her to play all her pieces, of which there are at least two hundred, without book. She is doubtful whether she has genius for composition —particularly with respect to thoughts or ideas; her father (who, between ourselves, is a little too much in love with her) affirms that she certainly has ideas, and that nothing but modesty and a want of confidence in herself prevent their appearing. We shall now see. If she really have no ideas, and I must say I have as yet seen no indication of them, it will be all in vain, for God knows I can give her none. It is not her father's intention to make any very great composer of her. 'I do not wish her,' he says, 'to write any operas, airs, concertos, or symphonies, but merely grand sonatas for her instrument, as I do for mine.'

"I gave her the fourth lesson to-day, and, as far as the rules of composition go, am tolerably satisfied with her; she put the bass to the first minuet which I placed before her, very correctly. We now commenced writing in three parts. She tried it, and fatigued herself in attempts, but it was impossible to help her; nor can we move on a step further, for it is too early, and in science one must advance by the proper gradations. If she had genius—but alas! there is none—she has no thoughts—nothing comes. I have tried her in every imaginable way; among others it occurred to me to place a very simple minuet before her, to see whether she could make a variation upon it. That was all to no purpose. Now, thought I, she does not know how to begin; so I varied the first bar for her, and told her to continue the variation pursuing that idea; and at length she got through tolerably well. I next requested her to begin something herself—the first part only—a melody; but after a quarter of an hour's cogitation nothing came. I then wrote four bars of a minuet, and said, 'What a stupid fellow I am! I have begun a minuet, and cannot finish the first part of it. Have the goodness to do it for me.' She distrusted her ability, but at last, with much labour, something came to light. I rejoiced that we got something at last. She had now to complete the entire minuet, that is to say, the melody only. On going away, I recommended her to alter my four bars for something of her own; to make another beginning even if she retained the same harmony, and only altered the melody. I shall see to-morrow how she has succeeded."

In the midst of this irksome labour, Mozart's beloved mother expired at Paris in the summer of 1778, after a fortnight's illness. He then wrote to his father that she was " very ill," and to a family friend at Salzburg, desiring him to prepare his father and sister for the truth. The whole correspondence at this time is interesting. The letter to the Abbé Bullinger is in these words :—

" Sympathize with me in this most wretched and melancholy day of my life. I write at two o'clock in the morning to inform you that my mother—my dearest mother—is no more! God has called her to himself. I saw clearly that nothing could save her, and resigned myself entirely to the will of God; he gave, and he can take away. Picture to yourself the state of alarm, care, and anxiety in which I have been kept for the last fortnight. She died without being conscious of anything—her life went out like a taper. Three days ago she confessed, received the sacrament and extreme unction; but since that time she has been constantly delirious and rambling, until this afternoon at twenty-one minutes after five, when she was seized with convulsions, and immediately lost all perception and feeling. I pressed her hand and spoke to her; but she neither saw me, heard me, nor seemed in the least sensible; and in this state she lay for five hours, namely, till twenty-one minutes past ten, when she departed, no one being present but myself, M. Haine, a good friend of ours whom my father knows, and the nurse. " I cannot at present write you the whole particulars of the illness; but my belief is, that she was to die—that it was the will of God. Let me now beg the friendly service of you, to prepare my poor father by gentle degrees for the melancholy tidings. I wrote to him by the same post, but told him no more than that she was very ill; and I now await his answer, by which I shall be

guided. May God support and strengthen him ! Oh, my friend ! through the especial grace of God I have been enabled to endure the whole with fortitude and resignation, and have long since been consoled under this great loss. In her extremity I prayed for two things : a blessed dying hour for my mother, and courage and strength for myself; and the gracious God heard my prayer, and richly bestowed those blessings upon me. Pray, therefore, dear friend, support my father. Say what you can to him, in order that when he knows the worst, he may not feel it too bitterly. I, commend my sister also to you from the bottom of my heart. Call on both of them soon, but say no word of the death—only prepare them. You can do and say what you will; but let me be so far at ease as to have no new misfortune to expect. Comfort my dear father and my dear sister, and pray send me a speedy answer."

This letter to his father is curiously circumstantial; but if on such occasions it is allowable to deceive at all, it is allowable to make the deception complete.

" The cause of my having left your letter of the 11th of June so long unanswered is, that I have very unpleasant and melancholy intelligence to communicate. My dear mother is very ill. At the beginning of her illness she was, as usual, bled, and this seemed to relieve and do her good; but in a few days she began to complain of sudden chills and heats, which were accompanied by headache and diarrhœa. We began now to use the remedy that we employ at home—the antispasmodic powder. We wished that we had brought the black, but had it not, and could not get it here, where even its name, *pulvis epilepticus*, is unknown. But as she got worse continually, spoke with difficulty, and so far lost her hearing, that it was necessary to call out in speaking to her, Baron Grimm sent us his physician She is still very weak, and is also feverish and delirious. They want to give me hope; but I have not much. I have been long already— for days and nights together—between hope and fear : but I have now entirely resigned myself to the will of God, and I hope that you and my dear sister will do the like. What are the means then to give us calm and peace, in a degree, if not absolutely? I am resigned, let the end be what it may, because I know that God, who, however mysteriously he may proceed to human eyes, ordains everything for the best, so wills it ; and I am not easily persuaded out of the belief, that neither physician nor any other man, neither misfortune nor accident can either take or give life, but God alone, though these are the means which he mostly employs; but even these not always. We see people constantly sinking and dying around us ; but I do not say, on that account, that my mother must and will die, or that we have lost all hope. She may recover, if it be the will of God. I, however, find consolation in these reflections, after praying to God as earnestly as I am able for my dear mother's health and life ; they strengthen, encourage, and console me, and you must needs think I require them. Let us now change the subject, and quit these melancholy thoughts. Let us hope, if not much, and put our trust in God, consoling ourselves with the reflection that everything is well ordered which the Almighty orders, and that he best knows what is essential to our temporal happiness and our eternal salvation."

The elder Mozart had, in the mean time, without knowing of her illness, begun a letter to his wife, designed to reach her on her name-day ; but, before its conclusion, he had received his son's letter, and seen the Abbé, and had thus learned not only her danger but its result.

" M. Bullinger found us, as every one else did, in deep affliction ; I handed him your letter without saying a word ; he dissembled very well ; and having read it, inquired what I thought about it. I said, that I firmly believed my dear wife was no more. He almost feared the same thing, he told me—and then, like a true friend, entered upon consolatory topics, and said to me everything that I had before said to myself. We finished our conversation, and our friends gradually left us with much concern. M. Bullinger, however, remained behind, and when we were alone, asked me whether I believed that there was any ground for hope after such a description of the illness as had been given. I replied, that I not merely believed her dead by this time—but that she was already so on the very day that the letter was written ; that I had

resigned myself to the will of God, and must remember that I have two children, who I hoped would love me, as I lived solely and entirely for them ; indeed, that I felt so certain, as to have taken some pains to write to, and remind you of the consequences, &c. Upon this he said, ' Yes, she is dead,' and in that instant the scales fell from my eyes ; for the suddenness of the accident had prevented my perceiving, what I else should have suspected, as soon as I had read your letter—namely, how probable it was that you had privately communicated the real truth to M. Bullinger. In fact, your letter stupified me—it was at first such a blow as to render me incapable of reflection. I have now no more to say. Do not be anxious on my account ; I shall bear my sorrow like a man. Remember what a tenderly loving mother you have had— now you will be able to appreciate all her care—as in your mature years, after my death, you will mine, with a constantly increasing affection. If you love me, as I doubt not but you do, take care of your health—on your life hangs mine, and the future support of your affectionate sister. How incomprehensibly bitter a thing it is, when death rends asunder a happy marriage—can only be known by experience."

In a few days, Mozart wrote to his father again :—

" I hope that you are now prepared to receive with firmness some intelligence of a very melancholy and distressing character ; indeed, my last letter, of the 3d, will not have encouraged you to expect anything very favourable. On the evening of the same day (the 3d), at twenty-one minutes after ten at night, my mother fell happily asleep in God, and was already experiencing the joys of heaven at the very moment that I wrote to you. All was over—I wrote to you in the night, and I trust that you and my sister will pardon this slight but very necessary artifice ;—for when, after all the distress that I had suffered, I turned my thoughts towards you, I could not possibly persuade myself to surprise you all at once with the dreadful and fatal news. Now, however, I hope that you have both prepared yourselves to hear the worst ; and after giving way to the reasonable and natural impulses of your grief, to submit yourselves at last to the will of

God, and to adore his inscrutable, unfathomable, and all-wise providence.

*	*	*	*

"I write this in the house of Madame d'Epinay and M. Baron de Grimm, with whom I am now staying, and where I have a pretty little room with a pleasant prospect, and am, as far as circumstances will permit, happy. It would be a great additional comfort were I to hear that my dear father and sister had resigned themselves with fortitude and submission to the will of God ; trusting him entirely, in the full conviction that everything is ordered for our good. Dear father,—be comforted ! Dearest sister— be comforted !—you know not the kind intentions of your brother towards you ; because, hitherto they have not been in his power to fulfil.

"I hope that you will both be careful of your health. Remember that you have still a son—a brother—who will exert himself to the utmost for your happiness, well knowing what sacrifices you are 'both ready to make for him, and that when the time shall come, neither of you will oppose the fulfilment of his honourable wishes. Oh ! then we will lead a life as peaceful and happy as is attainable in this world ; and at length, in God's time, meet all together again in the enjoyment of that object for which we were created."

We have given these letters at some length, as we think they show the worth, affection, and right feeling of the whole family.

The disconsolate state in which his father was thus left, decided Mozart, however reluctant, to return to the hated service of the Archbishop at Salzburg. The terms on which he was received back were somewhat improved, for his absence had 'rendered his value more perceptible ; and a greater latitude was allowed him in visiting and composing for other courts. In the winter of 1780–1, he made use of his leave of absence by writing and bringing out at Munich, with triumphant success, the splendid serious opera of *Idomeneo*, always so great a favourite with himself, and which is still regarded as a masterpiece.

"With this work, the most important in its influence on music, Mozart crowned his twenty-fifth year. The score is still a picture to the musician. It exhibits consummate knowledge of the theatre, displayed in an opera of the first magnitude and complexity ; which unites to a great orchestra the effects of a double chorus on the stage and behind the scenes; and introduces marches, processions, and dances, to various accompaniments in the orchestra, behind the scenes, or under the stage. This model opera, in which Mozart rises on the wing from one beauty to another through long acts, was completed, as we have seen, within a few weeks, and ever since has defied the scrutiny of musicians to detect in it the slightest negligence of style."

In March, 1781, Mozart followed the Salzburg court to Vienna, where he was subjected to such indignity by his patron, as finally to terminate their connexion. The author of *Idomeneo* was required to take his meals at the same table with his grace's valets, confectioner, and cooks. This was too much, even for Mozart's goodnature ; and, aggravated by the Archbishop's refusal to allow the display of his talents to the public, gave him courage to insist for his dismissal.

"The step, however, of resigning a pension, and of throwing himself entirely upon the public for fame and support, was a more important one than his sanguine imagination and excitement of feeling permitted him at the time to contemplate. How far his being an *unappointed* composer may have hastened the production of his immortal works, is open to question; but that his life was sacrificed in struggling against the difficulties in which he was thereby involved, is beyond a doubt.

"In the absence of any immediate design of a new dramatic composition, and delighted at the effect which his public performance on the pianoforte had created at Vienna, Mozart forgot all the fears he had expressed previously to his journey to Paris ; thought no more that teaching would interfere with the higher vocation of his muse ; and was content to become the fashionable performer, teacher, and pianoforte composer of the day. This mode of life for a time had its temptations and its success ; and he hoped that he might still better assist his father at Vienna than at Salzburg, as he was at intervals able to remit to him sums of from ten to thirty ducats. But here commenced the precarious existence which the composer was for the future destined to lead. For, not only was the taste of Vienna then, as now, proverbially variable and flippant—not only was concert-giving an uncertain speculation, and teaching an inconstant source of income—but in a man, who, like Mozart, had, from time to time, strong impulses to write for the theatre, it frequently happened that the order and regularity of his engagements were made to yield to the object which engrossed him; and that the profits of his time were sacrificed on the one hand, without any proportionate advantage on the other."

Let it be observed that Mozart's payment for teaching among the Austrian nobility, was at the rate of five shillings a lesson !

Mozart was distinguished for virtues which belong only to great or good men when labouring in the field of emulation—an absence of all envy and jealousy, of which he was himself too much the object, and a just and generous estimate of excellence in others. As observed by Mr. Holmes, good music, not his own, was his best relaxation from his toils; and his predecessors and contemporaries were alike sure of that sincere admiration which sprang from an unselfish love of the art. His regard and respect for Haydn, who was greatly his inferior in genius and power, is a pleasing illustration of what we have said.

"At this time, Joseph Haydn was established as kapell-meister in the service of Prince Nicholas Esterhazy, and enjoyed a very extensive reputation, which, indeed, the native energy of his genius, and the fortunate circumstances of his mature life, enabled him to earn with ease in a variety of compositions. He was frequently at Vienna, in the suite of his prince; and it was natural that Mozart, who had long lived on terms of mutual esteem with Michael Haydn, at Salzburg, should be predisposed to a regard for his brother;—but the simplicity, benevolence, and sincerity of Joseph Haydn's character, when united with the charming qualities of his genius, offered more than the materials for an ordinary friendship. The attachment of these two men remains accordingly one of the most honourable monuments of the virtuous love of art that musical history can produce. Haydn was at this period about fifty years of age. His constant habit of writing five

hours a day, had accumulated in a series of years a large collection of quartets, pianoforte music, church music, and symphonies, most of which were greatly admired for the spirit and elegance of their style, and the clearness and originality of their design. Mozart at once saw and acknowledged the excellence of Haydn: and in his future intercourse with that master, took the part which the difference of their age, if not of their genius, rendered graceful—by deferring to his judgment with all the meekness of a learner. To Haydn he submitted many of his compositions before publication; delighting often to call him his master and model in quartet writing, which he now began to cultivate in earnest; and omitting no circumstance which could gratify the veteran musician in possessing such an admirer. Haydn on his part repaid all this devotion with becoming generosity. However conscious that, in the universality of musical power, his own genius must be placed at a disadvantage in comparison with that of his friend, he harboured no envious or unworthy sentiment; and death alone interrupted the kind relation in which each stood to the other.

"At the musical parties which Mozart gave from time to time, when he had new compositions to try, and leisure to indulge his disposition for sociality, Haydn was a frequent guest, and no one more profoundly enjoyed the extraordinary beauty and perfection of Mozart's pianoforte playing. Years after, when those fingers, and the soul which animated them, were sought for in vain, a few touching words from Haydn spoke more feelingly to the imagination, in the description of that beauty, than the most laboured and minute criticism could have done. ' Mozart's playing,' said he, ' I can never forget ' "

Haydn's high estimate of his friend's superiority to himself, was always expressed with equal generosity. In a company of critics, who discovered that there were faults in Mozart's operas, Haydn, when appealed to, replied—" All I know is, that Mozart is the greatest composer now existing." When applied to, in 1787, to write a comic opera, Haydn thought a new subject, or *libretto*, would be necessary, and adds—

" Even then it would be a bold attempt, as scarcely any one can stand by the side of the great Mozart. For were it possible that I could impress every friend of music, particularly among the great, with that deep musical intelligence of the inimitable works of Mozart —that emotion of the soul with which they affect me, and in which I both comprehend and feel them, the nations would contend together for the possession of such a gem. Prague ought to retain him, and reward him well too; else the history of great genius is melancholy, and offers posterity but slight encouragement to exertion, which is the reason, alas! that many hopeful and aspiring spirits are repressed. I feel indignant that this *unique* Mozart is not yet engaged at some royal or imperial court. Forgive me if I stray from the subject—but I love the man too much."

Again, when engaged, along with Mozart, for Salomon's concerts in England—a plan which, so far as Mozart was concerned, was unhappily not carried out—Haydn's only stipulation was, that his compositions should precede those of his friend; and avowed, with unparalleled frankness, his feeling that he would otherwise have less chance of being heard with success.

The celebrity of Mozart, and the applause which attended some of his new compositions, procured him the notice, and ultimately the patronage of the Emperor Joseph—though somewhat unsteadily conferred, and divided with unworthy Italian rivals. The change, however, was tardy, and, when it came, did not much improve his external circumstances. The appointments he held made but a miserable sinecure, with a still more miserable salary; but the deficiency was supplied by soft words and familiar looks, which, with Mozart's kindly disposition, served to attach him to his imperial master, better than would have been done by a larger allowance ungraciously given.

In the mean time, relying upon his position as a composer, and hoping for the best, Mozart had formed the connexion, as to which Mr. Hogarth justly says, " that his fixing his affections on the admirable woman whom he married, was the wisest act, as it was the happiest event, of his life. Constance Weber was his guide—his monitress—his guardian angel. She regulated his domestic establishment

—managed his affairs—was the cheerful companion of his happier hours—and his never-failing consolation in sickness and despondency. He passionately loved her, and evinced his feelings by the most tender and delicate attentions."

It is remarkable that Mozart's attachment had at first been directed to his wife's elder sister, and seemed to be returned on her part. But after his absence in Paris, he was coldly received when they again met, and, fortunately for himself, he transferred his affections to Constance, who became his wife.

Rich as this union was in affection, and in all the happiness that affection can bestow, it was soon checkered by distress and difficulty. The health of the wife became precarious; and Mozart's ignorance of the world, as well as his generous and joyous disposition, joined to the precarious and varying amount of his earnings, and the disappointment in his prospects of imperial favour, involved him in debt, which, by overtaxing his mind and body, led to the errors and excesses, such as they were, of his latter life, and ultimately undermined his constitution, and brought him to an untimely tomb.

The " res angusta domi" stimulated the composer's pen, and the rapidity of his productions at this time is marvellous. The taste of Vienna, however, was capricious; and cabals among singers and critics succeeded in deadening the effect of his *Figaro,* when first brought out, and in thoroughly disgusting Mozart with the Viennese opera. How different the reception which it met from the true hearts and well-attuned ears of the Bohemian audiences! It was in February, 1787, after parting with the Storaces, on their leaving for England, with a hope that the mighty master would soon be allured to follow them, that his Bohemian visit was paid.

" In the very same week that he parted from his English friends, Mozart himself set out upon a journey to Prague, whither he had been very cordially invited by a distinguished nobleman and connoisseur, Count John Joseph Thun, who maintained in his service an excellent private band. This was the first professional expedition of any consequence in which he had engaged since his settlement in Vienna; it was prosecuted under the most favourable auspices, and with glowing anticipations of that pleasure for which he so ardently longed, but so imperfectly realized at home—the entire sympathy of the public. Nor was he disappointed. On the same evening that he alighted at the castle of his noble entertainer, his opera of 'Figaro' was given at the theatre, and Mozart found himself for the first time in the midst of that Bohemian audience of whose enthusiasm and taste he had heard so much. The news of his presence in the theatre quickly ran through the parterre, and the overture was no sooner ended than the whole audience rose and gave him a general acclamation of welcome, amidst deafening salvos of applause.

"The success of 'Le Nozze di Figaro,' so unsatisfactory at Vienna, was unexampled at Prague, where it amounted to absolute intoxication and frenzy. Having run through the whole previous winter without interruption, and rescued the treasury of the theatre from ruinous embarrassments, the opera was arranged in every possible form; for the pianoforte, for wind-instruments (garden music), as violin quintets for the chamber, and German dances; in short, the melodies of 'Figaro' re-echoed in every street and every garden; nay, even the blind harper himself, at the door of the beer-house, was obliged to strike up *Non più andrai* if he wished to gain an audience, or earn a kreutzer. Such was the effect of the popular parts of the opera on the public at large; its more refined beauties exercised an equal influence on musicians. The director of the orchestra, Strobach, under whose superintendence 'Figaro' was executed at Prague, often declared the excitement and emotion of the band in accompanying this work to have been such, that there was not a man among them, himself included, who, when the performance was finished, would not have cheerfully recommenced and played the whole through again.

"Finding himself, at length, in a region of sympathy so genial and delightful, a new era in the existence of the composer seemed to open, and he abandoned himself without reserve to its pleasures. In retracing a life so ill rewarded by contemporaries, and so checkered by calamity, it is pleasant to dally awhile in the primrose path, and enjoy the opening prospects of good fortune. "In a few days he was called upon to give a grand concert at the opera-house. This was in reality his first public appearance, and many circumstances conspire to render it memorable; but chiefly that every piece throughout the performance was of his own composition. The concert ended by an improvisation on the pianoforte. Having preluded and played a fantasia, which lasted a good half-hour, Mozart rose; but the stormy and outrageous applause of his Bohemian audience was not to be appeased, and he again sat down. His second fantasia, which was of an entirely different character, met with the same success; the applause was without end, and long after he had retired to the withdrawing-room, he heard the people in the theatre *thundering* for his re-appearance. Inwardly delighted, he presented himself for the third time. Just as he was about to begin, when every noise was hushed, and the stillness of death reigned throughout the theatre, a voice in the pit cried '*from Figaro.*' He took the hint, and ended this triumphant display of skill by extemporising a dozen of the most interesting and scientific variations upon the air *Non più andrai*. It is needless to mention the uproar that followed. The concert was altogether found so delightful, that a second, upon the same plan, soon followed. A sonnet was written in his honour, and his performances brought him one thousand florins. Wherever he appeared in public, it was to meet testimonies of esteem and affection. His emotion at the reception of 'Figaro' in Prague was so great, that he could not help saying to the manager, Bondini, 'As the Bohemians understand me so well, I must write an opera on purpose for them.' Bondini took him at his word, and entered with him, on the spot, into a contract to furnish his theatre with an opera for the ensuing winter. Thus was laid the foundation of 'Il Don Giovanni.'"

The greatest of Mozart's operas was composed at Prague, on a second visit thither in 1787, when he lived with a musical friend in the suburbs of the city. "Here, on an elevated site which commanded a view of the antique magnificence of Prague, its faded castles, ruined cloisters, and other majestic remains of feudal times, under the mild rays of an autumnal sun, and in the open air, *Don Giovanni* was written." It was immediately brought out at Prague with the success it deserves, and was afterwards performed at Vienna, but was badly got up, and but indifferently received. "Don Giovanni," said its author, "was rather written for Prague than Vienna, but chiefly for myself and my friends." It is a disgraceful fact, that it was eclipsed in popularity among the Viennese by the "Tarrare" of Salieri, of which no one now knows anything.

In 1787 Mozart's father died at Salzburg, less happy, it is to be feared, than his own worth and his son's genius should have made him. But he was ignorant of the great truth, that fame, and often merely posthumous fame, is the chief external blessing that awaits men of extraordinary mental powers in the arts, and that the appropriate reward of genius, any more than of virtue, is not always—"bread." On hearing of his father's illness, Mozart had written him in affectionate terms—

" I have just received some news which has given me a sad blow; the more so, as your last letter left me reason to suppose that you were in perfect health. I now, however, learn that you are really very ill. How anxiously I await and hope for some comforting intelligence from you I need hardly say, although I have long since accustomed myself in all things to expect the worst. As death, rightly considered, fulfils the real design of our life, I have for the last two years made myself so well acquainted with this true friend of mankind, that his image has no longer any terrors for me, but much that is peaceful and consoling; and I thank God that he has given me the opportunity to know him as the key to our true felicity. I never lie down in bed without reflecting that, perhaps (young as I am), I may never see another day; yet no one who knows me will say that I am gloomy or morose in society. For this blessing I daily thank my Creator, and from my heart wish it participated by my fellow-men."

In the autumn of the same year, he lost a valued and valuable friend in Dr. Barisani of Vienna, whose medical attentions had already been eminently useful to him, and might, if they had been continued, have saved him from

those irregularities of alternate labour and indulgence which so soon afterwards began to affect his health. Mozart made, on this occasion, an affecting entry in his memorandum-book, under some lines which his friend had written for him.

"To-day, the 2d of September, I have had the misfortune to lose, through an unexpected death, this honourable man, my best and dearest friend, and the preserver of my life. He is happy!—but I—we, and all who thoroughly knew him, cannot again be so—till we have the felicity to meet him in a better world, never again to separate."

In 1789, Mozart visited Prussia, where he was well received by every one, and seems to have been happy. We may here insert part of a well-known letter, written about this time, to an amateur baron, which gives a curious picture of Mozart's character and habits, as well as of the mixed tone of good humour and good sense with which he seems to have both written and conversed. The baron had sent him some tolerable music, and some better wine.

"TO THE BARON V——.

"Herewith I return you, my good baron, your scores; and if you perceive that in my hand there are more *nota benes* than notes, you will find from the sequel of this letter how that has happened. Your symphony has pleased me, on account of its ideas, more than the other pieces, and yet I think that it will produce the least effect. It is too much crowded, and to hear it partially or piecemeal (*stückweise*) would be, by your permission, like beholding an ant-hill (*Ameisen haufen*). I mean to say, that it is as if Eppes, the devil, were in it.

You must not snap your fingers at me, my dearest friend, for I would not for all the world have spoken out so candidly if I could have supposed that it would give you offence. Nor need you wonder at this; for it is so with all composers who, without having from their infancy, as it were, been trained by the whip and the curses (*Donnerwetter*) of the maestro, pretend to do everything with natural talent alone. Some compose fairly enough, but with other people's ideas, not possessing any themselves: others, who have ideas of their own, do not understand how to treat and master them. This last is your case. Only do not be angry, pray! for St. Cecilia's sake, not angry that I break out so abruptly. But your song has a beautiful cantabile, and your dear *Fraenzl* ought to sing it very often to you, which I should like as much to see as to hear. The minuet in the quartet is also pleasing enough, particularly from the place I have marked. The *coda*, however, may well clatter or tinkle, but it will never produce *music; sapienti sat*, and also to the *nihil sapienti*, by whom I mean myself. I am not very expert in writing on such subjects; I rather show at once how it ought to be done.

"You cannot imagine with what joy I read your letter; only you ought not to have praised me so much. We may get accustomed to the hearing of such things, but to read them is not quite so well. You good people make too much of me; I do not deserve it, nor my compositions either. And what shall I say to your present, my dearest baron, that came like a star in a dark night, or like a flower in winter, or like a cordial in sickness? God knows how I am obliged, at times, to toil and labour to gain a wretched livelihood, and Stänerl (Constance), too, must get something.

" To him who has told you that I am growing idle, I request you sincerely (and a baron may well do such a thing) to give him a good box on the ear. How gladly would I work and work, if it were only left me to write always such music as I please, and as I can write; such, I mean to say, as I myself set some value upon. Thus I composed three weeks ago an orchestral symphony, and by to-morrow's post I write again to Hoffmeister (the music-seller) to offer him three pianoforte quatuors, supposing that he is able to pay. Oh heavens! were I a wealthy man, I would say, 'Mozart, compose what you please, and as well as you can; but till you offer me something finished, you shall not get a single kreutzer. I'll buy of you every MS., and you shall not be obliged to go about and offer it for sale like a hawker.' Good God! how sad all this makes me, and then again how angry and savage, and it is in such a state of mind that I do things which ought not to be done. You see, my dear good friend, so it is, and not as stupid or vile wretches (*lumpen*) may have told you. Let this, however, go *a cassa del diavolo*.

" I now come to the most difficult part of your letter, which I would willingly pass over in silence, for here my pen denies me its service. Still I will try, even at the risk of being well laughed at. You say, you should like to know my way of composing, and what method I follow in writing works of some extent. I can really say no more on this subject than the following; for I myself know no more about it, and cannot account for it. When I am, as it were, completely myself, entirely alone, and of good cheer—say, travelling in a carriage, or walking after a good meal, or during the night when I cannot sleep; it is on such occasions that my ideas flow best and most abundantly. *Whence* and *how* they come, I know not; nor can I force them. Those ideas that please me I retain in memory, and am accustomed, as I have been told, to hum them to myself. If I continue in this way, it soon occurs to me how I may turn this or that morsel to account, so as to make a good dish of it; that is to say, agreeably to the rules of counterpoint, to the peculiarities of the various instruments, &c.

" All this fires my soul, and, provided I am not disturbed, my subject enlarges itself, becomes methodized and defined, and the whole, though it be long, stands almost complete and finished in my mind, so that I can survey it, like a fine picture or a beautiful statue, at a glance. Nor do I hear in my imagination the parts *successively*, but I hear them, as it were, all at once (*gleich alles zusammen*). What a delight this is I cannot tell! All this inventing, this producing, takes place in a pleasing lively dream. Still the actual hearing of the *tout ensemble* is after all the best. What has been thus produced I do not easily forget, and this is perhaps the best gift I have my Divine Maker to thank for.

" When I proceed to write down my ideas, I take out of the bag of my memory, if I may use that phrase, what has previously been collected into it in the way I have mentioned. For this reason the committing to paper is done quickly enough, for everything is, as I said before, already finished; and it rarely differs on paper from what it was in my imagination. At this occupation, I can therefore suffer myself to be disturbed; for whatever may be going on around me, I write, and even talk, but only of fowls and geese, or of Gretel or Bärbel, or some such matters. But why my productions take from my hand that particular form and style that makes them *Mozartish* and different from the works of other composers, is probably owing to the same cause which renders my nose so or so large, so aquiline, or, in short, makes it Mozart's, and different from those of other people. For I really do not study or aim at any originality; I should, in fact, not be able to describe in what mine consists, though I think it quite natural that persons who have really an individual appearance of their own, are also differently organized from others, both externally and internally. At least I know that I have constituted myself neither one way nor the other. . . . .

"Here, my best friend and well-wisher, the pages are full, and the bottle of your wine, which has done the duty of this day, is nearly empty. But since the letter which I wrote to my father-in-law, to request the hand of my wife, I hardly ever have written such an enormously long one. Pray take nothing ill. In speaking, as in writing, I must show myself as I am, or I must hold my tongue, and throw my pen aside. My last words shall be—my dearest friend, keep me in kind remembrance. Would to God I could one day be the cause of so much joy to you as you have been to me. Well! I drink to you in his glass: long live my good and faithful ——. "W. A. MOZART."

Before he left Prussia, the King offered him an appointment and a liberal pension. "Can I leave my good Emperor?" said Mozart with emotion. The proposal, however, made its impression, and shortly afterwards probably encouraged him, at Vienna, on occasion of fresh intrigues against him, to tender his resignation of his paltry situation there. But a kind-like appeal from his imperial patron drove him at once from his intention, and fixed him where he was. It was afterwards hinted to him that he might, at least, have taken this opportunity to stipulate for a better provision for himself. "Satan himself," he replied, "would hardly have thought of bargaining at such a moment."

The year 1789-90 seems to have been about the most disastrous in the situation of his affairs, and led to the most unhappy results.

"The music-shops, as a source of income, were almost closed to him, as he could not submit his genius to the dictates of fashion. Hoffmeister, the publisher, having once more advised him to write in a more *popular* style, or he could not continue to purchase his compositions, he answered with unusual bitterness, 'Then I can make no more by my pen, and I had better starve and go to destruction at once.' The fits of dejection which he experienced were partly the effect of bodily ailments, but more of a weariness with the perplexity of affairs, and of a prospect which afforded him but one object on which he could gaze with certainty of relief, and that was—death. Constant disappointment introduced him to indulgences which he had not before permitted himself.

"He became wild in the pursuit of pleasure; whatever changed the scene was delightful to him, and the more extravagant the better. His associates, and the frequent guests at his table, were recommended by their animal spirits and capacity as boon companions. They were stage-players and orchestral musicians, low and unprincipled persons, whose acquaintance injured him still more in reputation than in purse. Two of these men, Schickaneder, the director of a theatre (for whom Mozart wrote the 'Zauberflöte'), and Stadler, a clarionet-player, are known to have behaved with gross dishonesty towards the composer; and yet he forgave them, and continued their benefactor. The society of Shickaneder, a man of grotesque humour, often in difficulties, but of inexhaustible cheerfulness and good-fellowship, had attractions for Mozart, and led him into some excesses that contributed to the disorder of his health, as he was obliged to retrieve at night the hours lost in the day. A long-continued irregularity of income, also, disposed him to make the most of any favourable moment; and when a few rouleaus of gold brought the means of enjoyment, the Champagne and Tokay began to flow. This course is unhappily no novelty in the shifting life of genius, overworked and ill-rewarded, and seeking to throw off its cares in the pursuits and excitements of vulgar existence. It is necessary to know the composer as a man of pleasure, in order to understand certain allusions in the correspondence of his last years, when his affairs were in the most embarrassed condition, and his absence from Vienna frequently caused by the pressure of creditors. He appears at this time to have experienced moments of poignant self-reproach. His love of dancing, masquerades, masked-balls, &c., was so great, that he did not willingly forego an opportunity of joining any one of those assemblies, whether public or private. He dressed handsomely, and wished to make a favourable impression in society independently of his music. He was sensitive with regard to his figure, and was annoyed when he heard that the Prussian ambassador had said to some one, ' You must not estimate the genius of Mozart by the insignificance of his exterior.' The extremity of his animal spirits may occasion surprise. He composed pantomimes and ballets, and danced in them himself, and at the carnival balls sometimes assumed a character. He was actually incomparable in Arlequin and Pierrot. The public masquerades at Vienna, during the carnival, were supported with all the vivacity of Italy; the emperor occasionally mingled in them, and his example was generally followed. We are not, therefore, to measure these enjoyments by our colder northern notions."

It should be added, what Mr. Holmes tells us on good authority, that the vice of ebriety was not among Mozart's failings. " He drank to the point of exhilaration, but not beyond." His fondness for ballet-dancing may seem strange to us, who have almost a Roman repugnance to such exhibitions in men of good station. But it is possible that in some minds the love of graceful motion may be a refined passion and an exalted art; and it is singular that Mozart's wife told of him, that, in his own estimation, his taste lay in dancing rather than in music.

" That these scenes of extravagant delight seduced him into occasional indulgences, which cannot be reconciled with the purity of his earlier life, it would be the worst affectation in his biographer to deny. Nor is it necessary to the vindication of Mozart that such temporary errors should be suppressed by a feeling of mistaken delicacy. Living in such a round of excitements, and tortured by perpetual misfortunes, there is nothing very surprising in the fact, that he should sometimes have been drawn into the dangerous vortex; but he redeemed the true nobility of his nature by preserving, in the midst of his hasty inconstancies, the most earnest and unfailing attachment to his home. It is a curious illustration of his real character, that he always confessed his transgressions to his wife, who had the wise generosity to pardon them, from that confidence in his truth which survived alike the troubles and temptations of their checkered lives."

Let none lightly dare either to condemn or to imitate the irregularities of life of such wondrous men as Mozart and our own Burns. Those who may be gifted with equally strong and exquisite sensibilities as they, as fine and flexible affections, as bright an imagination, beautifying every object on which its rainbow colours rest, and who have been equally tried by affliction and misconstruction, and equally tempted by brilliant opportunities of pleasure in the intervals of penury and pain—these, if they stand fast, may be allowed to speak, and they will seldom speak uncharitably, of their brethren who have fallen; or, if they fall, they may be heard to plead a somewhat similar excuse. But let ordinary men, and men less extraordinary than those we speak of, beware how they either refer to them as a reproach, or follow them as an example.

The excesses of men of genius are always exaggerated by their enemies, and often overrated even by their friends and companions. With characteristic fervour they enter enthusiastically into everything in which they engage; and, when they indulge in dissipation, delight to sport on the brink of all its terrors, and to outvie in levity and extravagance the most practised professors of their new art. Few that see or hear them think, that even in the midst of their revels their hearts are often far away, or are extracting good from the evil spread before them; and that all the waste of time and talent, so openly and ostentatiously exhibited, is compensated in secret by longer and intenser application to the true object of their pursuit, and by acts of atonement and self-denial, of which the conscious stars of heaven are the only created witnesses. The worst operation of dissolute indulgences on genius is not, perhaps, in producing depravity of heart or habits, for its pure plumes have a virtue about them that is a preservative against pollution; but in wearing out the frame, ruffling the temper, and depressing the spirits, and thus embittering as well as shortening a career that, even when most peaceful and placid, is often destined to be short and sad enough.

The good-natured sympathy which Mozart always felt in the welfare of the very humblest of his brethren of the lyre, is highly creditable to him. But the extent to which he sacrificed his own interests to serve them, was often anything but prudent. He was devoid of every sordid and avaricious feeling, and indeed carried his generosity to an excess.

" The extreme kindness of his nature was grossly abused by artful performers, music-sellers, and managers of theatres. Whenever any poor artists, strangers in Vienna, applied to him for assistance, he offered them the use of his house and table, introduced them to the persons whom he thought could be of use to them, and frequently composed for their use concertos, of which he did not even keep a copy, in order that they might have the exclusive advantage of playing them. But, not content with this, they sold these pieces to music-publishers; and thus repaid his kindness by robbing him. He seldom received any recompense for his pianofore compositions, but generally wrote them for his friends, who were, of course, anxious to possess some work of his for their own use, and suited to their powers of playing Artaria, a music-seller of Vienna, and other members of the trade, contrived to get possession of many of these pieces, and published them without obtaining the author's consent, or making him any remuneration for them. A Polish count, who was invited to a concert at Mozart's house, heard a quintet performed for the first time, with which he was so greatly delighted that he asked Mozart to compose for him a trio for the flute. Mozart agreed, on condition that he should do it at his own time. The count next day sent a polite note, expressive of his thanks for the pleasure he had enjoyed, and along with it, one hundred gold demi-sovereigns (about £100 sterling). Mozart immediately sent him the original score of the quintet that had pleased him so much. The count returned to Vienna a year afterwards, and calling upon Mozart, inquired for the trio. Mozart said that he had never found himself in a disposition to write anything worthy of his acceptance. ' Perhaps, then,' said the count, 'you may find yourself in a disposition to return me the hundred demi-sovereigns I paid you beforehand.' Mozart instantly handed him the money, but the count said not a word about the quintet; and the composer soon afterwards had the satisfaction of seeing it published by Artaria, arranged as a quartet, for the pianoforte, violin, tenor, and violoncello. Mozart's quintets for wind instruments, published also as pianofore quartets, are among the most charming and popular of his instrumental compositions for the chamber; and this anecdote is a specimen of the manner in which he lost the benefit he ought to have derived, even from his finest works. The opera of the ' Zauberflöte' was composed for the purpose of relieving the distresses of a manager, who had been ruined by unsuccessful speculations, and came to implore his assistance. Mozart gave him the score without price, with full permission to perform it in his own theatre, and for his own benefit; only stipulating that he was not to give a copy to any one, in order that the author might afterwards be enabled to dispose of the copyright. The manager promised strict compliance with the condition. The opera was brought out, filled his theatre and his pockets, and, some short time afterwards, appeared at five or six different theatres, by means of copies received from the grateful manager."

Mozart's career, when hastening to its close, was illumined by gleams of prosperity that came but too late. On returning from Prague, in Nov. 1791, from bringing out the *Clemenza di Tito*, at the coronation of Leopold, the new Emperor—

" He found awaiting him the appointment of kapell-meister to the cathedral church of St. Stephen, with all its emoluments, besides extensive commissions from Holland and Hungary for works to be periodically delivered. This, with his engagement for the theatres of Prague and Vienna, assured him of a competent income for the future, exempt from all necessity for degrading employment. But prospects of worldly happiness were now phantoms that only came to mock his helplessness, and embitter his parting hour."

" Now must I go," he would exclaim, "just as I should be able to live in peace; now leave my art, when, no longer the slave of fashion, nor the tool of speculators, I could follow the dictates of my own feeling, and write whatever my heart prompts. I must leave my family—my poor children, at the very instant in which I should have been able to provide for their welfare."

The story of his composing the requiem for a mysterious stranger, and his melancholy forebodings during its composition, are too well known to require repetition here. The incident, to all appearance, was not extraordinary in itself, and owed its imposing character chiefly to the morbid state of Mozart's mind at the time.

On the 5th of December, 1791, the ill-defined disease under which he had for some time laboured, ended in his dissolution ; and subsequent examination showed that inflammation of the brain had taken place. He felt that he was dying—" The taste of death," he said to his sister-in-law, " is already on my tongue—*I taste death ;* and who will be near to support my Constance if you go away ?"

" Süssmayer (an assistant) was standing by the bedside, and on the counterpane lay the ' Requiem,' concerning which Mozart was still speaking and giving directions. As he looked over its pages for the last time, he said, with tears in his eyes, ' Did I not tell you that I was writing this for myself !' "

It should be added that this " Süssmayer, who had obtained possession of one transcript of the ' Requiem,' the other having been delivered to the stranger immediately after Mozart's decease, published the score some years afterwards, claiming to have composed from the *Sanctus* to the end. As there was no one to contradict this extraordinary story, it found partial credit until 1839, when a full score of the ' Requiem' in Mozart's handwriting was discovered."

We have now done. The life and character that we have been considering, speak for themselves. Mozart is not perhaps the greatest composer that ever lived, but Handel only is greater than he ; and to be second to Handel, seems now to us the highest conceivable praise. Yet, in some departments, Mozart was even greater than his predecessor. It is not our intention to characterize his excellences as a composer. The millions of mankind that he has delighted in one form or other, according to their opportunities and capacities, have spoken his best panegyric in the involuntary accents of open and enthusiastic admiration ; and his name will for ever be sweet in the ear of every one who has music in his soul.

Two remarks only we will make upon Mozart's taste and system as a master. The first is, that he invariably considered and proclaimed, that the great object of music was, not to astonish by its difficulty, but to delight by its beauty. Some of his own compositions are difficult as well as beautiful, and in some the beauty may be too transcendental for senses less exalted than his own. But, the production of *pleasure* in all its varied forms and degrees, was his uniform aim and effort; and no master has been more successful. Our next remark is, that with all his genius, he was a laborious and learned musician; and the monument to his own fame which he has completed in his works, was built upon the most anxious, heartfelt, and humble study of all the works of excellence that then existed, and without knowing and understanding which, he truly felt that he could never have equalled or surpassed them.

TO THE EDITOR OF BLACKWOOD'S MAGAZINE.

SIR,—The accompanying narrative was originally sent from the Sandwich Islands in the shape of a letter. Since my return to England, it has been suggested to me that it would suit your pages. If you think so, I shall be happy to place it at your disposal. The ground-plan annexed is intended merely to assist the description : it has no pretensions to strict accuracy, the distances have been estimated, not measured. I remain, Sir, your obedient servant,

AN OFFICER OF THE ROYAL NAVY.

ACCOUNT OF A VISIT TO THE VOLCANO OF KIRAUEA, IN OWHYHEE, SANDWICH ISLANDS, IN SEPTEMBER, 1844.

THE ship being about to proceed to Byron's Bay (the Hilo of the natives), on the N E. side of Owhyhee, to water, the captain arranged, that to give an opportunity to all those who wished to visit the volcano, distant from the anchorage forty miles, the excursion should be made in two parties. Having anchored on Wednesday the 11th of September, he and several of the officers left Hilo early on the 12th ; they travelled on horseback, and returned on the ensuing Monday, highly delighted with their trip, but giving a melancholy description of the road, which they pronounced to be in some places impassable to people on foot. This latter intelligence was disheartening to the second division, some of whom, and myself of the number, had intended to walk. These, notwithstanding, adhered to their resolution ; and the second party, consisting of eight, left the ship at 6 A.M. on Tuesday. Some on horseback, and some on foot, we got away from the village about eight o'clock, attended by thirteen natives, to whose calabashes our prog and clothing had been transferred ; these calabashes answer this purpose admirably ; they are gourds of enormous size, cut through rather above their largest diameter, which is from eighteen inches to two feet ; the half of another gourd forms the lid, and keeps all clean and dry within ; when filled, they are hung by network to each end of the pole thrown across the shoulders of a native, who will thus travel with a load of fifty or sixty pounds about three miles an hour. The day was fine and bright, and we started in high spirits, the horsemen hardly able to conceal their exultation in their superiority over the walkers, whilst they cantered over the plain from which our assent commenced ; this, 4000 feet almost gradual in forty miles, is not fatiguing ; and thus, although we found the path through a wood about three miles long, very deep, and the air oppressive, we all arrived together without distress at the " half-way house," by 1 P.M. Suppose a haystack hollowed out, and some holes cut for doors, and windows, and you have a picture of the " half-way house," and the ordinary dwellings of the natives of these islands ; it is kept by a respectable person, chiefly for the accommodation of travellers, and in it we found the comfort of a table, a piece of furniture by these people usually considered superfluous. Here we soon made ourselves snug, commencing by throwing ourselves on the mats, and allowing a dozen vigorous urchins to " rumi rumi " us. In this process of shampooing, every muscle is kneaded or beaten ; the refreshing luxury it affords can only be perfectly appreciated by those who have, like us, wakled twenty miles on a bad road, in a tropical climate. Here we were to stay the night, and our first object was to prepare dinner and then to eat it ; all seemed disposed to assist in the last part of this operation, and where every one was anxious to please, and determined to be pleased, sociability could not be absent. After this we whiled away our time with books and conversation, till one by one dropping asleep, all became quiet, except a wretched child belonging to our hostess, who, from one corner of the hut, every now and then set up its shrill pipe to disturb our slumbers. We were on the march the next morning at six, the walkers more confident than the horsemen, some of whose beasts did not seem at all disposed for another day's work. Our road lay for the most part through immense seas of lava, in the crevices of which a variety of ferns had taken root, and, though relieving the otherwise *triste* appearance, in many places shut out our view of anything besides. Two of the walkers, and some of the horsemen, came in at the journey's end, shortly after eleven o'clock; the remainder, some leaving their horses behind them, straggled in by two P.M. Here we were at the crater! Shall I confess that my first feeling was disappointment? The plan shows some distance between the outer and inner rims, immediately below the place where the house (F) is situated; this is filled up by another level, which shuts out a

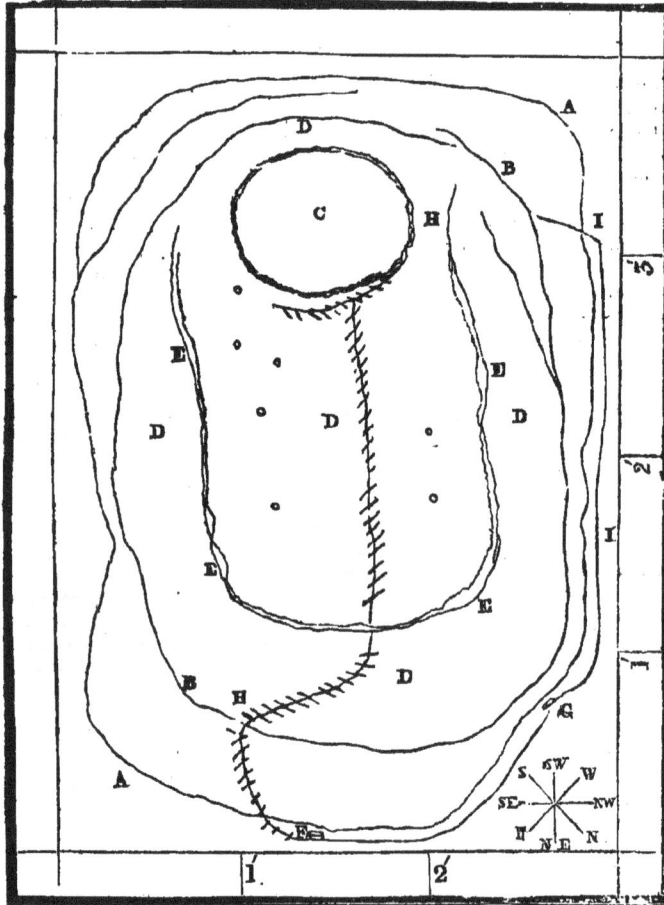

Explanation of Plan :—

A A The outer rim.
B B The inner rim.
C The active crater.
D D D D The surface of
the larger crater.
E E E E The dike.

F The house.
G The hut.
H H Track to and from crater.

I I Track of party on Wednesday night.
. *o o o o o o o* Cones in larger crater.

great part of the prospect; the remainder was too distant, and the sun's rays too powerful, to allow of our seeing more than a quantity of smoke, and an occasional fiery ebullition from the further extremity. It was not until we had walked to the hut (G) that we became sensible of the awful grandeur of the scene below; from this point we looked perpendicularly down on the blackened mass, and felt our insignificance. The path leads between many fissures in the ground, from which sulphurous vapour and steam issue; the latter, condensing on the surrounding bushes, and falling into holes in the compact lava, affords a supply of most excellent water. As evening set in, the active volcano assumed from the house an appearance of a city in flames; long intersecting lines of fire looked like streets in a blaze; and when here and there a more conspicuous burst took place, fancy pictured a church or some large building a prey to the element. Not contented with this distant view, three of our party started for the hut, whence in the afternoon we had so fine a prospect. When there, although our curiosity was highly gratified, it prompted us to see more; so pressing a native into our service, we proceeded along the brink of the N. W. side, until, being nearly half-way round the outer circle of the crater, we had hoped to obtain almost a bird's-eye view of the active volcano; we were therefore extremely chagrined to find, that as we drew nearer our object, it was completely shut out by a ridge below the one on which we stood. Our walking had thus far been very difficult, if not dangerous, and this, with the fatigues of the morning, had nearly exhausted our perseverance. We determined, however, to make another effort before giving it up, and were repaid by the discovery of a spur which led us down, and thence through a short valley to the point, where our track (I) terminates. We came in sight of the crater as we crested the hill; the view from hence was most brilliant. The crater appeared nearly circular, and was traversed in all directions by what seemed canals of fire intensely bright; several of these radiated from a centre near the N. E. edge, so as to

form a star, from which a coruscation, as if of jets of burning gas, was emitted. In other parts were furnaces in terrible activity, and undergoing continual change, sometimes becoming comparatively dark, and then bursting forth, throwing up torrents of flame and molten lava. All around the edge it seemed exceedingly agitated, and a noise like surf was audible; otherwise the stillness served to heighten the effect upon the senses, which it would be difficult to describe. The waning moon warned us to return, and reluctantly we retraced our steps; it required care to do this, so that we did not get back to the house before midnight. Worn out with the day's exertions, we threw ourselves on the ground and fell asleep, but not before I had revolved the possibility of standing at the brink of the active crater after nightfall. In the morning we matured the plan, which was to descend by daylight, so as to reconnoitre our road, to return to dinner, and then, if we thought it practicable, to leave the house about 5 P. M., and to remain in the large crater till after night set in. The only objection to this scheme (and it was a most serious one) was, that when we mentioned it to the guides, they appeared completely horror-struck at the notion of it. Here, as elsewhere in the neighbourhood of volcanic activity, the common people have a superstitious dread of a presiding deity; in this place, especially, where they are scarcely rescued from heathenism, we are not surprised to find it. This, and their personal fears (no human being ever having, as the natives assured us, entered the crater in darkness), we then found insuperable: all we could do was to take the best guides we were able to procure with us by daylight, so that they should refresh their memories as to the *locale*, and ascertain if any change had taken place since their last visit, and trust to being able during our walk to persuade one to return with us in the evening. Accordingly we all left the house after breakfast, following the track marked (H), which led us precipitously down, till we landed on the surface of the large crater, an immense sheet of scoriaceous lava cooled suddenly from a state of fusion; the upheaved waves and deep hollows evidencing that congelation has taken place before the mighty agitation has subsided. It is dotted with cones 60 or 70 feet high, and extensively intersected by deep cracks, from both of which sulphurous smoke ascends. It is surrounded by a wall about twelve miles in circumference, in most parts 1000 feet deep. I despair of conveying an idea of what our sensations were, when we first launched out on this fearful pit to cross to the active crater at the further end. With all the feeling of insecurity that attends treading on unsafe ice, was combined the utter sense of helplessness the desolation of the scene encouraged: it produced a sort of instinctive dread, such as brutes might be supposed to feel in such situations. This, however, soon left us, and attending our guides, who led us away to the right for about a mile, we turned abruptly to the left, and came upon a deep dike, which, running concentric with the sides, terminates near the active crater, with which I conceive its bottom is on a level. The lava had slipped into it where we crossed, and the loose blocks were difficult to scramble over. In the lowest part where these had not fallen, the fire appeared immediately beneath the surface. The guides here evinced great caution, trying with their poles before venturing their weight; the heat was intense, and made us glad to find ourselves again on *terra firma*, if that expression may be allowed where the walking was exceedingly disagreeable, owing to the hollowness of the lava, formed in great bubbles, that continually broke and let us in up to our knees. This dike has probably been formed by the drainage of the volcano by a lateral vent, as the part of the crater which it confines has sunk lower than that outside it, and the contraction caused by loss of heat may well account for its width, which varies from one to three hundred yards. In support of this opinion, I may mention, that in 1840 a molten river broke out, eight miles to the eastward, and in some places six miles broad, rolled down to the sea, where it materially altered the line of coast. From where we crossed, there is a gradual rise until within 200 yards

of the volcano, when the surface dips to its margin. Owing to this we came suddenly in view of it, and, lost in amazement, walked silently on to the brink. To the party who had made the excursion the previous evening, the surprise was not so great as to the others; moreover, a bright noonday sun, and a floating mirage which made it difficult to discern the real from the deceptive, robbed the scene of much of its brilliancy; still it was truly sublime, as a feeble attempt at description will show. This immense caldron, two and three-quarter miles in circumference, is filled to within twenty feet of its brim with red molten lava, over which lies a thin scum resembling the slag on a smelting furnace. The whole surface was in fearful agitation. Great rollers followed each other to the side, and, breaking, disclosed deep edges of crimson. These were the canals of fire we had noticed the night before diverging from a common centre, and the furnaces in equal activity; while what had appeared to us like jets of gas, proved to be fitful spurts of lava, thrown up from all parts of the lake (though principally from the focus near the N. E. edge) a height of thirty feet. Most people probably would have been satisfied with having witnessed this magnificent spectacle; but our admiration was so little exhausted, that the idea continually suggested itself, "How grand would this be by night!" The party who had encountered the difficulties of the walk the night before, were convinced that no greater ones existed in that of to-day; and therefore, if it continued fine, and we could induce the guide to accompany us, the project was feasible. The avarice of one of these ultimately overcame his fears, and, under his direction, we again left the house at 5 P. M., and, returning by our old track, reached the hill above the crater about the time the sun set, though long after it had sunk below the edge of the pit. Here we halted, and smoking our cigars lit from the cracks (now red-hot) which we had passed unnoticed in the glare of the sunlight, waited until it became quite dark, when we moved on; and, great as had been our expectations, we found them faint compared with the awful sublimity of the scene before us. The slag now appeared semi-transparent, and so extensively perforated as to show one sheet of liquid fire, its waves rising high, and pouring over each other in magnificent confusion, forming a succession of cascades of unequalled grandeur; the canals, now incandescent, the restless activity of the numerous vents throwing out great volumes of molten lava, the terrible agitation, and the brilliancy of the jets, which, shooting high in the air, fell with an echoless, lead-like sound, breaking the otherwise impressive stillness; formed a picture that language (at least any that I know) is quite inadequate to describe. We felt this; for no one spoke except when betrayed into an involuntary burst of amazement. On our hands and knees we crawled to the brink, and lying at full length, and shading our faces with paper, looked down at the fiery breakers as they dashed against the side of the basin beneath. The excessive heat, and the fact that the spray was frequently dashed over the edge, put a stop to this fool-hardiness; but at a more rational distance we stood gazing, with our feelings of wonder and awe so intensely excited, that we paid no regard to the entreaties of our guide to quit the spot. He at last persuaded us of the necessity of doing so, by pointing to the moon, and her distance above the dense cloud which hung, a lurid canopy, above the crater. Taking a last look, we "fell in" in Indian file, and got back to the house, with no further accident than a few bruises, about ten o'clock. The walk had required caution, and it was long after I had closed my eyes ere the retina yielded the impressions that had been so nervously drawn on them. The next morning at nine, we started on our return to the ship, sauntering leisurely along, picking strawberries by the way, and enjoying all the satisfaction inherent to the successful accomplishment of an undertaking. With health and strength for any attempt, we had been peculiarly favoured by the weather, and had thus done more than any who had preceded us. Our party, under

these circumstances, was most joyous; so that, independent of the object, the relaxation itself was such as we creatures of habit and discipline seldom experience.

To make this narrative more intelligible, it will be necessary to describe briefly the position and general features of this volcano, which does not, like most others, spring from a cone, but has excavated for itself a bed in the side of Mowna Roa, which rises 14,000 feet above the level of the sea; it is about sixteen miles distant from the summit of the mountain, wherein is an enormous extinct crater, from which this is probably the outlet; it is 4000 feet above the level of the sea, and twenty miles from the nearest coast line. Several distinct levels in the present crater prove that it has eaten its way to its present depth. On the most elevated of these, large trees now grow, evidences of many years' tranquillity; lower down we come to shrubs, and lastly to the fern, apparently the most venturesome of the vegetable kingdom; it seems to require nothing but rest and water, for we found it shooting out of crevices where the lava appeared to have undergone no decomposition. Nowhere, I conceive (not even in Iceland), can be seen such stupendous volcanic efforts as in Owhyhee. The whole island, eighty-six miles long by seventy broad, and rising, as it does at Mowna Keah, more than 15,000 feet above the sea, would seem to have been formed by layers of lava imposed at different periods. Some of these have followed quickly on each other; while the thickness of soil, made up of vegetable mould and decomposed lava, indicates a long interval of repose between others. The present surface is comparatively recent, though there is no tradition of any but partial eruptions.

"O Lord! how manifold are Thy works: in wisdom hast Thou made them all!"

We reached the village the next day at 1 P.M., and after a refreshing bathe, returned on board to find the ship prepared for sea, to which we proceeded the following morning at four o'clock.

THE DAYS OF THE FRONDE.

AT the beginning of the present year, and upon the authority of M. Alexandre Dumas, we laid before the readers of this Magazine a sketch of certain incidents in the lives of three French guardsmen, who, in company with a young cadet of Gascony, fought, drank, loved, and plotted under the reign of Louis the Thirteenth and the rule of Richelieu. The sketch was incomplete: contrary to established practice, M. Dumas neither married nor killed his heroes; but after exposing them to innumerable perils, out of all of which they came triumphant, although from none did they derive any important benefit, he left them nearly as he found them—with their fortunes still to make, and with little to rely upon save their good swords and their dauntless courage. He promised, however, a continuation of their history, and that promise he has kept, but with a difference. Passing over a score of years, he again introduces us to the guardsmen, whom he left in the heyday of youth, and who have now attained, most of them passed, the sober age of forty.

Twenty years later, then, we find D'Artagnan, the young Gascon gentleman aforesaid, alone upon the scene. His three friends, influenced by various motives, have retired from the corps of mousquetaires: Athos to reside upon a small estate in Poitou, Porthos to marry a rich widow, Aramis to become an abbé. D'Artagnan alone, having no estate to retire to larger than a cabbage garden, no widow to marry, or inclination for the church, has stuck to the service with credit, but with small profit to himself; and the lieutenancy bestowed upon him by the Cardinal-Duke in 1628, is still a lieutenancy in 1648, under Richelieu's less able, but equally ambitious successor, Cardinal Mazarine. Moreover, deprived, during the greater part of these twenty years, of the society of his three friends, who had in some measure formed his character, and from the example of two of whom he had caught much of what chivalry and elegance he possessed—deprived also of opportunities of dis-playing those peculiar talents for bold intrigue, which had once enabled him to thwart the projects of Richelieu himself, D'Artagnan has degenerated into a mere trooper. His talents and shrewdness have not deserted him; on the contrary, the latter has increased with his experience of the world; but instead of being employed in the service of queens and princes, their exercise has been for some years confined to procuring their owner those physical and positive comforts which soldiers seek and prize—namely, a good table, comfortable quarters, and a complaisant hostess.

Although thus making the best of his position, and only occasionally grumbling at the caprice of Dame Fortune, who seems entirely to have forgotten him, it is with a lively sensation of joy that D'Artagnan, one evening when on guard at the Palais Royal, hears himself summoned to the presence of Mazarine. It is at the commencement of the Fronde; the exactions of the cardinal have irritated the people, who show symptoms of open resistance; his enemies, already sufficiently numerous, are daily increasing and becoming more formidable. Mazarine trembles for his power, and looks around him for men of head and action, to aid him in breasting the storm and carrying out his schemes. He hears tell of the four guardsmen, whose fidelity and devotion had once saved the reputation of Anne of Austria, and baffled the most powerful minister France ever saw; these four men he resolves to make his own, and D'Artagnan is dispatched to find his three former companions, and induce them to espouse the cause of the cardinal. The mission is but partially successful. D'Artagnan finds Porthos, whose real name is Du Vallon, rich, flourishing, and a widower, but, notwithstanding all these advantages, perfectly unhappy because he has no title. Vanity was always the failing of Porthos. Aramis, otherwise the Chevalier—now the Abbé—d'Herblay, is up to the ears in intrigues of every description. Athos, Count de la Fère, has abandoned the wine-flask, formerly the deity of his adoration, and is busied in the education of a natural son, a youth of sixteen, of whom the beautiful Duchess of Chevreuse is the mother. By the promise of a barony, D'Artagnan easily induces Porthos to follow him to Paris; but with his other two friends he is less successful. Athos and Aramis put him off with excuses, for both have already pledged themselves to the cause of the Fronde and of the Duke of Beaufort.

This prince, the grandson of Henry the Fourth, and of the celebrated Gabrielle D'Estrées, is a prisoner in the fortress of Vincennes, and a constant subject of uneasiness to Mazarine. Brave as steel, but of limited capacity, the idol of the people, who, by the use of his name, are easily roused to rebellion, the duke has beguiled his long captivity by abuse of the Facchino Mazarini, as he styles the cardinal, and by keeping up a constant petty warfare with the governor of Vincennes, Monsieur de Chavigny. On his way to prison, he boasted to his guards that he had at least forty plans of escape, some one of which would infallibly succeed. This was repeated to the cardinal; and so well is the duke guarded in consequence, that five years have elapsed and he is still at Vincennes. At last his friends find means of communicating with him, and Grimaud, the servant of the Count de la Fère, is introduced, in the capacity of an under jailer, into the fortress, where, by his taciturnity and apparent strictness, he gains the entire confidence of La Ramée, an official who, under M. de Chavigny, is appointed to the especial guardianship of the Duke of Beaufort. An attempt to escape is fixed for the day of the Pentecost. Upon the morning of that day, Monsieur de Chavigny starts upon a short journey, leaving the castle in charge of La Ramée, whom the duke invites to sup with him upon a famous pasty, that has been ordered for the occasion from a confectioner who has recently established himself at Vincennes. Here is what takes place at the repast.

La Ramée, who, at the bottom of his heart, entertained a considerable degree of regard and affection for M. de Beaufort, made himself a great treat of this tête-à-tête supper. His chief foible was gluttony, and for this grand occasion the confectioner had promised to outdo himself. The pastry was to be of pheasants, the wine of the best vintage of Chambertin. By adding to the agreeable images which this promise called up in his mind, the society of the duke, who in the main was such an excellent fellow, who played Monsieur de Chavigny such capital tricks, and made such biting jokes against the cardinal, La Ramée had composed a picture of a perfectly delightful evening, which he looked forward to with proportionate jubilation, and with an impatience almost equalling that of the duke. His first visit that morning had been to the pastrycook, who had shown him the crust of a gigantic pasty, decorated at the top with the arms of Monsieur de Beaufort. The said crust was still empty, but beside it were a pheasant and two partridges, so minutely and closely larded, that each of them looked like a cushion stuck full of pins. La Ramée's mouth watered at the sight.

Early in the day, M. de Beaufort went to play at ball with La Ramée; a sign from Grimaud warned him to pay attention to everything. Grimaud walked before them, as if to point out the road that he and the duke would have to take that evening. The place where they were in the habit of playing was the smaller court of the fortress—a solitary enclosure, where sentinels only were stationed when the duke was there; even that precaution seeming unnecessary, on account of the great height of the ramparts. There were three doors to open before reaching this court, and each door was opened with a different key. All three keys were kept by La Ramée. When they reached the court, Grimaud seated himself negligently in one of the embrasures, his legs dangling outside the wall. The duke understood that the rope-ladder was to be fixed at that place. This, and other manœuvres, comprehensible enough to M. de Beaufort, and carefully noted by him, had, of course, no intelligible meaning for La Ramée.

The game began. M. de Beaufort was in play, and sent the balls wherever he liked; La Ramée could not win a game. When they had finished playing, the duke, whilst rallying La Ramée on his ill success, pulled out a couple of louis-d'ors, and offered them to his guards, who had followed him to the court to pick up the balls, telling them to go and drink his health. The guards asked La Ramée's permission, which he gave, but for the evening only. Up to that time he had various important matters to arrange, some of which would require him to absent himself from his prisoner, whom he did not wish to be lost sight of.

Six o'clock came, and although the dinner hour was fixed for seven, the table was already spread, and the enormous pie placed upon the sideboard. Everybody was impatient for something : the guards to go and drink, La Ramée to dine, and Monsieur de Beaufort to escape. Grimaud was the only one who seemed to be waiting for nothing, and to remain perfectly calm; and at times when the duke looked at his dull, immoveable countenance, he almost doubted whether that could be the man who was to aid his projected flight.

At half-past six La Ramée dismissed the guards, the duke sat down at the table, and signed to his jailer to take a chair opposite to him. Grimaud served the soup, and stationed himself behind La Ramée. The most perfect enjoyment was depicted on the countenance of the latter, as he commenced the repast from which he had been anticipating so much pleasure. The duke looked at him with a smile.

"Ventre St Gris! La Ramée," cried he, "if I were told that at this moment there is in all France a happier man than yourself, I would not believe it."

"And you would be quite right not to do so, Monseigneur," said La Ramée. "I confess that, when I am hungry, I know no pleasure equal to that of sitting down to a good dinner ; and when I remember that my Amphitryon is the grandson of Henry the Fourth, the pleasure is at least doubled by the honour done to me."

The duke bowed. "My dear La Ramée," said he, "you are unequalled in the art of paying compliments."

"It is no compliment, Monseigneur," said La Ramée ; "I say exactly what I think."

"You are really attached to me, then ?" said the duke.

"Most sincerely," replied La Ramée ; "and I should be inconsolable if your highness were to leave Vincennes."

"A singular proof of affection that !" returned the duke.

"But, Monseigneur," continued La Ramée, sipping at a glass of Madeira, "what would you do if you were set at liberty ? You would only get into some new scrape, and be sent to the Bastile instead of to Vincennes."

"Indeed !" said the duke, considerably amused at the turn the conversation was taking, and glancing at the clock, of which the hands, as he thought, advanced more slowly than usual.

"M. de Chavigny is not very amiable," said La Ramée, "but M. de Tremblay is a great deal worse. You may depend, Monseigneur, that it was a real kindness to send you here, where you breathe a fine air, and have nothing to do but to eat and drink, and play at ball."

"According to your account, La Ramée, I was very ungrateful ever to think of escaping."

"Exceedingly so," replied La Ramée ; "but your highness never did think seriously of it."

"Indeed did I, though !" said the duke ; "and what is more, folly though it may be, I sometimes think of it still."

"Still by one of your forty plans, Monseigneur ?"

The duke nodded affirmatively.

"Monseigneur," resumed La Ramée, "since you have so far honoured me with your confidence, I wish you would tell me one of the forty methods of escape which your highness had invented."

"With pleasure," replied the duke. "Grimaud, give me the pasty."

"I am all attention," said La Ramée, leaning back in his chair, and raising his glass so as to look at the setting sun through the liquid amber which it contained. The duke glanced at the clock. Ten minutes more and it would strike seven, the hour for which his escape was concerted. Grimaud placed the pie before M. de Beaufort, who took his silver-bladed knife—steel ones were not allowed him—to cut it; but La Ramée, unwilling to see so magnificent a pasty mangled by a dull knife, passed him his own, which was of steel.

"Well, Monseigneur," said he, "and this famous plan?"

"Do you wish me to tell you," said the duke, "the one on the success of which I most reckoned, and which I intended to try the first?"

"By all means," said La Ramée.

"Well," said M. de Beaufort, who was busy in the dissection of the pie, "in the first place I hoped to have for my guardian some honest fellow like yourself, Monsieur La Ramée."

"Your hope was realized, Monseigneur. And then?"

"I said to myself," continued the duke, "if once I have about me a good fellow like La Ramée, I will get a friend, whom he does not know to be my friend, to recommend to him a man devoted to my interests, and who will aid my escape."

"Good!" said La Ramée. "No bad idea."

"When I have accomplished this," said the duke, "if the man is skilful, and manages to gain the confidence of my jailer, I shall have no difficulty in keeping up a communication with my friends."

"Indeed!" said La Ramée; "how so?"

"Easily enough," replied M. de Beaufort; "in playing at ball, for instance."

"In playing at ball!" repeated La Ramée, who was beginning to pay great attention to the duke's words.

"Yes. I strike a ball into the moat; a man who is at hand, working in his garden, picks it up. The ball contains a letter. Instead of throwing back the same ball, he throws another, which contains a letter for me. My friends hear from me and I from them, without any one being the wiser."

"The devil!" said La Ramée, scratching his head, "you do well to tell me this, Monseigneur. In future I will keep an eye on pickers up of balls. But, after all, that is only a means of correspondence."

"Wait a little. I write to my friends—'On such a day and at such an hour, be in waiting on the other side of the moat with two led horses.'"

"Well," said La Ramée, with some appearance of uneasiness, "but what then? Unless, indeed, the horses have wings and can fly up the rampart to fetch you."

"Or that I have means of flying down," said the duke, carelessly. "A rope-ladder for instance."

"Yes," said La Ramée, with a forced laugh; "but a rope-ladder can hardly be sent in a tennis-ball, though a letter may."

"No; but it may be sent in something else. Let us only suppose, for argument's sake, that my cook, Noirmont, has purchased the pastrycook's shop opposite the castle. La Ramée, who is a bit of an epicure, tries his pies, finds them excellent, and asks me if I would like to taste one. I accept the offer on condition that he shall help me to eat it. To do so more at his ease, he sends away the guards, and only keeps Grimaud here to wait upon us. Grimaud is the man whom my friend has recommended, and who is ready to second me in all things. The moment of my escape is fixed for seven o'clock. At a few minutes to seven"——

"At a few minutes to seven!" repeated La Ramée, perspiring with alarm.

"At a few minutes to seven," continued the duke, suiting the action to the word, "I take the crust off the pie. Inside it, I find two poniards, a rope-ladder, and a gag. I put one of the poniards to La Ramée's breast, and I say to him—'My good friend, La Ramée, if you make a motion or utter a cry, you are a dead man'!"

The duke, as we have already said, whilst uttering these last sentences, had acted in conformity. He was now standing close to La Ramée, to whom his tone of voice, and the sight of the dagger levelled at his heart, intimated plainly enough that M. de Beaufort would keep his word. Meanwhile Grimaud, silent as the grave, took out of the pie the second poniard, the rope-ladder, and the gag. La Ramée followed each of these objects with his eye with a visibly increasing terror.

"Oh, Monseigneur!" cried he, looking at the duke with an air of stupefaction, which, at any other time would have made M. de Beaufort laugh heartily, "you would not have the heart to kill me?"

"No, if you do not oppose my flight."

"But, Monseigneur, if I let you escape, I am a ruined man."

"I will pay you the value of your office."

"And if I defend myself, or call out?"

"By the honour of a gentleman, you die upon the spot!"

At this moment the clock struck.

"Seven o'clock," said Grimaud, who had not yet uttered a word.

La Ramée made a movement. The duke frowned, and the unlucky jailer felt the point of the dagger penetrate his clothes, and press against his breast.

"Enough, Monseigneur," cried he; "I will not stir. But I entreat you to tie my hands and feet, or I shall be taken for your accomplice."

The duke took off his girdle, and gave it to Grimaud, who tied La Ramée's hands firmly behind his back. La Ramée then held out his legs; Grimaud tore a napkin into strips, and bound his ankles together.

"And now the gag!" cried poor La Ramée; "the gag! I insist upon it; or they will hang me for not having given the alarm."

In an instant La Ramée was gagged, and laid upon the ground; two or three chairs were overturned, to make it appear that there had been a struggle. Grimaud took from La Ramée's pockets all the keys that they contained, opened the room-door, shut and double locked it when the duke and himself had passed out, and led the way to the court. This the fugitives reached without accident or encounter, and found it entirely deserted; no sentinels, nor anybody at the windows that overlooked it. The duke hurried to the rampart, and saw upon the further side of the moat three horsemen and two led horses. He exchanged a sign with them; they were waiting for him. Meanwhile Grimaud was fastened to the rope by which the descent was to be effected. It was not a ladder but a silken cord rolled upon a stick, which was to be placed between the legs, and becomes unrolled by the weight of the person descending.

"Go," said the duke.

"First, Monseigneur?" asked Grimaud.

"Certainly," was the reply; "if I am taken, a prison awaits me; if you are caught, you will be hung."

"True," said Grimaud; and putting himself astride the stick, he commenced his perilous descent. The duke followed him anxiously with his eyes. About three quarters of the distance were accomplished, when the cord broke, and Grimaud fell into the moat. M. de Beaufort uttered a cry; but Grimaud said nothing, although he was evidently severely hurt, for he remained motionless upon the spot on which he had fallen. One of the three horsemen slid down into the moat, fastened the noose of a rope under the arms of Grimaud, and his two companions, who held the other end, pulled him up.

"Come down, Monseigneur," cried the cavaliers; "the fall is only about fifteen feet, and the grass is soft."

The duke was already descending. His task was difficult; for the stick was no longer there to sustain him, and he was obliged to lower himself along the slender rope from a height of fifty feet by sheer force of wrist. But his activity, strength, and coolness came to his aid; in less than five minutes he was at the end of the cord. He then let go his hold, and fell upon his feet without injury. Climbing out of the moat, he found himself in the company of Count Rochefort, and of two other gentlemen with whom he was unacquainted. Grimaud, whose senses had left him, was fastened upon a horse.

"Gentlemen," said the duke, "I will thank you and by; just now we have not an instant to lose. Forward then, and let who loves me follow."

And springing upon his horse, he set off at full gallop, breathing as if a load were removed from his breast, and exclaiming in accents of inexpressible joy—

"Free! Free! Free!"

The two cavaliers who accompany the Duke and the Count de Rochefort, are Athos and Aramis. D'Artagnan and Porthos are sent in pursuit of the cardinal, and in the obscurity by night the four friends, who have so often fought side by side, find themselves at sword's point with each other. Fortunately a recognition ensues before any harm is done. A strong party of the Duke of Beaufort's adherents comes up, and D'Artagan and Porthos are taken prisoners, but immediately set at liberty by the duke.

The readers of the *Three Mousquetaires* will not have forgotten a certain Lady de Winter, having a *fleur-de-lis* branded on her shoulder, who plays an important part in that romance, and who, after committing innumerable crimes, at last meets her death at the hands of a public executioner, but without form of trial. This latter, indeed, might be considered almost superfluous, so numerous and notorious were her offences; but nevertheless, D'Artagnan and his three friends, by whose order and in whose presence the execution took place, sometimes feel pangs of remorse for the deed, which none of the many lives they have taken in fair and open fight ever occasion them. Athos especially, the most reflecting and sensitive of the four, continually reproaches himself with the share he took in that act of illegal justice. This woman has left a son, who inherits all her vices, and who, having been proved illegitimate, has been deprived of Lord De Winter's estates, and passes by the name of Mordaunt. He is now. brought upon the scene. Raoul, Viscount of Braguelonne, the son of Athos, is proceeding to Flanders, in company with the young Count de Guiche, to join the army under the Prince of Condé, when, on the last day of his journey, and whilst passing through a forest, he falls in with, and disperses a party of Spanish marauders, who are robbing and ill-treating two travellers. Of these latter, one is dead, and the other, who is desperately wounded, implores the aid of a priest. Raoul and his friend order their attendants to form a litter of branches, and to convey the wounded man to a neighbouring forest inn, whilst they hasten on to the next village to procure him the spiritual consolation he is so urgent to obtain.

The two young men had ridden

more than a league, and were already in sight of the village of Greney, when they saw coming towards them, mounted upon a mule, a poor monk, whom, from his large hat and grey woollen gown, they took to be an Augustine friar. Chance seemed to have sent them exactly what they were seeking. Upon approaching the monk, they found him to be a man of two or three and twenty years of age, but who might have been taken for some years older, owing probably to long fasts and severe penances. His complexion was pale, not that clear white paleness which is agreeable to behold, but a bilious yellow; his hair was of a light colour, and his eyes, of a greenish grey, seemed devoid of all expression.

" Sir," said Raoul, with his usual politeness, " have you taken orders?"

" Why do you ask?" said the stranger, in a tone so abrupt as to be scarcely civil.

" For our information," replied the Count de Guiche haughtily.

The stranger touched his mule with his heel, and moved onwards. With a bound of his horse De Guiche placed himself before him, blocking up the road. " Answer, sir," said he. " The question was politely put, and deserves a reply."

" I am not obliged, I suppose, to inform the first comer who and what I am."

With considerable difficulty De Guiche repressed a violent inclination to break the bones of the insolent monk.

" In the first place," said he, " we will tell you who *we* are. My friend here is the Viscount of Braguelonne, and I am the Count de Guiche. It is no mere caprice that induces us to question you; we are seeking spiritual aid for a dying man. If you are a priest, I call upon you in the name of humanity to afford him the assistance he implores; if, on the other hand, you are not in orders, I warn you to expect the chastisement which your impertinence merits."

The monk's pale face became livid, and a smile of so strange an expression overspread it, that Raoul, whose eyes were fixed upon him, felt an involuntary and unaccountable uneasiness.

"He is some spy of the Imperialists," said the viscount, putting his hand upon his pistols. A stern and menacing glance from the monk replied to the accusation.

"Well, sir," said De Guiche, "will you answer?"

"I am a priest," replied the young man, his face resuming its former calm inexpressiveness.

"Then, holy father," said Raoul, letting his pistol fall back into the holster, and giving a tone of respect to his words, "since you are a priest, you have now an opportunity of exercising your sacred functions. A man wounded to death is at the little inn which you will soon find upon your road, and he implores the assistance of one of God's ministers."

"I will go to him," said the monk calmly, setting his mule in motion.

"If you do not, sir," said De Guiche, "remember that our horses will soon overtake your mule, that we possess sufficient influence to have you seized wherever you go, and that then your trial will be very short. A tree and a rope are to be found everywhere."

The eyes of the monk emitted an angry spark, but he merely repeated the words, "I will go to him," and rode on.

"Let us follow," said De Guiche; "it will be the surest plan."

"I was about to propose it," said Raoul. And the young men followed the monk at pistol-shot distance.

On arriving in sight of the roadside tavern, they saw their servants approaching it from the opposite direction, leading their horses, and carrying the wounded man. On perceiving the monk, an expression of joy illuminated the countenance of the sufferer.

"And now," said Raoul, "we have done all we can for you, and must hasten onwards to join the prince's army. There is to be a battle tomorrow, it is said, and we would not miss it."

The host had got everything ready, a bed, lint and bandages, and a messenger had been dispatched to Lens, which was the nearest town, to bring back a surgeon.

"You will follow us," said Raoul to the servants, "as soon as you have

conveyed this person to his room. A horseman will arrive here in the course of the afternoon," added he to the innkeeper, "and will probably inquire if the Viscount de Braguelonne has passed this way. He is one of my attendants, and his name is Grimaud. You will tell him that I have passed, and shall sleep at Cambrin."

By this time the litter had reached the door of the inn. The monk got off his mule, ordered it to be put in the stable without unsaddling, and entered the house. The two young men rode away, followed by the benedictions of the wounded man.

The litter was just being carried into the inn, when the hostess hurried forward to receive her guests. On catching sight of the sufferer, she seized her husband's arm with an exclamation of terror.

"Well," said the host, "what is the matter?"

"Do you not recognize him?" said the woman, pointing to the wounded man.

"Recognize him! No—yet—surely I remember the face. Can it be?"——

"The former headsman of Bethune," said his wife, completing the sentence.

"The headsman of Bethune!" repeated the young monk, recoiling with a look and gesture of marked repugnance.

The chief of Raoul's attendants perceived the disgust with which the monk heard the quality of his penitent.

"Sir," he said, "although he may have been an executioner, or even if he still be so, it is no reason for refusing him the consolations of religion. Render him the service he claims at your hands, and you will have the more merit in the sight of God."

The monk made no reply, but entered a room on the ground-floor, in which the servants were now placing the wounded man upon a bed. As he did so, every one left the apartment, and the penitent remained alone with his confessor. The presence of Raoul's and De Guiche's followers being no longer required, the latter remounted their horses, and set off at a sharp trot to rejoin their masters, who were already out of sight.

They had been gone but a few

minutes, when a single horseman rode up to the door of the inn.

"What is your pleasure, sir ?" said the host, still pale and aghast at the discovery his wife had made.

"A feed for my horse, and a bottle of wine for myself," was the reply. "Have you seen a young gentleman pass by," continued the stranger, "mounted on a chestnut horse, and followed by two attendants ?"

"The Viscount de Braguelonne ?" aid the innkeeper.

"The same."

"Then you are Monsieur Grimaud ?"

The traveller nodded assent.

"Your master was here not half an hour ago," said the host. "He has ridden on, and will sleep at Cambrin."

Grimaud sat down at a table, wiped the dust and perspiration from his face, poured out a glass of wine, and drank in silence. He was about to fill his glass a second time, when a loud shrill cry was heard, issuing from the apartment in which the monk and the patient were shut up together. Grimaud started to his feet.

"What is that ?" exclaimed he.

"From the wounded man's room," replied the host.

"What wounded man ?"

"The former headsman of Bethune, who has been set upon and sorely hurt by Spanish partisans. The Viscount de Braguelonne rescued and brought him hither, and he is now confessing himself to an Augustine friar. He seems to suffer terribly."

"The headsman of Bethune," muttered Grimaud, apparently striving to recollect something. "A man of fifty-five or sixty years of age, tall and powerful; of dark complexion, with black hair and beard ?"

"The same; excepting that his beard has become grey, and his hair white. Do you know him ?"

"I have seen him once," replied Grimaud gloomily.

At this moment another cry was heard, less loud than the first, but followed by a long deep groan. Grimaud and the innkeeper looked at each other.

"It is like the cry of a man who is being murdered," said the latter.

"We must see what it is," said Grimaud.

Although slow to speak, Grimaud was prompt in action. He rushed to the door, and shook it violently; it was secured on the inner side.

"Open the door instantly," cried he, "or I break it down."

No answer was returned. Grimaud looked around him, and perceived a heavy crowbar standing in a corner of the passage. This he seized hold of, and before the host could interfere, the door was burst open. The room was inundated with blood, which was trickling from the mattrass ; there was a hoarse rattling in the wounded man's throat ; the monk had disappeared. Grimaud hurried to an open window which looked upon the court-yard.

"He has escaped through this," said he.

"Do you think so ?" said the host. "Boy, see if the monk's mule is still in the stable."

"It is gone," was the answer.

Grimaud approached the bed, and gazed upon the harsh and strongly marked features of the wounded man.

"Is he still alive ?" said the host.

Without replying, Grimaud opened the man's doublet to feel if his heart beat, and at the same time the innkeeper approached the bed. Suddenly both started back with an exclamation of horror. A poniard was buried to the hilt in the left breast of the headsman.

What had passed between the priest and his penitent was as follows.

It has been seen that the monk showed himself little disposed to delay his journey in order to receive the confession of the wounded man ; so little, indeed, that he would probably have endeavoured to avoid it by flight, had not the menaces of the Count de Guiche, and afterwards the presence of the servants, or perhaps his own reflections, induced him to perform to the end the duties of his sacred office.

On finding himself alone with the sufferer, he approached the pillow of the latter. The headsman examined him with one of those rapid, anxious looks peculiar to dying men, and made a movement of surprise.

"You are very young, holy father," said he.

"Those who wear my dress have no age," replied the monk severely.

"Alas, good father, speak to me more kindly! I need a friend in these my last moments."

"Do you suffer much?" asked the monk.

"Yes, but in soul rather than in body."

"We will save your soul," said the young man; "but, tell me, are you really the executioner of Bethune, as these people say."

"I was," replied the wounded man hurriedly, as though fearful that the acknowledgment of his degrading profession might deprive him of the assistance of which he stood in such imminent need. "I was, but I am so no longer; I gave up my office many years ago. I am still obliged to appear at executions, but I no longer officiate. Heaven forbid that I should!"

"You have a horror of your profession, then?"

The headsman groaned.

"So long as I only struck in the name of the law and of justice," said he, "my conscience was at rest, and my sleep untroubled; but since that terrible night when I served as instrument of a private vengeance, and raised my sword with hatred against one of God's creatures—since that night"——

The headsman paused, and shook his head despairingly.

"Speak on," said the monk, who had seated himself on the edge of the bed, and began to take an interest in a confession that commenced so strangely.

"Ah!" exclaimed the dying man, "what efforts have I not made to stifle my remorse by twenty years of good works! I have exposed my own existence to preserve that of others, and have saved human lives in exchange for the one I had unwarrantably taken. I frequented the churches, sought out the poor to console and relieve them; those who once avoided became accustomed to see me, and some have even loved me. But God has not pardoned me; for, do what I will, the memory of my crime pursues me, and each night in my dreams the spectre of that woman stands menacing before me."

"A woman! Was it a woman, then, whom you assassinated?" cried the monk.

"And you, too," exclaimed the headsman—"you, too, use that word, assassinated. It *was* an assassination, then, not an execution, and I am a murderer!"

He shut his eyes and uttered a hollow moan. The monk feared probably that he would die without completing his confession, for he hastened to console him.

"Go on," said he. "I cannot yet know how far you are guilty. When I have heard all, I will decide. Tell me, then, how you came to commit this deed."

"It was night," resumed the headsman, in faltering accents: "a man came to my house to seek me, and showed me an order. I followed him. Four other gentlemen were waiting for him; they put a mask upon my face, and led me with them. I was resolved to resist, if what they required me to do appeared unjust. We rode on for five or six leagues almost without uttering a word; at last we halted—and they showed me, through the window of a cottage, a woman seated at a table. 'That,' said they, 'is she whom you are to decapitate.'"

"Horrible!" exclaimed the monk. "And you obeyed?"

"Father, that woman was a monster; she had poisoned her husband, had tried to assassinate her brother-in-law, who was one of the men that now accompanied me; she had murdered a young girl whom she thought her rival; and, before leaving England, has instigated the assassination of the king's favourite."

"Buckingham?" exclaimed the monk.

"Yes, Buckingham—that was the name."

"She was an Englishwoman, then?"

"No—a Frenchwoman, but she had been married to an English nobleman."

The monk grew pale, passed his hand across his forehead, and, rising from the bed, approached the door and bolted it. The headsman thought that he was leaving him, and implored him to return.

"I am here," said the monk, resuming his seat. "Who were the five men who accompanied you?"

"One was an Englishman; the other four were French, and wore the uniform of the mousquetaires."

"Their names?" demanded the monk.

"I do not know them. But the four Frenchmen called the Englishman 'My lord.'"

"And the woman; was she young?"

"Young and beautiful, most beautiful, as she kneeled before me imploring mercy. I have never been able to understand how I had the courage to strike off that pale and lovely head."

The monk seemed to be under the influence of some violent emotion; his limbs trembled, and he appeared unable to speak. At last, mastering himself by a strong effort—"The name of this woman?" said he.

"I do not know it. She had been married twice, once in France and once in England."

"And you killed her!" said the monk, vehemently. "You served as instrument to those dastardly villains who dared not kill her themselves. You had no pity on her youth, her beauty, her weakness! You killed her!"

"Alas! holy father," said the headsman, "this woman concealed, under the exterior of an angel, the vices of a demon; and when I saw her, when I remembered all that I had myself suffered from her"——

"You? And what could she have done to you?"

"She had seduced my brother, who was a priest, had fled with him from his convent, lost him both body and soul."

"Your brother?"

"Yes, my brother had been her first lover. Oh, my father! do not look at me thus. I am very guilty, then! You cannot pardon me!"

The monk composed his features, which had assumed a terrible expression during the latter part of the dying man's confession.

"I will pardon you," said he, "if you tell me all. Since your brother was her first lover, you must know her maiden name. Tell it me."

"Oh, my God! my God!" exclaimed the headsman—"I am dying! Absolution, holy father! absolution!"

"Her name," said the monk, "and I give it to you."

The headsman, who was convulsed with agony, both physical and moral, seemed scarcely able to speak. The monk bent over him as if to catch the smallest sound he should utter.

"Her name," said he, "or no absolution." The dying man seemed to collect all his strength.

"Anne de Bueil," murmured he.

"Anne de Bueil!" repeated the monk, rising to his feet, and lifting his hands to heaven, "Anne de Bueil! Did you say Anne de Bueil?"

"Yes, yes, that was her name; and now absolve me, for I am dying."

"*I* absolve you?" cried the monk, with a laugh that made the sufferer's hair stand on end; "*I* absolve you? I am no priest!"

"You are no priest!" cried the headsman; "but who and what are you, then?"

"I will tell you, miscreant! I am John de Winter, and that woman"——

"And that woman" —— gasped the executioner.

"Was my mother!"

The headsman uttered a shriek, the long and terrible one which Grimaud and the innkeeper had heard.

"Oh, pardon, pardon!" murmured he—"forgive me, if not in God's name, at least in your own. If not as a priest, as a son."

"Pardon you!" replied the pretended monk; "pardon you! God may perhaps do it, but I never will. Die, wretch, die! unabsolved, despairing, and accursed." And, drawing a dagger from under his gown, he plunged it into the breast of the headsman "Take that," said he, "for my absolution."

It was then that the second cry, followed by a long moan, had been uttered. The headsman, who had partially raised himself, fell back upon the bed. The monk, without withdrawing his dagger from the wound, ran to the window, opened it, jumped out into the little flower-garden below, and hurried to the stable. Leading out his mule, he plunged into the thickest part of the adjacent forest, stripped off his monk's garb, took a horseman's dress out of his valise, and put it on. Then, making all haste to the nearest post-house, he took a horse, and continued with the utmost speed his journey to Paris.

The headsman lives long enough to inform Grimaud of what has passed; and Grimaud, who was present at the decapitation of Lady de Winter, returns to Paris, to put Athos and his friends on their guard against the vengeance of her son. Mordaunt, *alias* De Winter, is one of Cromwell's most devoted and unscrupulous agents, and is proceeding to the French capital to negotiate with Mazarine on the part of the Parliamentary general. Guided by what he has heard from the executioner of Bethune, he discovers who the men are by whose orders his mother was beheaded, and he vows their destruction. The four friends soon afterwards meet in England, whither D'Artagnan and Porthos have been sent on a mission to Cromwell; whilst Athos and Aramis have repaired thither to strive to prop the falling fortunes of Charles the First. We cannot say much in favour of that portion of the book of which the scene is laid on English ground. M. Dumas is much happier in his delineations of Frondeurs and Mazarinists than of Puritans and Cavaliers; and his account of Charles the First, and of the scenes prior to his execution, is horribly Frenchified.

After numerous narrow escapes from Mordaunt, who pursues them with unrelenting rancour, and succeeds in assassinating their friend and his uncle Lord de Winter, the four guardsmen embark on board a small vessel to return to France. Mordaunt discovers this, gets the captain and crew out of the way, replaces them by one Groslow and other creatures of his own, and conceals himself on board. His plan is, so soon as the vessel is a short distance out at sea, to escape in a boat with his confederates, after firing a train communicating with some barrels of powder in the hold. There is some improbability in this part of the story; but,

gunpowder plots have special privilege of absurdity. The guardsmen, however, discover the mischief that is brewing against them, just in time to escape through the cabin windows, and swim off to the boat, which is towing astern.

Scarcely had D'Artagnan cut the rope that attached the boat to the ship, when a shrill whistle was heard proceeding from the latter, which, as it moved on whilst the boat remained stationary, was already beginning to be lost to view in the darkness. At the same moment a lantern was brought upon deck, and lit up the figures of the crew. Suddenly a great outcry was heard; and just then the clouds that covered the heavens split and parted, and the silver light of the moon fell upon the white sails and dark rigging of the vessel. Persons were seen running about the deck in bewilderment and confusion; and Mordaunt himself, carrying a torch in his hand, appeared upon the poop.

At the appointed hour, Groslow had collected his men, and Mordaunt, after listening at the door of the cabin, and concluding from the silence that reigned that his intended victims were buried in sleep, had hurried to the powder barrels and set fire to the train. Whilst he was doing this, Groslow and his sailors were preparing to leave the ship.

"Haul in the rope," said the former, "and bring the boat alongside."

One of the sailors seized the rope and pulled it. It came to him without resistance.

"The cable is cut!" exclaimed the man; "the boat is gone."

"The boat gone?" repeated Groslow; "impossible!"

"It is nevertheless true," returned the sailor. "See here; nothing in our wake, and here is the end of the rope."

It was then that Groslow uttered the cry which the guardsmen heard from their boat.

"What is the matter?" demanded Mordaunt, emerging from the hatchway, his torch in his hand, and rushing towards the stern.

"The matter is, that your enemies

have escaped you. They have cut the rope, and saved themselves in the boat."

With a single bound Mordaunt was at the cabin door, which he burst open with his foot. It was empty.

"We will follow them," said Groslow; "they cannot be far off. We will give them the stem; sail right over them."

"Yes; but the powder—I have fired the train!"

"Damnation!" roared Groslow, rushing to the hatchway. "Perhaps there is still time."

A horrible laugh and a frightful blasphemy were Mordaunt's reply; and then, his features distorted by rage and disappointed hate rather than by fear, he hurled his torch into the sea, and precipitated himself after it. At the same moment, and before Groslow had reached the powder barrels, the ship opened like the crater of a volcano, a gush of fire rose from it with a noise like that of fifty pieces of artillery, and blazing fragments of the doomed vessel were seen careering through the air in every direction. It lasted but an instant; the red glow that had lit up the sea for miles around vanished; the burning fragments fell hissing into the water; and with the exception of a vibration in the air, all was calm as before. The felucca had disappeared; Groslow, and his men were annihilated.

Our four guardsmen had witnessed this terrible spectacle with mute awe and horror, and when it was over, they remained for a moment downcast and silent. Porthos and D'Artagnan, who had each taken an oar, forgot to use them, and sat gazing at their companions, whilst the boat rocked to and fro at the will of the waves.

"*Ma foi!*" said Aramis, who was the first to break the pause, "this time I think we are fairly rid of him."

"Help, gentlemen, help!" just then cried a voice that came sweeping in piteous accents over the troubled surface of the sea. "Help! for heaven's sake, help!"

The guardsmen looked at each other. Athos shuddered.

"It is his voice!" said he.

All recognized the voice, and strained their eyes in the direction in which the felucca had disappeared. Presently a man was seen swimming vigorously towards them. Athos extended his arm, pointing him out to his companions.

"Yes, yes," said D'Artagnan; "I see him."

"Will nothing kill him?" said Porthos.

Aramis leaned forward and spoke in a whisper to D'Artagnan. Mordaunt advanced a few yards, and raised one hand out of the water in sign of distress.

"Pity! gentlemen," cried he; "pity and mercy! My strength is leaving me, and I am about to sink."

The tone of agony in which these words were spoken awakened a feeling of compassion in the breast of Athos.

"Unhappy man!" he murmured.

"Good!" said D'Artagnan. "I like to see you pity him. On my word, I think he is swimming towards us. Does he suppose we are going to take him in? Row, Porthos, row."

And D'Artagnan plunged his oar into the water. Two or three long strokes placed twenty fathoms between the boat and the drowning man.

"Oh! you will have mercy!" cried Mordaunt. "You will not let me perish!"

"Ah! my fine fellow," said Porthos, "we have you now, I think, without a chance of escape."

"Oh, Porthos!" murmured the Count de la Fère.

"For heaven's sake, Athos," replied Porthos, "cease your eternal generosity, which is ridiculous under such circumstances. For my part I declare to you, that if he comes within my reach, I will split his skull with the oar."

D'Artagnan, who had just finished his colloquy with Aramis, stood up in the boat.

"Sir," said he to the swimmer, "be so good as to betake yourself in some other direction. The vessel which you intended for our coffin is scarcely yet at the bottom of the sea, and your present situation is a bed of roses compared to that in which you intended to put us."

"Gentlemen!" said Mordaunt in despairing accents, "I swear to you that I sincerely repent. I am too young to die. I was led away by a natural resentment; I wished to revenge my mother. You would all have acted as I have done."

"Pshaw!" said D'Artagnan, who saw that Athos was becoming more and more softened by Mordaunt's supplications. The swimmer was again within three or four fathoms of the boat. The approach of death seemed to give him supernatural strength.

"Alas!" said he, "I am going to die, then. And yet I was right to avenge my mother. And besides, if it were a crime, I repent of it, and you ought to pardon me."

A wave that passed over his head, interrupted his entreaties. He again emerged, and made a stroke in the direction of the boat. D'Artagnan took his oar in both hands. The unhappy wretch uttered a groan of despair. Athos could bear it no longer.

"D'Artagnan!" cried he, "my son D'Artagnan, I entreat of you to spare his life. It is so horrible to let a man die when you can save him by stretching out your hand. I cannot witness such a deed; he *must* be saved."

"Mordieu!" replied D'Artagnan, "why do you not tie our hands and feet, and deliver us up to him at once? The thing would be sooner over. Ha! Count de la Fère, you wish to perish at his hands: well, I, whom you call your son—I will not suffer it."

Aramis quietly drew his sword, which he had carried between his teeth when he swam off from the ship.

"If he lays a hand upon the boat," said he, "I sever it from his body, like that of a regicide, as he is."

"Wait a moment," said Porthos.

"What are you going to do?" said Aramis.

"Jump overboard and strangle him," replied the giant.

"Oh, my friends!" said Athos, in a tone of entreaty that was irresistible; "remember that we are men and Christians! Grant me the life of this unhappy wretch!"

D'Artagnan hung his head: Aramis lowered his sword: Porthos sat down.

"Count de la Fère," exclaimed Mordaunt, now very near the boat, "it is you whom I implore. Have

pity upon me, and that quickly, for my strength is exhausted. Count de la Fère, where are you?"

"I am here, sir," replied Athos, with that noble and dignified air that was habitual to him. "Take my hand and come into our boat."

"I cannot bear to witness it," said D'Artagnan; "such weakness is really pitiable." And he turned towards his two remaining friends, who, on their part, recoiled to, the other side of the boat as if unwilling to touch the man to whom Athos alone did not fear to give his hand. Mordaunt made an effort, raised himself up, and seized the arm extended to him.

"So," said Athos, leaning over the gunwale of the boat—"now place your other hand here;" and he offered him his shoulder as a support, so that his head nearly touched that of Mordaunt; and for a moment the two deadly foes seemed to embrace each other like brothers. Mordaunt grasped the count's collar with his cold and dripping fingers.

"And now, sir, you are saved," said Athos; "compose yourself."

"Ah, my mother!" exclaimed Mordaunt, with the look of a demon, and an accent of hatred impossible to render, "I can offer you but one victim, but it is the one you would yourself have chosen!"

D'Artagnan uttered a cry; Porthos raised his oar; Aramis sprang forward, his naked sword in his hand. But it was too late. By a last effort, and with a yell of triumph, Mordaunt dragged Athos into the water, compressing his throat, and winding his limbs round him like the coils of a serpent. Without uttering a word, or calling for help, Athos strove for a moment to maintain himself on the surface of the water. But his movements were fettered, the weight that clung to him was too great to bear up against, and little by little he sank. Before his friends could get to his assistance, his head was under water, and only his long hair was seen floating; then all disappeared, and a circle of foam, which in its turn was rapidly obliterated, alone marked the spot where the two men had been engulfed. Struck dumb by horror, motionless, and almost suffocated with grief and indignation, the three guardsmen remained, with dilated eyes and extended arms, gazing down upon the dark waves that rolled over the body of their friend, the brave, the chivalrous, the noble-hearted Athos. Porthos was the first to recover his speech.

"Oh, Athos!" said he, tearing his hair, and with an explosion of grief doubly affecting in a man of his gigantic frame and iron mould; "Oh, Athos! are you indeed gone from us?"

At this moment, in the midst of the vast circle which the rays of the moon lit up, the agitation of the water which had accompanied the absorption of the two men, was renewed, and there appeared, first a quantity of fair hair, then a pallid human face, with eyes wide open, but fixed and glazed, then a body, which, after raising its bust out of the water, fell softly backwards, and floated upon the surface of the sea. In the breast of the corpse was buried a dagger, of which the golden hilt sparkled in the moonbeams.

"Mordaunt! Mordaunt!" cried the three friends; "it is Mordaunt! But Athos! where is he?"

Just then the boat gave a lurch, and Grimaud uttered an exclamation of joy. The guardsmen turned, and saw Athos, his face livid with exhaustion, supporting himself with a trembling hand upon the gunwale of the boat. In an instant he was lifted in, and clasped in the arms of his friends.

"You are unhurt?" said D'Artagnan.

"Yes," replied Athos. "And Mordaunt?"

"Oh! thank God, he is dead at last. Look yonder."

And D'Artagnan forced Athos to look in the direction he pointed out, where the body of Mordaunt, tossed upon the wave, seemed to pursue the friends with a look of insult and mortal hate. Athos gazed at it with an expression of mingled pity and melancholy.

"Bravo! Athos," cried Aramis, with a degree of exultation which he rarely showed.

"A good blow," exclaimed Porthos.

"I have a son," said Athos, "and I wished to live. But it was not I who killed him. It was the hand of fate."

Soon after the escape of Monsieur de Beaufort, the Parisians, stirred up by various influential malcontents—one of the chief of whom is the famous Jean de Gondy, Coadjutor of Paris, and afterwards Cardinal de Retz—break out into open insurrection. Mazarine's life is menaced; the queen-mother and the young king are virtually prisoners of the Frondeurs. The Prince of Condé, with the laurels he has gained on the battle-field of Lens yet fresh upon his brow, hurries to Paris to take part against the Fronde; the queen and Mazarine are anxious to escape from the capital in order to carry on the war in the open field instead of in the narrow streets, fighting in which latter, or from behind their barricades, the ill-disciplined troops of the insurgents are nearly as efficient as the most practised veterans. How to manage the escape is the difficulty. The gates of the city are guarded by armed citizens; there appears no possibility of egress. In this dilemma, Anne of Austria bethinks her of the man to whose address and courage she had, twenty years previously, been so deeply indebted; D'Artagnan is called in to her assistance. He succeeds in smuggling the cardinal out of Paris, and then returns to fetch Louis XIV. and the queen-mother.

Instead of re-entering Paris by the gate of St. Honoré, D'Artagnan, who had time to spare, went round to that of Richelieu. The guard stopped him, and when they saw by his plumed hat and laced cloak that he was an officer of mousquetaires, they insisted upon his crying out, "Down with Mazarine." This he did with so good a grace, and in so sonorous a voice, that the most difficult were fully satisfied. He then walked down the Rue Richelieu, reflecting how he should manage the escape of the queen, for it would be impossible to take her away in one of the royal carriages, with the arms of France painted upon it. On passing before the hotel of Madame de Guéménée, who passed for the mistress of Monsieur de Gondy, he perceived a coach standing at the door. A sudden idea struck him.

"Pardieu!" said he, "it would be an excellent manœuvre." And stepping up to the carriage, he examined the arms upon the panels, and the livery of the coachman, who was sleeping on the box.

"It is the Coadjutor's carriage," said D'Artagnan to himself. "Providence is decidedly in our favour."

He opened the door without noise, got into the coach, and pulled the check-string.

"To the Palais Royal," cried he to the coachman.

The man, waking in a fright, made no doubt that the order came from his master, and drove off at full speed to the palace. The gates of the court were just closing as he drove in. On pulling up at the steps, the coachman perceived that the footmen were not behind the carriage, and, supposing that M. de Gondy had sent them somewhere, he got off his box and opened the door. D'Artagnan jumped out, and just as the coachman, alarmed at seeing a stranger instead of his master, made a step backwards, he seized him by the collar with his left hand, and with his right put a pistol to his breast.

"Not a word," said D'Artagnan, "or you are a dead man."

The coachman saw that he had fallen into a snare. He remained silent, with open mouth and staring eyes. Two mousquetaires were walking up and down the court; D'Artagnan called them, handed over the coachman to one of them, with orders to keep him in safe custody, and desired the other to get on the box of the carriage, drive it round to the door of the private staircase leading out of the palace, and there to wait till he came. The coachman's livery coat and hat went with the carriage. Those arrangements completed, D'Artagnan entered the palace, and knocked at the door of the queen's apartments. He was instantly admitted; Anne of Austria was waiting for him in her oratory.

"Is everything prepared?" said she.

"Everything, madam."

"And the cardinal?"

"He has left Paris without accident, and waits for your majesty at Cours la Reine."

"Come with me to the king."

D'Artagnan bowed, and followed the queen. The young king was already dressed, with the exception of his shoes and doublet. He seemed greatly astonished at being thus roused in the middle of the night, and overwhelmed his valet-de-chambre, Laporte, with questions, to all of which the latter replied—"Sire, it is by order of her majesty." The bedclothes were thrown back, and the sheets were seen worn threadbare and even into holes. This was one of the results of Mazarine's excessive parsimony. The queen entered, and D'Artagnan remained at the door of the apartment. As soon as the child saw his mother, he escaped from Laporte's hand and ran up to her. She signed to D'Artagnan to approach.

"My son," said Anne of Austria, showing him the mousquetaire, who stood with his plumed hat in his hand, calm, grave, and collected, "this is M. D'Artagnan, who is brave as one of those knights of old whose histories you love to hear repeated. Look at him well, and remember his name, for he is about to render us a great service."

Louis XIV. gazed at D'Artagnan with his large proud eyes; then, slowly lifting his little hand, he held it out to the officer, who bent his knee and kissed it.

"Monsieur D'Artagnan," repeated the young king. "It is well, madam; I shall remember it."

At this moment a loud murmuring noise was heard approaching the palace.

"Ha!" said D'Artagnan, straining his ears to distinguish the sound—"The people are rising."

"We must fly instantly, said the queen.

"Madam," said D'Artagnan, "you have deigned to give me the direction of this night's proceedings. Let your majesty remain and learn what the people want. I will answer for everything."

Nothing is more easily communicated than confidence. The queen, herself courageous and energetic, appreciated in the highest degree those two virtues in others.

"Do as you please," said she. "I trust entirely to you."

"Does your majesty authorize me to give orders in your name?"

"I do, sir."

D'Artagnan hurried from the room. The tumult was increasing; the mob seemed to surround the Palais Royal. On all sides were heard seditious cries and clamours. Presently M. de Comminges, who was on guard that night at the Palais Royal, craved admittance to the queen's presence. He had about two hundred men in the court-yard and stables, and he placed them at her majesty's disposal.

"What do the people want?" said Anne of Austria to D'Artagnan, who just then re-appeared.

"A report has been spread, madam, that your majesty has left the Palais Royal, taking the king with you. The mob demand a proof of the contrary, or threaten to demolish the palace."

"Oh! this time it is too bad," said the queen. "I will soon show them that I am not gone."

D'Artagnan saw by the expression of Anne's face, that she was about to give some violent order. He hastened to interfere.

"Madam," said he, in a low voice, "have you still confidence in me?"

"Entire confidence, sir," was the reply.

"Then let your majesty send away M. de Comminges, and order him to shut himself up with his men in the guard-room and stables. The people wish to see the king, and the people must see him."

"See him! But how? On the balcony?"

"No, madam; here in his bed, sleeping."

The queen reflected a moment, and smiled. There was a degree of duplicity in the course proposed that chimed in with her humour.

"Let it be as you will," said she.

"Monsieur Laporte," said D'Artagnan; "go and announce to the people, that in five minutes they shall see the king in his bed. Say also that his majesty is sleeping, and that the queen requests them to be silent, in order not to awaken him."

"But they cannot all come," said Anne. "A deputation of two or four persons."

"All of them, madam."

"But it will last till to-morrow morning."

"In a quarter of an hour it will be over. I know the mob, madam; it is a great baby that only wants flattery and caresses. Before the king, these noisy rioters will be mute and timid as lambs."

"Go, Laporte," said the queen. The young king approached his mother.

"Why do you do what these people ask?" said he.

"It must be so, my son," said Anne of Austria.

"But if they can tell me that it *must* be so, I am no longer king."

The queen remained silent.

"Sire," said D'Artagnan, "will your majesty permit me to ask you a question?"

"Yes, sir," replied Louis, after a moment's pause, occasioned by surprise at the guardsman's boldness.

"Does your majesty remember, when playing in the park at Fontainebleau, or the gardens at Versailles, to have seen the heavens become clouded, and to have heard the thunder roll?"

"Certainly I do," answered Louis.

"Well, the noise of that thunder told your majesty, that, however disposed you might be to play, you *must* go in-doors."

"Certainly, sir; but I have been told that the voice of the thunder is the voice of God."

"Well, sire, let your majesty listen to the voice of the people, and you will perceive that it greatly resembles that of the thunder."

As he spoke, a low deep roar, proceeding from the multitude without, was borne upon the night breeze to the windows of the apartment. The next instant all was still and hushed.

"Hark, sire," said D'Artagnan, "they have just told the people that you are sleeping. You see that you are still king."

The queen looked with astonishment at this singular man, whose brilliant courage made him the equal of the bravest; whose keen and ready wit rendered him the equal of all. Laporte entered the room, and announced that the message he had taken to the people had acted like oil upon the waves, and that they were waiting in respectful silence, till the five minutes, at the expiration of which they were to see the king, should have elapsed. By the queen's order, Louis was put into bed, dressed as he was, and covered up to the throat with the sheets. His mother stooped over him, and kissed his forehead.

"Pretend to sleep, Louis," said she.

"Yes," said the king, "but not one of those men must touch me."

"Sire," said D'Artagnan, "I am here; and if one of them had that audacity, he should pay for it with his life."

The five minutes were over. Laporte went out to usher in the mob; the queen remained standing near the door; D'Artagnan concealed himself behind the curtains of the bed. Then was heard the march of a great multitude of men, striving to step lightly and noiselessly. The queen raised with her own hand the tapestry that covered the doorway, and placed her finger on her lips. On beholding her, the crowd paused, struck with respect.

"Come in, gentlemen—come in," said the queen.

There was apparent in the mob a degree of hesitation which resembled shame; they had expected resistance, had anticipated a contest with the guards, bloodshed and violence; instead of that, the gates had been peaceably opened, and the king, ostensibly at least, was unguarded save by his mother. The men in front of the throng stammered out an excuse, and attempted to retire.

"Come in, gentlemen," said Laporte, "since the queen desires it."

Upon this invitation, a man, bolder than the rest, entered the room, and advanced on tiptoe towards the bed. He was followed by others, and the chamber was rapidly filled, as silently as if the new comers had been the most humble and obsequious courtiers. D'Artagnan saw everything through a hole he had made in the curtain. In the man who had first entered, he recognized his former servant Planchet, who, since he had left his service, had been a sergeant in the regiment of Piedmont, and who was now a confectioner in the Rue des Lombards, and an active partisan of the Fronde.

"Sir," said the queen, who saw that Planchet was a leader of the mob,

"you wished to see the king, and the king is here. Approach, and look at him, and say if we resemble persons who are going to escape."

"Certainly not, your majesty," said Planchet, a little astonished at the honour done to him.

"You will tell my good and loyal Parisians," continued Anne of Austria, with a smile of which D'Artagnan well understood the meaning, "that you have seen the king in bed, and sleeping, and the queen about to go to bed also."

"I will tell them so, madam, and those who accompany me will also bear witness to it, but"——

"But what?" said the queen.

"I beseech your majesty to pardon me," said Planchet; "but is this really the king?"

The queen trembled with suppressed anger.

"Is there one amongst you who knows the king?" said she. "If so, let him approach, and say if this be his majesty or not"

A man, muffled in a cloak, which he wore in such a manner as to conceal his face, drew near, and stooping over the bed, gazed at the features of Louis. For a moment D'Artagnan thought that this person had some evil design, and he placed his hand upon his sword; but as he did so, the cloak slipped partially from before the man's face, and the guardsman recognized the Coadjutor, De Gondy.

"It is the king himself," said the man. "God bless his majesty!"

"God bless his majesty!" murmured the crowd.

"And now, my friends," said Planchet; "let us thank her majesty, and retire."

The insurgents bowed their thanks, and left the room with the same caution and silence with which they had entered it. When the last had disappeared, followed by Laporte, the remaining actors in this strange scene remained for a moment looking at each other without uttering a word: the queen standing near the door; D'Artagnan half out of his hiding-place; the king leaning on his elbow, but ready to fall back upon his pillow at the least noise that should indicate the return of the mob. The noise of footsteps, however, grew rapidly more remote, and at last entirely ceased. The queen drew a deep breath of relief; D'Artagnan wiped the perspiration of anxiety from his brow; the king slid out of his bed.

"Let us go," said Louis.

Just then Laporte returned.

"I have followed them to the gates, madam," said the valet-de-chambre; "they informed their companions that they had seen the king, and spoken to the queen, and the mob has dispersed, perfectly satisfied."

"The wretches!" murmured Anne of Austria; "they shall pay dearly for their insolence." Then, turning to D'Artagnan, "Sir," said she, "you have this night given me the best advice I ever received in my life. What is next to be done?"

"We can set out when your majesty pleases. I shall be waiting at the foot of the private staircase."

"Go, sir," said the queen. "We will follow you."

D'Artagnan descended the stairs, and found the carriage at the appointed place, with the guardsman sitting on the box. He took the hat and coat of M. de Gondy's coachman, put them on himself, and took the guardsman's place. He had a brace of pistols in his belt, a musquetoon under his feet, his naked sword behind him. The queen appeared, accompanied by the king, and by his brother the Duke of Anjou.

"The Coadjutor's carriage!" exclaimed she, starting back in astonishment.

"Yes, madam," said D'Artagnan, "but be not alarmed. I shall drive you."

The queen uttered a cry of surprise, and stepped into the coach. The king and his brother followed, and sat down beside her. By her command, Laporte also entered the vehicle. The mantelets of the windows were closed, and the horses set off at a gallop along the Rue Richelieu. On reaching the gate at the extremity of the street, the chief of the guard advanced at the head of a dozen men, and carrying a lantern in his hand. D'Artagnan made him a sign.

"Do you recognize the carriage?" said he to the sergeant.

"No," was the reply.

"Look at the arms."

The sergeant put his lantern close to the pannel.

"They are those of M. le Coadjuteur," said he.

"Hush!" said d'Artagnan. "Madam de Guéménée is with him."

The sergeant laughed. "Open the gate," said he; "I know who it is." Then, approaching the mantelet— "Much pleasure, Monseigneur," said he.

"Hold your tongue!" cried D'Artagnan, "or you will lose me my place."

The gate creaked upon its hinges; D'Artagnan, seeing the gate open, flogged his horses, and set off at a rapid trot. In five minutes he had rejoined the cardinal's coach.

"Mousqueton," cried D'Artagnan to M. du Vallon's servant, "open the door of his majesty's carriage."

"It is he!" exclaimed Porthos, who was waiting for his friend.

"In a coachman's livery!" cried Mazarine.

"And with the Coadjutor's carriage," said the queen.

"*Corpo di Dio*, Monsieur d'Artagnan!" said the cardinal, "you are worth your weight in gold!"

We cannot attempt to give more than these slight glimpses of the eight volumes now lying before us, in which the extravagance and exaggeration of many of the incidents are only redeemed by the brilliant diction and animated narrative of their clever but unscrupulous author. It would be too lengthy to give even a sketch of the chain of incidents that succeeds those above detailed, or to show how, according to M. Dumas, D'Artagnan and his friends became instrumental to the conclusion of the treaty by which the hostilities between Frondeurs and Mazarinists are for the time brought to a close. The first act of the war of the Fronde is over; Louis XIV., now within a year of his majority, re-enters the capital with Anne of Austria and Mazarine, D'Artagnan, now captain of mousquetaires, riding on one side of his carriage, and Porthos, now Baron du Vallon, on the other. Baron Porthos goes back to his estates, happy and glorious; Aramis and Athos return to the seclusion whence the stirring times had called them forth, the latter leaving his son in charge of D'Artagnan, who is to take the young man with him to the Flemish wars. The restless spirit of the Gascon abhors the idea of repose.

"Come, D'Artagnan," said Porthos, as he got upon his horse to depart, "take my advice; throw up your commission, hang up your sword, and accompany me to Du Vallon. We will grow old together, whilst talking of our past adventures."

"Not so," replied D'Artagnan. "*Peste!* the campaign is just opening, and I mean to make it. I hope to gain something by it."

"And what do you hope to, become?"

"*Pardieu!* who can tell? Marshal of France, perhaps."

"Ab, ah!" said Porthos, looking at D'Artagnan, to whose gasconading he had never been able quite to accustom himself. And the two friends parted.

"You will prepare your best apartment for me, Madeleine," said D'Artagnan to his handsome hostess, as he re-entered his hotel. "I must keep up appearances, now that I am Captain of Mousquetaires."

THE GRAND GENERAL JUNCTION AND INDEFINITE EXTENSION RAILWAY RHAPSODY.

By a Provisional Committee of Contributors.

THOUGH the farmer's hope may perish,
　While in floods the harvest lies,
Speculation let us cherish,
　Let the Railway market rise!

Honest trader, whosoever,
　Sick with losses, sad with cares,
Quit your burden now or never,
　Cut the shop and deal in shares.

Spendthrift—short of drink and dinners,
　Half-pay captain, younger son,
Boldly throw while all are winners,
　Laugh henceforth at debt and dun.

Come, ye saints, whose skill in cavilling,
　Shock'd at skittles, cards and dice,
Thinks, except for Sunday travelling,
　Railway gaming is no vice.

Hither haste, each black-leg fellow,
　Quit the turf or loaded bone;
Like your brother-black Othello.
　Own your occupation's gone.

Tribes that live by depredation—
　"Bulls" and "Bears," and birds of prey,
See the coming spoliation,
　Scent the premiums far away.

"Stags!" your rapid forms revealing,
　Show awhile your front so bright,
Then from your pursuers stealing,
　Vanish sudden out of sight.

Leave all meaner things, my St. John,
  For the locomotive race;
Post your tin upon the engine,
  Go ahead, and keep the pace.

At a Railway Monarch's splendour
  Envious squires and nobles stare;
Even the Hebrew gewgaw vender
  Turns sharebroker in despair.

Now no more the Ragfair dealer
  Hints with horrid breath, " Old Clo';"
Putting forth another feeler,
  " Any shares?" he whispers low.

Every paper's a prospectus,
  Nostrums, news, are at an end;
" Easy shaving" don't affect us,
  Silent even " The Silent Friend."

Morison resigns his bubbling,
  Lazenby has lost his zest;
Widow Welch has ceased from troubling,
  Weary Moses is at rest.

Every station, age, and gender,
  Deep within the torrent dip;
Even our children, young and tender,
  Play at games of nursery scrip.

Over meadows, moors, and mosses,
  Quagmires black, and mountains grey,
Careless where or how it crosses,
  Speculation finds the way.

Every valley is exalted,
  Every mountain is made low;
Where we once were roughly jolted,
  Light and lively now we go.

Speed along with fire and fury!
  Hark! the whistle shrilly shrieks!
Speed—but mark! we don't insure ye
  'Gainst the boiler's frolic freaks.

But before a trip is ventured,
  This precaution prudence begs:
When you've seen your luggage enter'd,
  Also book your arms and legs.

Ask not if yon luckless stoker,
  Blown into the air, survive—
These are trifles while the broker
  Quotes our shares at Ninety-five.

Vainly points some bleeding spectre
  To his mangled remnants;—still
Calmly answers each Director,
  " Charge the damage to the bill."

All the perils which environ
   (As the poet *now* would sing)
Him who meddles with *hot* iron,
   Seem to us a pleasant thing.

Countless lines, from Lewes to Lerwick,
   Cross like nets the country soon ;
Soon a railway (Atmospheric)
   Speeds our progress to the moon.

Traversing yon space between us,
   Soon the rapid trains will bring,
Ores from Mars, and fires from Venus,
   Lots of lead from Saturn's Ring.

Belts from Jupiter's own factory,
   Mercury from Maia's Son ;
And when summers look refractory,
   Bottled sunbeams frum the sun.

If too soaring, too seraphic,
   Seems to some that heavenward track,
T'other way there's much more traffic,
   Though not many travel back.

What a gradient through Avernus !
   What a curve will Hades take !
When with joy the Shades discern us,
   How Hell's terminus will shake !

How the Pandemonium Junction,
   With the Central will combine,
Rattling both without compunction
   Down the Tartarus incline !

Phlegethon no more need fright us,
   For we've bridged its fiery way ;
And the steamer on Cocytus
   Long ago has ceased to pay.

Charon—under sequestration—
   Does the Stygian bark resign,
Glad to find a situation
   As policeman to the line.

Thoughts of penance need not haunt us ;
   Who remains our sins to snub ?
Pluto, Minos, Rhadamanthus,
   All have joined the " Railway Club."

Fortune's gifts, then, catch and cherish ;
   Follow where her currents flow ;
Sure to prosper—or to perish,
   Follow, though to Styx we go !

SKETCHES OF ITALY—LUCCA.

THE records of travellers in the *Livres des Etrangers* at Modena, had prepared us to expect nothing tolerable at the night halts in our journey through the Apennines to our projected place of *séjour* during the great heats of summer, the *Bagni di Lucca.* At the *mountain* locandas, we were always prepared, not to say resigned, to encounter those various distresses which seem light evils at a distance—knowing that we could not starve as long as eggs and maccaroni were to be found, and even as to lodging we were too old travellers to flinch at trifles. The rural inn at Piave, which looked more inviting than the great one of the small place, was delighted to receive us, and gave us good trout, tolerable bread, and excellent honey: we were in the midst of a lovely country, we heard a limpid stream running within a few yards of our window; and what had we to fear? But night came, and with it more annoyances than one bargains for even in Italy. A floor of thin planks which had never fitted, and of which the joinings, which had never been of the kind called *callidæ*, were now widened by time, was all that parted our small bedroom from that of the horses. Through these, and also through large rat-holes, there came up copious ammoniacal smells, which our mucous membrane resented from the first; and well it had fared with us had this been all. We had never been so near horses at night, and had no idea they made such an incessant noise. One horse stabled and littered for the night were bad enough, but we had a whole stableful; and just as we were forgetting the fleas, and forgiving the mosquitos, and sleep led on by indigestion was heavy on our eyelids, a snort, loud as a lion's roar, made us start. Then there came a long succession of chump, chump, from the molar teeth, and a snort, snort, from the wakeful nostril of our mute companions (*equo ne credite, Teucri !*)—one stinted quadruped was ransacking the manger for hay, another was

cracking his beans to make him frisky to-morrow, and more than one seemed actually rubbing his moist nose just under our bed! This was not all; not a whisk of their tails escaped us, and when they coughed, which was often, the hoarse *roncione* shook the very tressels of our bed; in short, we never suffered such real nightmare before. We dreamt *stethoscopes* and racks. But morning came, and, with it, morning freshness and morning sound. The wood-pigeons are cooing, the green hills just opposite seem to have come closer up to our window to wish us good-day; so we throw open our little casement, to let out the gaseous compounds from bed and stable. How elegantly do the dew-bedded vines take hold of the poplars and elms, and hang their festoons of ripening fruit from branch to branch! But the sun begins to break a brilliant pencil of rays over the hill-top, nor will he take long to leave the screen and uncover himself; indeed, in less than a quarter of an hour, he will have stared us quite out of countenance, and, long before the hour of his advent shall have been completed, the birds, which till now have been all activity, will become torpid, the pigeons will have given over their cooing, and the sparrow his chirp; so the fish that has not yet breakfasted had better make haste, for his are chariot-wheels which have been looked after overnight, and linchpins that never came out; nor has he had one break-down or overturn since he first set off on his *Macadamized* way. In haste to escape from the heat of the plains of Tuscany, we were not sorry when we saw the douaniers of *Pistoia*, the last of its cities. This town is dullness, not epitomized, but extended over a considerable space; its streets are many, long, and, what is not usual in Italy, wide. There is no population stirring; the very piazza is without activity; and, if you leave it, you may walk a mile between very large houses, churches, convents, and palaces, without meeting any one. Pistoia, in short, is an improvement on *Oxford* in the long vacation—the place, however, has its ancient fame, has given birth to two or three distinguished literati, and figured in the civil wars. The fifteenth century records among others the name of *Cini*, whose epitaph we saw in the cathedral ; and the author of the *Riciardetto* was, we believe, also one of its citizens. In its immediate vicinity fell *Catiline.* They say the Italian language is spoken here with great purity of *accent*, which is remarkable, as it is only twenty miles from the guttural and inharmonious speech of Florence. It was not our purpose to explore its decayed manufactures, if such there still exist at all, of fire-arms and organs; indeed, we know not if pistols and organ-pipes have anything particular to do with it; so, after refreshment of the cattle, we passed on through a beautiful country at its most beautiful season, and thought we had seldom seen anything more striking than the views from *Serravalle,* or those about *Pescia* and *Monte Catino.* The high, almost the highest Apennines were right a-head ; and could we have taken the wings of the bird, or of the morning, and lighted on any of those peaks at no great distance, we should have looked directly down on to the Mediterranean, and almost into the gulf of *La Spezzia ;* we should have seen the long Ligurian promontory in the distant horizon to the right, and have embraced Leghorn, Elba, Gorgona, and the coast as far as *Piombino,* in the opposite direction. An imperceptible ascent conducts from the *town of Lucca* towards its *baths ;* and you may expect, in about three hours, to have accomplished its sixteen miles. The road follows the long windings and beautiful valleys of the *Serchio,* of which, harmless as it looks, we read on all the bridges records of its occasional violence, and of their repeated destruction. After a morning's ride, to which there are few equals even in Italy or Switzerland, we begin to get our books, and paper, and light luggage, out of the nets and pockets of the carriage—for there are the *Bagni Caldi,* about a mile before us. It is not our purpose

to describe the humours of an Italian watering-place ; but let it not be supposed that this retreat is the happy thought of our own restless population. The English have had nothing to do with bringing the baths of Lucca into notice or fashion, although they are at present among its principal inhabitants from June to September. Hither flock in summer the families who have established themselves in winter-quarters at Florence or Pisa ; and here they soon get possession of all the cracked pianos, and strolling music-masters who come on speculation, and forthwith begin a series of screaming lessons, called singing, executed by English young women, studious of cheap accomplishments, to the infinite distress of all who pass by their open windows, at whatever hour ! As the baths are frequented by the little court of Lucca, there is a *residenza*, a *casino*, and tables for play. There are two or three good hotels or *tables-d'hôtes*, and there is a shabby little coffee-house, and a handful of *Balzacs and Paul de Kocks* at one circulating library. There is one butcher and one baker at each of the villages, privileged dispensers of their respective commodities. There is a scarcity of poultry, of fresh butter, and vegetables; but there is abundance of maccaroni. There are two grocers, who both supply amateurs with English pickles, Harvey's sauce, Warren's blacking, Henry's Magnesia, James's powder, and the other necessaries of life. The houses are generally let for the season, and the rent of the best is as high as £4 a-week. The furniture is old and bad, but tolerably clean. Ascend any of the hills, and you look down on roofs that have scarcely any chimneys. Whenever you ride or walk, you have a hill on the right and left of you, and a river making its way against the opposition of huge masses of stone, and angular impediments from the turns of the valley itself. On these hills, you have uniformly vines below ; and when you get above the vines, you walk entirely among the chestnut trees which constitute the real riches of the country. The best office, however, of the hills, is not the production of fruit-trees, but the screen they afford against the Italian sun. The early sunset here is worth all the wine of the territory, which is scarce and very bad. In the evenings of July and August, there is a turn-out of equipages that have figured on the Boulevards and in Hyde Park, which commonly make a halt opposite the little shabby coffee-house, to eat bad ices, and do the agreeable to each other—the rush-bottomed chairs at the door being occupied the while by a set of *intelligent* young men, with mustache, who smoke bad cigars, and cultivate as elsewhere the charm of each other's classical conversation. Montaigne was here in the 15th century, and Fallopius, he of the trumpets, came here to be cured of deafness—which is one of the infirmities which the Latin inscription declares to have yielded to the use of the waters. Lorenzo di Medici came to talk platonism and the fine arts at a place which will never know either any more; and, from a Latin letter extant, was summoned from the Bagni to the death-bed of his wife. Ladies have often been recommended to the baths to be cured of sterility; and, from what we have seen, we think there are far more unpromising places. Doctors, whose names only are known, but who were probably men of learning, have written on these salutary springs, and modern flippancy has at present forborne them. We have no quack to patronize them; the " *numen aquæ* " is not violated

in *print* at least by jobbing apothecaries; but there is Gentile di Foligno, and Ugolino di Monte Catino, and Savonarola, and Bandinelli (1483), and Fallopio (1569), and Ducini (1711), who have written books, of which the object, as they are in Latin, is not assuredly what there is too much reason to believe it *is,* when such books are now presented to the world. Of the waters (which, like those of Bath, contain minute portions of silex and oxide of iron), the temperature differs at the different establishments—and there are three; 43° Reaumur is assigned as the highest, and 35° 24' to two others.

We were stranded at this pleasant place of endurable ennui for three long months, during which there was no going out from nine to five P.M. Our society afforded little resource, our reading less. When the weather permitted—that is, in the delicious, incomparable month of October — we made little excursions to Barga, Ponte Nero, &c., &c., and always returned delighted; nor were our walks of shorter distance unproductive of interest. The Lucchese are the most industrious people in the world, and their agriculture made us, *pro tempore,* amateurs of rural economy. We will not bore the reader with *Georgics* such as ours; but if he will accept, in place of picture galleries and churches, the " *quid faciat lætas segetes* " of this far from miserable population, we will cheerfully take him with us in our walks.

AGRICULTURE ROUND LUCCA.

The *bearded* wheat, or *triticum,* not the *siligo,* or common wheat of our English culture, was the plant which, whenever the attributes of Ceres were to be represented on ancient coins, was selected for that purpose; but the Lucchese territory, where the *Cerealia* in general abound, offers few specimens of either kind. These productions seem afraid of their *ears* in the neighbourhood of the *Great Turk,* who is the great tyrant here, and, together with the rice, monopolizes three-fourths of all the land devoted to the culture of grain; the

millet (*miglio*), the *panixa* (*panico*), Indian wheat (*sagena*), together with the lupins, and a variety of peas, beans, and lentiles, occupy the remainder. "The Great Turk is a great eater, is he not?" "Yes," replied the peasant who cultivated him, " *mangia come Christiano,*"—he eats like a Christian all he can get out of the ground; only, the more he gets the better he looks for it—which is not always the case with Christians." There are two kinds of *Gran Turco,* or *maize;* that sown in May is of rather better quality than the other, and produces on an average 10 lbs. more per sack in weight than that which is sown afterwards in June. In order to secure a good crop, it is necessary that the ground should be well manured with lupins, which are either grown for this single purpose the year before, and left to rot, or boiled to prevent their germination, and then scattered over the field. The Grand Turk commonly carries but one head on his shoulders, but occasionally we have remarked two or more on the same stem. In the year 1817, the sack (160 lbs.) fetched fifty-eight pauls; while wheat was seventy-eight, and even the chestnut flour sold at fifty; so that, even in the Lucchese territory, they have their approach to famine in bad years.

SAGENA.

Pliny mentions the *Sagena*, under the name of Saracenic millet, as a thing which came from India, and was first brought into Italy in his own time. Herodotus speaks of its cultivation by the Babylonians. The Saracens used it in the fourteenth century for making bread, as do the Lucchese to this day; it is, however, lightly esteemed, and not used at all when other corn abounds, but thrown into the hencoop to fatten poultry. It is a beautiful thing to see the high jungle of this most elastic plant bending to the breeze, and displaying, as it moves, its beaded top, looking at a distance like so many flowers; but, when seen nearer, exhibiting *racemes* (on highly polished stems) of small pedunculated berries, in mitre-looking capsules. When the seed has been shaken from the plant, the tops are brought together, and form those excellent besoms which, throughout southern Europe, supply the place of birchbroom, than which they are more elastic, not so brittle, and much cleaner. The ultimate fibrils of this plant are sometimes sold in little bundles for the purpose of being slit, and receiving the small Neapolitan firework called *gera foletti*, which scintillates like a fire-fly. Other kinds of millet and pannick are also grown here; care being taken to plant them far from the vine and mulberry, as they make considerable demands on the soil. Rice is said to have constituted the sole aliment of the republicans of early Rome, and it is still largely cultivated in many parts of Italy. In the lowland about Viareggio, it monopolizes the ground almost as much as the Grand Turk in the more interior parts of the country.

LUPINS.

Lupins are largely cultivated, both for their own intrinsic value, and to induce the growth of other plants. "We are bitter," say the Lupins in an Italian work on agriculture; "but we enrich the earth which lacks other manure, and by our bitterness kill those insects which, if not destroyed, would destroy our successors in the soil. You owe much, O husbandmen! to us Lupins."

HEMP.

Invaluable plant—pride of intelligent agriculture—that tendest thine own fibre—and strength to him that rightly cultivates thee—and constitutest the greatest element of mechanical power! What does not England —the world itself—owe to that growth which we now contemplate! Armies are encamped within thy walls—thou towest forth the ship of discovery on her venturous way, and carriest man and his merchandise to the Equator and to the Pole! Vain were the auspicious breeze unless it blew upon thy opening sails; and what were the sheet-anchor, but for that cable of thine which connects it with the ship. Vegetable iron! incomparable hemp! Extemporaneous memory can scarcely follow thy services. Talk of the battering-ram—but what propelled it forward? The shot, whizzing in the teeth of adverse winds, carries thy coil to snatch the sailor from the rock where he stands helpless and beyond aid from all the powers or productions of man and nature but thine ! Thy ladder, and thine alone, can rescue from the house on fire ! Look at the fisheries all over the world — the herrings of Scotland, and the cod of the Baltic, might defy us but for thee. What were wells and windlasses without thee ? useless as corkscrews to empty bottles. Thou art the strong arm of the pulley and the crane. Gravitation itself, that universal tyrant, had bound all things to the earth but for thy opposition. The scaffolds were thine from which grew the *Colosseum*, and the Pyramids have arisen in thine arms. The kite of science, which went cruising among thunder-clouds to bring down to a modern Prometheus the spark which ignites the storm, was held by fibres of thine. The *diver* and the *miner* cling to thee for safety, and they that hunt the wild-bird's egg on the sea-shaken cliff, as they swing over the frightful abyss. With the lasso the bold Matador, like the *Retiarius* of the ancient arena, makes the cast that is for life. Then the fine arts !—Carrara sends her block for the Laocoon by aid of thine : and what were all the galleries in Europe but a collection of gilt frames, but for thy backing and support ! By thy subserviency alone (for what were *panel* or *laminated copper* for such gigantic works ?) did Raffaelle bequeath so many legacies of his immortal genius. It is the strength of thy fibres that is the strength of the loaded supper-tables of Paul Veronese ; and the velvets, the furs, the satins of Titian and Vandyke, are quilted upon thee. Nor disdainest thou to render to man, who bruises thee to try thy virtue, a thousand humbler services. Thou preservest our horses from flies, our fruit from birds ; and who has not felt how thou cheerest the weary length of continental travelling, by the crack of thy whipcord at the approach of a new relay ?

Here our friend *Anamnesis* seemed fatigued, as if he thought he had spun a sufficiently *long yarn* on the subject ; so we prevailed on him to prosecute the walk, as evening was beginning to close in — not, indeed, without apprehension that he would make a stand at several other interesting plants on which it might suit him to prelect.

Hemp, when cut, is left to dry for a week ; it is then immersed for another week in water ; after which it is flayed of its skin—a process which is conducted either by the hand, leaving the stem in this case entire ; or by subjecting the whole plant to a bruising process, conducted by a machine.

Besides the above-mentioned grain, the ground produces plenty of vegetables, but of an inferior quality; as are all Italian fruits, and most of the leguminous productions also, from want of care. Even as to flowers, you would find it difficult to make up a bouquet, unless of ferns, which here abound. The only cultivated flower, except a few dahlias and sunflowers, are the yellow petals of the lucchini, a kind of vegetable marrow, which creeps and creeps till its twisted tendrils and broad leaves occupy, by continual encroachment, the whole field where they germinate. Besides the *fruit* of this plant, which we begin to be supplied with about August, its young leaf and stalk are boiled like kail for common greens ; and its yellow flower, a little later, makes a *frittura*, which is in request. Fruits are plentiful, and some of them good ; but, for the greater part, of a very inferior quality. Strawberries, and particularly raspberries (*lampóni*), are found throughout the season ; which, commencing with these, and a scanty supply of currants and gooseberries (the latter very poor indeed, and the first quite inferior to our own), brings us fine figs of many species and in vast quantities. Apples and pears have their kinds, and many distinctive names, but are without flavour. The great supply of the raspberry and small Alpine strawberry is about midsummer. The next-door-hood of all the *Scotch* families is now fragrant, " on all lawful days," with the odour of boiling down fruit for jams and marmalades for winter consumption. As autumn comes on, heaps of watermelons, piled like cannon-balls under the chestnut-trees, display their promising purple flesh, and look cooling and desirable, but are not to be attempted twice under penalty of gastric inconvenience. Plums and nuts abound, and are followed by a second course of hard, unripe, and tasteless nectarines and peaches. The season is closing fast, for the prickly pods of the ripening chestnut now begin to gape, and the indifferent grapes of the district attain their imperfect maturity, and are gathered for the wine-press. September is in its last week, and in less than another month we must all migrate somewhere for the winter. The baths, on the 15th of October, are quite empty.

TREES.

A good walnut-tree is as good to a poor man as a milk-cow. " I would not sell either of those walnut-trees in my garden for thirty scudi a-piece," said a peasant to us; and, observing that we looked as if we would not like to tempt him, asked us if we had seen the large walnut-tree of *Teraglia* (we had, and had *pic-nicked* very nearly under it), " because," added he, " the proprietor of *that* tree refused sixty *scudi* for it last week, *e ha ragione*, for it is a nonpareil. A good tree like those in my garden yields me eight *sacks of shelled fruit* on an average every year; and a sack of walnuts fetches from a scudo to ten pauls (four shillings and sixpence) in the market. So that my trees, between them, bring me in one hundred and sixty pauls (*i. e.* £4 English) every year." Indeed! and the chestnut-trees opposite? Oh! in this land of chestnut-trees we don't pay *prezzi d'affezione* for them — a good tree standing in the *plain* may cost about eight or ten scudi, and may yield about four sacks of shelled fruit in a good year; but it is a capricious tree even in the *plain;* while those on the *mountain*, the roots of which derive a precarious subsistence from the uncertain soil, are liable to be blown down, and are made pollards of at an early age to prevent this mishap; also, they are frequently burned down by bonfires kindled under them to destroy the furze. The chestnut shoot is only four years old before it begins to bear. Three pounds of fresh chestnuts fetch about one penny—*dried*, or in flour, about double that price. The peasants bake a little cake of the chestnut flour called " *netche*," about the thickness of a crimpet, and having much the flavour and appearance of potato scones. This paste they bake between two hot stones, with a couple of the leaves of the chestnut (dried for the purpose by the peasants) interposed. The baking takes scarcely a minute, and the cakes are then piled and packed, and sent far and wide. The arms and the tops of the chestnuts are made into charcoal, so that no part of this important tree is lost. We are here in the very midst of forests of chestnut only — far as the eye can reach in every direction, and as far as vegetation will go up every mountain side, its grateful green forms a pleasing contrast to those gloomy frequenters and favourites of the mountain, the sombre pine, and the dusky olive.

Several fine-sized olive-trees were shown to us for sale, and said to be good fruit-bearers (no olive bears fruit under ten years), for twenty-five scudi per tree. These trees were computed to yield about two and a quarter to three sacks of berries; whereof every sack yielded a profit of three scudi for one hundred to one hundred and ten pounds of oil, which represents about the quantity generally expressed. In retail, Lucca oil, at the present moment, is about one paul, and olives about three farthings per pound.

OAKS.

We observe three kinds of oaks which here both flourish and abound. The *Farnia*, the *Querci*, and the *Leccio* — the last evidently a corruption of Ilex. The first kind grows with amazing rapidity; in twenty years it is a head and shoulders above all the other trees which began life with it. It has very long acorns, which are less astringent than those of either of the other trees, and very much preferred by pigs. A common oak felled for ship timber costs, where it stands, from ten to fourteen scudi, and they are in great request for the Leghorn market.

INSECTS.

Insects do not greatly abound in the neighbourhood about Lucca. Even the mosquito winds his horn less frequently in our valley, than his universality elsewhere would lead you to expect. Our beds are free from bugs, and fleas are not very troublesome. Of the out-of-doors insects, those which live upon the vegetable kingdom are not very numerous, nor of much variety. The *Cassida*, who rejoices in lettuce, brings up his family in other districts where the lettuce abounds. Wanting the tamarisk, we miss our little *Curculio*, who thrives upon its leaves; and the *Bruchus pisi*, for want of peas, is frequently caught in the bean-tops. But the republican armies of ants are immense, and the realm of bees is uncircumscribed; as no birds of prey, neither the audacious robin, nor the woodpecker, tapping away on the hollow beech-tree, diminish their hordes. But if the fowls of the air be few, the nets of entomologists abound. *Slaters* of an immense kind, and spotted, and small mahogany-coloured *Blattidæ*, are found under stones, which also conceal hordes of predatory *beetles* and *scorpions*, which bristle up at you as you expose them; and nests of tiny *snakes*, that coil and cuddle together, from the size of crowquills to the thickness of the little finger. During June and July, the monotonous *Cicadæ* spring their rattles in the trees around, and one comes at last even to like their note, in spite of its sameness. A little later, flies and wasps send their buzzing progeny into our dining-rooms, to tease us over our dessert, like troublesome children: at the same period, some of the larger families of *Longicorns* abound, and one of them, *Hamaticherus moschatus*, musks your finger if you lay hold of him. In the July and August evenings, fire-flies scintillate on a thousand points around you, and swarm along the hedges, lighting each other to bed, till about midnight, which is their curfew; for you seldom meet one of these lantern-bearers later, though you may still, in returning from a late party, be stopped with momentary admiration at beholding a magnificent glow-worm burning her tail away at a great rate, and lighting up some dark recess unvisited by star or moon, herself a star, and giving sufficient light to enable you to read the small print of a newspaper a foot off! But who shall attempt to describe his first acquaintance with the fire-fly; We have seen birthday illuminations in London and in Paris; we have seen the cupola of St. Peter's start into pale yellow light, as the deepening shadows of night shrouded all things around; we have seen the Corso, on *Moccoletti* night, a long fluctuating line of ever renewed light, from the street to the fourth story— an illumination *sui generis*, and " beautiful exceedingly ;" but noise and confusion are around all these as you approach them. But, oh! to plunge suddenly into an atmosphere filled with *Lucciole* in the quiet gloaming of an Italian sky, amidst the olive groves and plantations of Indian corn, with no noise but the drowsy hum of the huge *stag beetle* (the only patrole of the district), or the yet fainter sounds of frogs complaining to each other of the sultriness of the night, or the monotonous hymn, at the peasant's door, addressed to the Virgin! Your first impression is unmixed delight— your next, a wish probably that you could introduce the fire-fly into England. Could one empty a few hatfuls along Pall-Mall or Bond Street, on opera nights, what an amazement would seize the people! We swept them up into the crown of our hat, and could not get enough of them; then we set them flying about our room, putting out the lights and shutting the shutters; and then we caught them, and began to look more closely at the sources of our delight, and to examine the acts and deeds of these wonderful little creatures. As to the light itself, we soon perceived that, in reality, the fire-fly emitted it from *two sources;* for, besides his *steady* light, which never varied, there came, we saw, at intervals, flicks or sparks of far greater brilliancy, like the revolving light of the beacon on the sea-shore, only that the light here was never wholly eclipsed, but merely much abated. We soon perceived, too, that those sudden jets of light came and went at vastly IRREGULAR intervals; sometimes in very quick succession, sometimes less frequently —from which observation, we concluded that this dispensation of his rich endowment did not proceed from any motion of the *fluids* in the animal economy analogous to our own circulation—it being far too irregular and inconstant to depend on any such regulated movement. On removing the head of a *Lucciola*, this intermitting light *immediately* ceased; but the other—the permanent, steady, and equable light—remained unchanged, and was not extinguished for from *sixty to seventy hours after the death of the insect*, unless the body was immersed in oil or alcohol, which extinguished it presently. We found, that though oil and alcohol quickly extinguished the light, it became suddenly much brighter when fading, by plunging the insect into hot water; but we did not find that it could be restored when it had once *entirely* ceased, by this or any other means, as some French naturalists have affirmed; and as to its exploding a jar of hydrogen, as others have written, we disbelieve it, because the temperature of the insect is far too low. We think, then, for the present, that there are two distinct repositories, or two different sources, of light in the firefly; and that while *one* depends on the *head*, and is a strictly *vital phenomenon*, the other is altogether independent of any physiological law of the nervous or circulating system.

———

We have a great respect for *ants;* but we do not go the length of some of their historians, or believe them to be, any more than ourselves, *infallible.* We have seen a laborious ant (*magni Formica laboris*) tugging a snail-shell (for some reason only known to himself) up a hill, stopping to take breath, and going cheerily to work again till he had nearly accomplished his ascent, and found himself on the very edge of its summit. Here he has been surrounded by friends, officious busy-bodies, who, *intending* no doubt to help him, have got *into* the shell, in place of lending him a hand, till their added load was too much, and the unfortunate ant has been obliged to loose his hold and let them go, shell and all! Then off they would scud, very much frightened, no doubt, at the overturn; while he, having remained stationary a moment as if to watch its results, takes his resolution, and proceeds on his journey without his load. In brushing the grass for insects, we have constantly found that the ants, *with their mouths full*, fight with each other, or with their brother captives, and are quite unaware of their bondage. For while most other insects, on opening the net, are glad to escape by flying or leaping, these will remain as if to secure their booty, and turn even misfortunes to account. Often have we watched their battles, which are battles indeed!—battles, in which every man of them seems to think the day depends on his own courage and activity. We have never been able to make out which were the best battalions of these variously coloured troops; for all of them fight to the death, and *show no quarter.* We have seen on some large tree the ants running up and down, and picking off individual enemies from a horde of smaller kind and reddish colour below. We have occasionally knocked off one or two of the giants, who, falling alive into the midst of their enemies, were surrounded, spread-eagled, trampled upon, and either lacerated to death, or killed by their own *formic acid*, in a very short space of time indeed. We have seen all this and marvelled; but we were never sufficiently in the confidence of either the invaders or the invaded to know their motives for fighting. It could not be for territory, for they had all the world before them; it could not be for food, for they were full.

We never could make out why flies seem *fond of walking over dead spiders*, for we will not impute to them our unworthy feelings of enduring hatred and hostility. That insects had no brains in their heads to direct and guide their progressive movements, or form focuses for their passions, had long ago to us been plain. Besides all that we once committed ourselves by writing on the subject, we

have done many other cruel things;
such as dividing insects (whether at
the union of the head with corselet, or
of the corselet with the abdomen), and
we have found that the segments to
which the members were articulated
carried on their functions *without the
head.* The Elytra would open the
wings, and the legs would move, as
by association they had moved in the
perfect insect. The guidance of the
head was destroyed, yet the legs
pushed the abdomen and corselet on ;
so that a disapproving friend had to
divide his sympathy, and to *feel for
each of the pieces.* And what appeared to us worthy of remark was, that
whereas, when a snake was decollated,
it was only the tail that continued to
wriggle—when a *worm* was divided,
all the segments writhed in the same
way, and manifested an equal irritability ; showing the difference between creatures of annulated structure, according as they have or have
not a *brain.* A new argument against
the brain as the organ of sensation,
was afforded to us by the conduct of
many insects of voracious propensi-
ties. We took *locusts* and *grilli ;* we
held them by their wings, and we
presented them *with their own legs*
for dinner ; and on our veracity we
can affirm, that on no single occasion
did the animal fail to seize his foot ;
and having demolished the toes and
the tibia, with all the meat upon it,
proceed to demolish up to the very
end of the *trochanter !* Nor were
they more tender of their own *an-
tennæ,* of which, when we had duly
convinced a sceptical friend, he exclaimed — It *seems impossible ;* but
there is no doubting the fact !

Insects (who would have thought
it ?) lose a great deal by insensible
transpiration ; from one-tenth to one-
quarter of their whole weight, as we
have abundantly ascertained by a
series of experiments, for which we
have the tables to show. A very interesting fact respecting the difference
of irritability of insects from that of
the higher animals, is this : the temperature of man and the mammalia is
in health always the same, and varies
very inconsiderably in disease. *External* heat and *external* cold do not produce a blood, in man, warmer at the
equator than at the pole. This is not the
case with insects, whose mean temperature may be about 80° ; but the
thermometer inserted into their bodies
may be made to *rise* or *fall* by bringing any cold or warm body in contact
with their external surface. You may
thus sink the temperature of an insect
to 50° or raise it to 100° and the
insect continue alive. This is a very
curious fact, and shows the inaccuracy
of Hunter's description or definition of
life—" That it was *that* which *resisted*
the physical agency of cold and heat."
Insectorum duorum (e genere Cantha-
ridum) in coitu deprehensorum, ex-
tincto a nobis uno, alterum per dies
plures, nullo alio quàm organorum
sexus vinculo sibi adstrictum, amicæ
suæ corpus sursum et deorsum trahen-
tem, mirantes vidimus !—*Spanish* flies,
you exclaim !—as if he had not taken
a dose of his own powder ; but after
the joke is over, we think this *is*
another *poser* for the advocates of
insect intelligence. We found that
if either of two insects was destroyed in coition, that state was not
interrupted for two or three days.
The insects on which are observed
this remarkable circumstance, were
the *Cantharis oclemero,* and some
others. Spanish flies, you will say !
That accounts for it ; but at present
we are not mystifying our indulgent
readers.

SHOOTING FISH.

Long before the middle of September we are frequently startled, before
we have proceeded a hundred yards,
by the popping of guns amongst the
vineyards and chestnut woods, but
more frequently in the direction of
the stream that winds along our valley—and the sight of one or two
of the chasseurs on the road may well
surprise any not accustomed to the
sports of the Lucchese.—Here are two
of them, each with a gun on his
shoulder, coming up the stream. One
has shot three four-ounce dace, which
dangle by his side ; the other has a bag
full of *small fry,* shot as they frisked
about in shoals near the water's edge !
an ounce of *sand* exploded to receive

about the same amount of fish! The man who has shot the dace is proud of his exploit, and keeps turning them round and round to gauge their dimensions, as if they were partridges! Don't think, however, they have killed off all the fish of the stream. Besides that string of four-ounce dace, we have every now and then a sample of barbel and trout. One man has purchased the monopoly of the fishery within two miles, and for which he pays twelve crowns by the year. He sells his trout at two, and two and a half, pauls per pound, and we should have thought that he made a good thing of it; but they lose their fish: the torrents come and empty the holes, and they have nothing for it but to stock them again—an event which, he assured me, frequently took place. Besides, fly-rods and flies have been introduced by an English shopkeeper, and there is no legal provision against them.

Owls.

There comes a man with an owl in a basket, and another tied by the leg on a pole covered with red cloth; another accompanies him with a bundle of reeds, through which a rod runs, smeared all the way down with bird-lime. This apparatus he disposes on a hedge or cover of any kind—the little owl (*Civetta*) sits opposite on his pole—the birds come to tease him, and fly on the birdlime twig, when, if it be a sparrow, he is effectually detained by the viscus only—if a blackbird, pop at him goes an old rusty gun. "We sometimes catch twenty tomtits before breakfast," said a modest-looking sportsman, modestly, but not shamefacedly, showing us one thrush and one linnet.

An image-man told me to-day, that after the trade for classical models—Apollos and Venuses—had gone out, and nobody would buy, *Tam o' Shanter* and *Souter Johnny* operated a good *revival* of the fine arts for several months. How much, then, the models from the antique, do towards improving our taste! and how absurd to set up institutions with the expectation of making the populace other than the gross, unideal, matter-of-fact thing it is, and always was, no doubt, even in Athens itself!

The Improvisatore.

We heard one of these monsters last night. The arena for his exhibition might, but for the known liberality of society, be thought objectionable—being none other than the English place of worship. But *tout est sain aux sains*—or *aux saints*, if you please. Charity covereth many sins; and if there be a place upon earth where charity reigns, it is at what you call *watering-places*. Pindar was right, αριστον μεν υδωρ. If we were inquired of, and propitiated by a fee, as to the effects of the waters here, we should give it as our opinion that they act directly on the *picrochole*, or bitter principle of bile, and carry it, soft as milk, through the duodenal passages. Our Improvisatore has, we understand, been six times *painted* (we know not what saloons are so fortunate as to possess his portrait), but we believe he has not been described. When we saw him, his hair danced wildly over his shoulders, as if electrified: he had a quick eye, and wore enviably well-fitting ducks: his neck, besides supporting his head and all its contents, supported an inextricable labyrinth of gold chains; from every buttonhole of his waistcoat the chains they came in, and the chains they came out, like the peripatetic man on the Boulevards who sells them: his gloves, well-fitting, and buttoning at the wrist, were of the whitest kid, and grasped a yet whiter and highly-scented cambric: his boots shone bright with varnish, and his face with self-complacency. As the room filled, he went round, giving the girls permission to write *subjects* on bits of waste (wasted!) paper, which set them *thinking* at a great rate. Presently, a second circuit round the room, to collect the orders payable at sight—a title such as the *Lucciola, Italia, The Exile, Woman's Love, Man's Ingrati-*

tude; after which he proceeds to fold up and puts them into a large glass vessel. Presently a small hand, properly incited, dives down for a second into the interior of the vase, and brings up, between two of its fair, round, turquoise-encircled fingers, the scrap of paper. Its pretty owner blushes, and timidly announces, " Bellini's Tomb; *Bellini's Tomb* is buzzed about the room. At this juncture the Duke, who has been *expected,* sends a messenger to announce that we are not to wait for him—a sly fellow the Duke! The bard now concentrates himself for inspiration, but begs us to talk on, and not mind him. While he waits for the *afflatus divinus,* and consults the muses—and in fact his eyes soon begin to betray *possession* — he passes his hand over his parturient forehead, while the *os magno sonaturum* is getting ready; the labour-pains are evidently on him; he hurls back his hair, and fixes his eyes upon the moon (who has been looking at *him* for several minutes through the window opposite). Full of her influence, and not knowing there is such a place as bedlam in the world, he starts upon his legs, makes two or three rapid strides up and down the room, like a lion taking exercise, or a lord of council and session in Scotland preparing to pronounce sentence, and means to be delivered (mercy on us!) exactly opposite our chair! All are attentive to the god-like man; you might hear a pin drop; the subject is announced once and again in a very audible voice; the touch-paper is ignited, the magazine will blow up presently! Incontinently we are rapt off to *Père la Chaise,* where the great composer lies buried, and a form of communication is made to us on this suitable spot, that Bellini is *dead;* then comes, in episode, a catalogue of all the operas he ever wrote, with allusions to each, and not a little vapouring and pathos, whilst a host of heroes and heroines we never before heard of, is let loose upon us; presently a marked pause, and some by-play, makes it evident that he sees something, and cannot see what the thing is; he shortly, however, imparts to us in confidence, though in a very low tone, for fear of disturbing it — he sees, he assures us, a female form stealing to the young man's tomb—the form of a widowed lady—who is she? *e la sua madre!* This was startling, no doubt; though we, or many of us, were like the cat in Florian, to whom the monkey was showing a magic lantern *without a light,* and describing what she ought to have seen. Believing her, however, to be there on such good authority, we were getting very sorry for Bellini's mother, when we were unexpectedly relieved, by finding it was only a bit of make-believe; for it was now divulged, *che questa madre che piangea il suo figlio,* was not in fact his personal mother, but " *Italy*" dressed up *like* his mother, and gone to Paris on purpose to weep and put garlands on the composer's tomb, amaranth and crocus, and whatever else was in season. Thunders of applause—we hope the new chapel is insured!—for the *assidua ruptæ lectore columnæ* is as old as earthquake in Italy. He now mopped his forehead, and prepared for a new effort. The English girls are already in raptures, and their Italian masters, sitting by, " ride on the whirlwind and direct the storm." The next subject which destiny assigned to him and inflicted on us, was *The Exile.* A nicely manured field or common place to sow and reap on—and what a harvest it yielded accordingly!—the dear friends! the dear native hill! the honour of suffering for the truth! (political martyrdom!) the mother that bore him— (and a good deal besides)—his helpless children! (a proper number for the occasion)—all these fascinating themes were dwelt on one by one till moved apparently at our emotion he dropt his menacing attitude, and, mitigating his voice, assumed a resigned demeanour, of which many of his audience had long since set him the example. He began to look down mournfully, whereas he had a minute ago looked up fiercely—a smile, to the relief of the young ladies, stole over his countenance, and having thrice shaken his head to dispel whatever gloomy thoughts might still be lingering there, he carried us to the Exile's return, which brought of course the natal soil and a second service of the mother, sire, and son, with the addition of a dog, a clump of trees, a church, and a steeple. He compresses between his hands the yielding cambric into a very small space, his body is fixed, his legs are slightly apart, his head wags, like a wooden mandarin's, with thoughts too big for utterance, till the moment arrives for the critical start, then, " *Duplices tendens ad sidera palmas*," he becomes quite Virgilian. The unfurled cambric flutters to the breeze of his own creation, and coruscations of white kid and other white materials pass and repass before our eyes. He gives vent to his emotions in tears, after a reasonable indulgence in which, as he cannot (as Tilburina's *confidante* very properly observes) stay crying there all night, he gradually comes right again. Besides all which, it is eight o'clock, and he has still to *do*, and we to *suffer*, *Napoleon*—whose ashes were just then being carried to Paris, as we had read in all the papers of last week. Glad were we when they reached the *Octroi*, and when the indulgent *Barrière* passed them all with the honours of the *Douane*. An old lady has twice yawned, and many would follow her example but that the performer fascinates his audience by staring at them—like the boa at the poor bird in the wood—and frightens them to their seats for a few minutes longer. At length one *resolute* chair moves; two others are out of the ranks; new centres of movements are establishing; several shawls are seen advancing to the door. The rout is complete, there will be no rally, and the efforts of the artist have been *crowned* (one hundred and fifty scudi) with success. We meet him everywhere. He honours our table-d'hôte daily, where he stays an hour and a half to bait—

after which we see him lounging in the carriage of some fair *compatriote* with herself and daughters. If we are paying a morning visit, in he comes, "glissading it" into the drawing-room, and bowing like a dancing-master; nor does he disdain to produce a small book of testimonials, in which the subscribers have agreed to give him a poetic *character*, and compare him to a torrent, to a nightingale, to an eagle, to an avalanche. They who love flattery as a bee loves honey, are all captivated, and almost make love to him. Their albums are rich in the spoils of his poetry, and she is happy who, by her blandishments, can detain him in conversation for five minutes. Yet they own they understand less than half of what he says. Vexed with one to whom we were talking, we thought rationally, for permitting herself to be "so pestered by a popinjay," — "He *is* so clever," was the reply; "such an odd creature, too. I wish you knew him. He is in such a strange humour to-night. Do you know he tells me he wishes to marry an English girl? See! he is gone into the balcony yonder to look at the moon." To be sure he was. He came back looking somewhat wild, and, walking in like a modern Prometheus, down he sits, and then new inspiration is presently bespoken for the fly page of virgin scrap-book. Smoothly flows the immortal verse, without care, correction, or halt, for the lines are the result of power that works unerringly (Pope *blotted* most disgracefully), and goes right *ahead*. The precious *morçeau* is concluded, and the improvisatore's name appears in a constellation of zig-zags.

TABLES D'HÔTES—MR. SNAPLEY.

Did you never meet Mr. Snapley? —Mr. Snapley was the greatest of bores—he bored holes in your self-complacency, and riddled your patience through and through; to put up with him was hard, to put him down was impossible (your long tolerated nuisance of fifty is always incorrigible). His bore was surprising considering the smallness of his calibre; like a meagre gimlet he would drill a small hole in some unimportant statement, and then gather up

his *opima spolia*, and march off to the sound of his own trumpet. For instance, on convicting you of assigning a fine picture to a wrong church or gallery, he denied all your pretensions to judge of the picture itself. He had a reindeer's length of tongue (how often did we wish it salted and dried)! and the splutter of words it sent forth, took off, as it often happens, sufficient observation of the miserably small stock of ideas that he had to work upon. He enjoyed, as we all do, the blameless pleasure of dining out as often as he could; when, though he did not consume all the provisions, he would willingly have taken possession of the whole of the talk (*that* being his notion of a conversation). When one had to dine at the same table with him, one contrived to take up a position as remote as possible from the interruption of his thin, wiry, ill-modulated voice—the *false* suavity of which in saying impertinent things was really so disagreeable, that one would have renounced the society of wit or beauty on the right hand, rather than have been flanked by Mr. Snapley on the *left*, and thankfully have accepted the companionship, *pro hac vice*, of the plainest woman or the dullest man of the party, to be only completely out of his reach. Your *soup* you *might* take in peace, for he was at this time studying the composition of the party, and the chances of endurance or resistance inscribed on the countenance of the guests; but the moment an opportunity occurred of correcting or cavilling with any of those unprecise and generally unchallenged observations, the interruption of which is at the cost of the quietness of the repast, Mr. Snapley's voice was heard! You were too glad, of course, to give up the trifling point out of which he had raised a discussion; but the earliest concession never saved you, nor did you ever afterwards escape the consciousness that he was still hovering like a harpy over the tablecloth and ready to fall foul of you again. Let the subject be what it might, you had only to make a remark in his presence, and without his permission, to *insure* its contradiction. "What a needless annoyance in travelling it is for a family to be stopped by douaniers, only to extort money for *not* doing a duty which would be absurd if *done?*" "Why, really I don't see that," &c. &c. "What a plague it is to send your servant (a whole morning's work) from one subaltern with a queer name, to another, for a lady's ticket to witness any of the functions at the Sistine!" Well, it did appear to him the simplest thing in the world; it was ten times more troublesome to see anything in London! "What nuisance it is on quitting an Italian

city to find the passport which' has already given you so much trouble only available for *three* days, leaving you liable to be stopped at the gate, if sickness or accident have made you transgress even *by an hour!*" "Why, it is *your own fault*, it is so easy to get it *viséd again* over night." All these impertinencies were only πιδακος εξ ιερης ολιγη λιβας. Besides all this, Mr. Snapley was a miserable monopolizer of pompously advanced no things. He would not willingly suffer any other man's goose to feed upon the common—he cared for nobody but himself, and everything that was or he esteemed to be *his* — his very joints were worked unlike those of another man — he must have had a set of *adductors* and *abductors*, of *flexors* and *extensors*, on purpose. He was stiff, priggish, precise, when he addressed any gentleman with light hair and an *English complexion;* but let him approach any foreign button-hole with a bit of riband in it, then worked he the muscles of his face into most grotesque expression of interest or pleasure — (*Tunc immensa cavi spirant mendacia folles!*)—and you had a famous display of grimace and deferential civility, in bad French or worse Italian. We have seen him sneering or leering as he made his way round a drawing-room at an evening party, and bowing like a French perruquier to some absurd fool of a foreigner; and we have seen him a minute after, holding up his head and cocking his chin in defiance, if an English voice approached. When any of us ventured to criticise *anything foreign*, he was up in arms, and cock-a-hoop for the climate, the customs, the constitution! He sneered awfully at a simple *gaucherie*, but to make amends, had ever an approving wink for the meanest *irreverence;* any intellect, however feeble, being secure of his praise if only tried to thwart the end for which it was given. When not talking about himself, which was seldom, he was evidently *occupied* about his *personel*, with which he was obviously satisfied. If you talked of books, he settled for you, in laconic sentences, works of acknowledged merit—put down men of uncontested superiority — but women of title and tainted reputation, if they would but ask him to their parties, became at once his favourites and his oracles. He cunningly contrives to get a good artist's opinion on works of art, and debits it as his own—a proceeding which makes Mr. Snapley *sometimes* formidable in sculpture and in painting. As to other topics, on which educated men and accomplished women converse, he would fain be as profound as *Locke* with the one, and as gallant as *Fontenelle* with the other. For ourselves, who meet him but too often, we would as soon approach without necessity a huxter's mongrel growling under his master's cart, as venture near enough to examine all the small-wares of one who "hates coxcombs," and is the very

prince of fops; laughs at pedants, and only wants a *little more learning* to attempt the character; with whom no repetition of familiar acts can reconcile you, and to whom no number of dinners can conquer your repugnance.—*Did* you ever meet Mr. Snapley?' We are sure you must — the Snapleys are a very old family—you may generally know them by the *nez retroussé* (which our acquaintance, however, had not). We never knew but one good-natured man with a *nez retroussé*, and he was. if ever man was — a philanthropist, Generally, however, *beware* of the *nez retroussé* except in women—you know its interpretation *chez elles;* — and if you do (on second thoughts), still beware.

HINTS FOR DOCTORS.

Esquilias, dictumque petunt a *Vimine* collem.—Juv.

* * * "I observed a gentleman in black," said our informant, "who seemed to fix me across the table-d'hôte, at dinner, in a way which soon showed me I was an object of interest to him. It was very odd! We were not in Austria! I could not have offended the police — nor in Spain, the Inquisition. If I *took* of a particular dish, his eye was on me again. They *did* use to *poison* people in Italy, but it was in the fifteenth century, and all the Borgias were gone! What could it mean? The very waiters seemed to watch the man in black, and signals of intelligence seemed to pass between them as they went their rounds with the dishes. After thus meeting the eye of the unknown at intervals for more than an hour, when the table was beginning to clear, I rose, and limped out of the room as well as my complaints would let me, and was sauntering a few steps from the door, when judge of my terror on turning round, to find him of the black coat at my elbow! "In pain, sir, I see." All my alarm ceased in a moment. It was pure philanthropy which had made me an object of so much interest. "Yes, sir, in great pain." "*You should take care of yourself, sir.* Rheumatic, are you not?" "Very rheumatic." "Well, sir, you have come to the best place in the world for rheumatism. The air, the water, and proper treatment, will

soon set you up." "Your report is encouraging; but I have suffered too long to hope much." "Well, at any rate, sir, let us not talk over your interesting case in this heat. Come and put your feet up on a chair in my rooms, and we will drink a glass of soda-water to your better health." What a kind-hearted man I had met with, and how kind Providence is to us! I now ventured to ask him his name. "My name is Dr. ——; and now, my dear friend, just tell me your whole case from the very beginning down to now, for I am really interested in you." I told my case. "Put out your tongue." "Brown," we thought we heard him say. "Wrist — pulse not amiss—but you *require care, sir! you require care!* Clear case for the medicine I gave so successfully last week." Finding myself thus fallen into professional hands *without intending it*, I said something introductory to the mention of a fee. "True, I was *forgetting* that; when one takes a proper interest in one's case, and hopes to do good, fees are the last thing one thinks of—two scudi if you please." So I found myself immediately booked in a small memorandum-book, and constituted his patient. Now came civil promises to introduce me, &c. &c. &c., and I took my leave delighted. It is almost needless to say, that in a very short time I found that my acquaintance had, like so many more, commenced physician on the soil of Italy. What will become of London if all her apothecaries desert her at this rate? For ourselves, reflecting on the accomplishments of many of these patriotic men, their learning, their modesty, their disinterestedness, we have often had a twinge of the philanthropic extorted by the loss inflicted on our native city—she may come to want a dose of jalap, and have nobody to mix it!—and have said to ourselves, as we have looked more than one of these worthies in the face,

Ω κλειν' Αθηναι, Παλλαδος θ' ωρισματα,
Οἱον στερησεσθ' ανδρος !

One day after dinner a little bit of gold rolled over the table to the doctor, from a bluff-looking gentleman opposite—it was well aimed—" There, doctor! *there's your fee;* but don't you begin again prating a parcel of stuff to my wife about her complaints—she is quite well—and if you frighten her into illness, take notice, you will get a different sort of fee next time !" All this, half joke half earnestly, must have been very agreeable to the guests.

PRIVATE MUSIC PARTY.

Let us try to describe the last musical party at which we assisted. A scramble amid piles of unbound music; the right *cahier* found, snatched up, and opened at the well-thumbed solo with which she had already contended for many a long hour, and now hopes to execute for our applause. Alas! the piano sounds as if it had the pip; the paralytic keys halt, and stammer, and tremble, or else run into each other like ink upon blotting paper, and the pedals are the only part of the instrument which do the work for which they were intended. We should be sorry that our favourite dog had his paw between them and the lady's slipper. The dust which succeeds the concerto proves satisfactorily that it is possible to be frisky without being lively; its vulgarity is so pronounced that it offends you like low conversation. Another concerto follows—ten folio pages! whew!!—— Oh, ye ebony and ivory devils! oh, for an exorcist to put you to flight! Cramped fingers are crossing each other at a great rate; we really tremble for the glue, and the pegs, and the wires, and the whole economy of the instrument, at that critical juncture when the performers arrive at a piece of mysterious notation, where a great many tadpole-looking figures are huddled together under a black rainbow. At such a " passage" as this, it seems one would think the house were on fire, and no time to be lost; the black mittens and the white now *Rob-Royishly* invade each other's territory; each snatches up something and carries it off, like the old marauders of the Border country; and reprisals are made, and lines of discord and dissonance are establishing, which require the police, the magistrate, and the riot act. Bravo! bravo! bravo! and the battle ceases, and the *babble* commences. Place for the foreign train, the performers *par métier!* Full of confidence are they; amidst all their smiles and obsequiousness, there is a business air about the thing. As soon as the pianist has asked the piano how it finds itself, and the piano has intimated that it is pretty well, but somewhat out of tune, a collateral fiddler and a violoncello brace up their respective nerves, compare notes, and when their drawlings and crookings are in unison, a third piece of music of indefinite duration, and as it seems to us all about nothing, begins. Our violinist is evidently not long come out, and has little to recommend him—he employs but a second-rate tailor, wears no collar, dirty mustaches, and a tight coat; he is ill at ease, poor man, wincing, pulling down his coat-sleeves, or pulling up his braces over their respective shoulders. His strings soon become moist with the finger dew of exertion and trepidation; his bow draws out nothing but groans or squeals; and so, in order to correct these visceral complaints, a piece of rosin is awkwardly produced from his trousers' pocket, and applied to the rheumatic member, with some half-dozen brisk rubs in a parenthesis of music. The effect is painfully ludicrous !——

I am *sleepy, sleepy,* begins the piano! Sleepy, sleepy, *mews* Mr.

Violin—very, very, very sleepy, drones the drowsy four-stringed leviathan. Oh, do try if you can't say something, something, something to enliven one a bit! On this hint, the little violin first got excited upon one string, and then upon another, and then the bow rode a hand-gallop over two at once; then saw we four fingers flying as far up the finger-board as they could go, without falling overboard, near the *bridge*—a dangerous place at all times from the currents and eddies—and there provoking a series of sounds, as if the performer were pinching the tails of a dozen mice, that squeaked and squealed as he made the experiment. The bow (like the funambulist with the soles of his slippers fresh chalked) kept glancing on and off, till we hoped he would be off altogether and break his neck; and now the least harsh and grating of the cords snaps up in the fiddler's face, and a crude one is to be applied; and now—but what is the use of pursuing the description? Let us leave the old bass to snore away his lethargic accompaniment for ten minutes more, and the affair will end. The pianist, the Octavius of the triumvirs, thinks it necessary to excuse Signor ——, telling us, " He has bad violin, he play like one angel on good one"—but hisht, hisht! the evening-star is rising, and we are to be repaid, they say, for all we have gone through! Signor * * * is going to play. The *maestro* advances with perfect consciousness of his own powers; his gait is lounging, he does not mean to hurry himself, not he—his power of abstraction (from the company) is perfect; he is going to play in solitude before fifty people, and only for his own amusement. He places himself at least a foot from the piano, his knees touching the board, his body rises perpendicularly from the music-stool, his head turns for a moment to either shoulder as if he were glancing at epaulets thereon, and then he looks right ahead; he neither has nor needs a book; with the wide-extended fingers of both hands, down he pounces, like a falcon, on the sleeping keys, which, caught by surprise, now speak out and exert all their energies. Those keys, which a few minutes ago vibrated so feebly, and spoke so inarticulately, now pour forth a continuous swell of the richest melody and distinctest utterance. The little wooden parallelograms at first seemed to be keeping out of their ranks just to see what is going on, till the affair becomes warm, they can no longer stand it, but grow excited and take part in the general action. Relying fully on the perfect obedience of his light troops, and relaxing a little from his erect attitude of command, he gently inclines his body to the left, leads his disposable force rapidly upwards in that direction, where, having surprised the post against which they were dispatched, he recovers his swerve, and they retrace with equal precision and rapidity their course from the wings to the centre.

Come, *this* is playing! This is worth coming to; the instrument seems but the organ of the man's own feelings; its mournful tones are only a paraphrase of his sighs; its brilliant arabesques are but the playful expression of his own delight with everything and everybody! His cheek is warm, his eyes sparkle, his hands detonate thunder and lightnings from the keys, and he concludes as suddenly as he began; the very silence is felt, and the breathless guests, who have watched the fingers and been rapt by the tones, now burst forth simultaneously in expressions of delight and applause.

THE RAILWAYS.

We read, no later than yesterday, two very pungent original articles in the London daily journals, on the present all-absorbing subject of railway speculation. Both writers are evidently well versed in the details of the novel system; both possess some smattering of political economy, sufficient at least to enable them to form a judgment; and both consistent in their data and statistical information. Yet, agreeing in these points, it is somewhat singular to find that the *Coryphæi* have arrived at diametrically opposite conclusions. One of them is quite clear, that if the present railway *mania* (as he calls it) is permitted to go on unchecked for a short time further, the country will not only be on the verge of bankruptcy, but a general crash will be inevitable; that, vast as the resources of Britain undoubtedly are, she cannot, by any exertion short of crippling her staple commercial relations, furnish capital enough for the fulfilment of a moiety of the schemes already announced, and thrown into the public market; that the fact, which is incontestable, that a large proportion of these shares were originally, and are presently, held by parties who have no means of paying up the calls, but who are solely speculating for the rise, must very soon produce a reaction, and that such re-action will be of the absolute nature of a panic. Such are the opinions of this writer, who is clearly of the restrictive school. He holds that the government is bound, in such a crisis as that which he rather states than prophesies, to interfere at once with an arbitrary order, and to prevent the issue of any new schemes until those already before the public are either disposed of or exhausted.

How this is to be effected, the writer does not sufficiently explain. He points to immediate interference, from which expression we are led to believe he points at some such proceeding as an Order in Council, to be pronounced during the recess of Parliament. If so, we may dismiss this gentleman and his remedy in a very summary manner. Such an order in Council would be worse than useless, because it would be a manifest breach of the constitution. As well might an Order be issued to close our manufactories, to restrict the amount of any branch of produce, or to prevent parties from forming themselves into companies for the most blameless and legitimate purpose. It is a strange symptom of the credulousness of the age, or rather of the ignorance of the people in all matters relating to the science of government, that, towards the close of September last, some such rumour was actually circulated and believed, though its father was manifestly *a bear,* and its birthplace the Stock Exchange. But if this merely is meant, that there lies with the Imperial Parliament a controlling and interferential power, and that the great estates of the realm may be called upon to use it, we do not question the proposition. Whether, however, it would be wise to use that power so sweepingly as the journalist recommends, or whether, practically, it could be possible, are very serious considerations indeed.

But the existence of any evil is denied *in toto* by the other journalist. In the crowded columns of the morning prints, driven to supplement and even extra-supplement by the overwhelming mass of railway advertisements, he can see no topic of alarm, but "matter for high exultation, and almost boundless hope." His belief in superabundance of capital, and its annual enormous increment, is fixed and steadfast. He considers the railways as the most legitimate channel ever yet afforded for the employment of that capital, and the most fortunate in result for the ultimate destinies of the country. He compares—and very aptly too—the essential difference between the nature of the schemes in which the public are now embarking, and those which led to the disastrous results of 1825. His sole regret is, that he must regard the present direction of enterprise, "as an opportunity, that is, facility of investment, that from its nature can be but temporary, though the profit of the investment must, from the nature of things, be perpetual, and though even the temporary felicity may, and probably will last, for some years." This is a hopeful, sunny-minded fellow, with whose aspirations, did our conscience permit us, we should be thoroughly delighted to concur.

These writers may be taken as examples of two numerous classes. They are, in fact, the Trois Eschelles' and Petit Andrés of the railroads, The first consider every commercial exertion consequent on a new discovery, or the opening of a new channel for investment, doubtful in itself, and highly dangerous if hurriedly and unhesitatingly adopted. The social system, in their view, may suffer quite as much from plethora as from inanition. Too much blood is as unwholesome as too little, notwithstanding of any extraneous means to work it off. " Slow and sure," is their motto— " Carpe diem," essentially that of their antagonists. And yet in one thing, we believe, most individuals holding these opposite opinions will be found to concur. They all speculate. Heraclitus signs his contract with a shudder, and trembles as he places his realized premium in the bank. Democritus laughingly subscribes his name to thousands, and chuckles as he beholds his favourite stock ascending in the thermometer of the share-market. Heraclitus sells— Democritus holds; and thus the great point of wisdom at issue between them, is reduced to a mere question of time.

But it is with their opinions, not their practice, that we have to deal. As usual, truth will be found to lie somewhere between two opposite extremes. We neither entertain the timid fear of the one writer, nor the fearless enthusiasm of the other. The present state of matters presents, in a double sense, a vast field of speculation, through which we think it necessary to see our way a little more clearly. Rash interference may be as dangerous as the principle of " *laissez faire*," which in fact is no principle at all, but a blind abandonment to chance. Let us, therefore, endeavour to borrow some light from the experience of the past.

The desire of growing rapidly rich is a very old epidemic in this country. It is a disease which infests the nation

whenever capital, in consequence of the success of trade and prosperous harvests, becomes abundant; nor can it, in the nature of things, be otherwise. Capital will not remain unemployed. If no natural channel is presented, the accumulated weight of riches is sure to make an outlet for itself; and the wisdom or folly of the irruption depends solely upon the course which the stream may take. Of false channels which have conducted our British Pactolus directly to a Dead Sea, from which there is no return—we or our fathers have witnessed many. For example, there were the South American and Mexican mining companies, founded on the most absurd reports, and miserably mismanaged, in which many millions of the capital of this country were sunk. Again, Mr. Porter writes so late as 1843—" A very large amount of capital belonging to individuals in this country, the result of their savings, has of late years sought profitable investments in other lands. It has been computed that the United States of America have, *during the last five years*, absorbed in this manner more than TWENTY-FIVE MILLIONS of English capital, which sum has been invested in various public undertakings, such as canals, *railroads*, and banks in that country. Large sums have also been, from time to time, invested in the public securities of that and other foreign governments, not always, indeed, with a profitable result.". We need hardly remind our readers of the poignant testimony of the Rev. Sydney Smith as to the profit derived from such investments, or the probable fate of the actual capital under a repudiating system.

These may be taken as two great instances of the danger of foreign speculation. The capital of the mining companies was squandered with no other effect than that of providing employment, for a certain number of years, to the lowest of the Mexican peasantry; whereas the same amount, applied to a similar purpose in this country, would not only have produced a handsome return to the invester, but would have afforded work and wages to a considerable portion of the community. There is a reciprocity between labour and capital which never ought to be forgotten. Labour is the parent of all capital, and capital, therefore, should be used for the fostering and assistance of the power by which it is produced. Here, however, it was removed, and became, to all intents and purposes, as useless and irrecoverable as the bullion on board of a vessel which has foundered at sea. This, therefore, may be regarded as so much lost capital; but what shall we say to the other instance? Simply this—that whoever has lost by the failure of American banks, by repudiation, or by stoppages of dividends, need not claim one single iota of our compassion. With British money has the acute Columbian united state to state by more enduring ties than can be framed within the walls of Congress—with it he has overcome the gigantic difficulties of nature—formed a level for the western waters where none existed before— pierced the interminable forests with his railroads, and made such a rapid stride in civilisation as the world has never yet witnessed. What of all this could he have done on his own resources? Something, we must allow—because his spirit of enterprise is great, even to recklessness, and a young and forming country can afford to run risks which are impossible for an older state—but a very small part, unquestionably, without the use of British capital. We cannot, and we will not believe, that any considerable portion of these loans will be ultimately lost to this country. Great allowance must be made for the anger and vexation of the prospective sufferers at the first apparent breach of international faith, and it is no wonder if their lament was both loud, and long, and heavy. But we think it is but a fair construction to suppose that our Transatlantic brethren, in the very rapidity of their "slickness," have carried improvement too far, given way to a false system of credit among themselves, and so, having outrun the national constable, have found themselves compelled to suspend payment for an interval, which, in the present course of their prosperity, cannot be of long continuance. So at least we, having lent the American neither plack nor penny, do

in perfect charity presume; but in the meantime he has our capital—say now some thirty millions—he has used it most thoroughly and judiciously for himself, and even supposing that we shall not ultimately suffer, what gain can we qualify thereby?

If John Doe hath an estate of some twenty thousand acres in tolerable cultivation, which, nevertheless, in order to bring it to a perfect state of production, requires the accessaries of tile-draining, planting, fencing, and the accommodation of roads, it is quite evident that his extra thousand pounds of capital will be more profitably expended on such purposes than on lending it to Richard Roe, who has double the quantity of land in a state of nature. For Richard, though with the best intentions, may not find his agricultural returns quite so speedy as he expected, may shake his head negatively at the hint of repayment of the principal, and even be rather tardy with tender of interest at the term. John, moreover, has a population on his land whom he cannot get rid of, who must be clothed and fed at his expense, whether he can find work for them or no. This latter consideration, indeed, is, in political economy, paramount—give work to your own people, and ample work if possible, before you commit in loan to your neighbour that capital which constitutes the sinews alike of peace and of war.

We believe there are few thinking persons in this country who will dispute the truth of this position. Indeed, the general results of foreign speculation have been unfortunate altogether, as is shown by the testimony of our ablest commercial writers. One of them gives the following summary: —"Large sums have, from time to time, been lent to various foreign states by English capitalists, whose money has been put to great hazard, and, in some cases, lost. On the other hand, many foreign loans have been contracted by our merchants, which have proved highly profitable, through the progressive sale of the stock in foreign countries at higher than the contract prices. It is evidently impossible to form any correct estimate of the profit or loss which has resulted to the country from these various operations; the general impression is, that hitherto the losses have much exceeded the gains." In that general impression we most cordially concur—indeed, we never heard any man whose opinion was worth having, say otherwise.

But in the absence of home speculation it is little wonder that, for the chance of unfrequent gain, men should choose, rather than leave their capital unemployed, to run the risk of the frequent loss. It does not, however, follow, as a matter of course, that home speculation shall always prove profitable either to the invester or to the nation at large. We have said already, that the proper function of capital is to foster and encourage labour; but this may be carried too far. For example, it is just twenty years ago, when at a time of great prosperity in trade—the regular products of this country being as nearly as possible equal to the demand—a large body of capitalists, finding no other outlet for their savings, gave an unnatural stimulus to production, by buying up and storing immense quantities of our home manufactures. This they must have done upon some abstruse but utterly false calculation of augmented demand from abroad, making no allowance for change of season, foreign fluctuation, or any other of the occult causes which influence the markets of the world. The result, as is well known, was most disastrous. Trade on a sudden grew slack. The capitalists, in alarm, threw open the whole of their accumulated stock at greatly depreciated prices. There was no further demand for manufacturing labour, because the world was glutted with the supply, and hence arose strikes, panic, bankruptcy, and a period of almost unexampled hardship to the workman, and of serious and permanent loss to the master manufacturer. Speculation, therefore, in an old branch of industry, is peril-ous not only to the invester but to the prosperity of the branch itself. The case, however, is widely different when a new and important source of industry and income is suddenly developed in the country.

We shall look back in vain over our past history to find any parallel at all approaching to the present state and prospects of the railway system. Forty-four years have elapsed since the first public railway in Great Britain (the Wandsworth and Croydon) received the sanction of the legislature. Twenty-five years afterwards, at the close of 1826, when the Manchester and Liverpool bill was passed, the whole number of railroad acts amounted to thirty-five; in 1838 it had increased to one hundred and forty-two. The capital of these railways, with the sums which the proprietors were authorized to borrow, cannot be taken at less than SIXTY MILLIONS STERLING.

Now, it is very instructive to remark, that until the opening of the Liverpool and Manchester line in September, 1830, not one single railway was constructed with a view to the conveyance of passengers. The first intention of the railway was to provide for the carriage of goods at a cheaper rate than could be effected by means of the canals, and for the accommodation of the great coal-fields and mineral districts of England. In the Liverpool and Manchester prospectus—a species of document not usually remarkable for modesty or shyness of assumption—the estimate of the number of passengers between these two great towns was taken at the rate of one half of those who availed themselves of coach conveyance. Cotton bales, manufactures, cattle, coals, and iron, were relied on as the staple sources of revenue. Had it not been for the introduction of the locomotive engine, and the vast improvements it has received, by means of which we are now whirled from place to place with almost magical rapidity, there can be no doubt that the railways would, in most instances, have proved an utter failure. The fact is singular, but it is perfectly ascertained, that the railroads have not hitherto materially interfered with the canals in the article of transmission of goods. The cost of railway construction is incomparably greater than that attendant on the cutting of canals, and therefore the land carriage can very seldom, when speed is not required, compete with the water conveyance. But for passengers, speed is all in all. The facility and shortness of transit creates travellers at a ratio of which we probably have as yet no very accurate idea. Wherever the system has had a fair trial, the number of passengers has been quadrupled — in some cases quintupled, and even more ; and every month is adding to their numbers.

But 1838, though prolific in railways, was still a mere Rachel when compared with the seven Leahs that have succeeded it. The principle of trunk lines, then first recognized, has since been carried into effect throughout England, and adopted in Scotland, though here the system has not yet had full time for development. The statistics of the railways already completed, have fully and satisfactorily demonstrated the immense amount of revenue which in future will be drawn from these great national undertakings, the increase on the last year alone having amounted to upwards of a million sterling. That revenue is the interest of the new property so created ; and, therefore, we are making no extravagant calculation when we estimate the increased value of these railways at twenty millions in the course of a single year. That is an enormous national gain, and quite beyond precedent. Indeed, if the following paragraph, which we have extracted from a late railway periodical, be true, our estimate is much within the mark. " The improvement in the incomes of existing railways still continues, and during the last two months has amounted to upwards of £200,000 in comparison with the corresponding two months of 1844. The lines which have reduced their fares most liberally, are the greatest gainers. At this rate of increase of income, the value of the railway property of the country is becoming greater by upwards of £2,000,000 sterling per month. It is, therefore, by no means wonderful that as much of the available capital of the country as can be withdrawn from its staple sources of income should be eagerly invested in the railways, since no other field can afford the prospect of so certain and increasing a return.

The question has been often mooted, whether government ought not in the first instance to have taken the management of the railways into its own hands. Much may be said upon one or other side, and the success of the experiment is, of course, a very differ-ent thing from the mere prospect of success. Our opinion is quite decided, that, as great public works, the government ought most certainly to have made the trunk railways, or, as in France, to have leased them to companies who would undertake the construction of them for a certain term of years, at the expiry of which the works themselves would have become the property of the nation. Never was there such a prospect afforded to a statesman of relieving the country by its own internal resources, of a great part of the national debt. Public works are not unknown or without precedent in this country ; but somehow or other they are always unprofitable. At the cost of upwards of a million, government constructed the Caledonian Canal, the revenue drawn from which does not at the present moment defray its own expenses, much less return a farthing of interest on this large expenditure of capital. Now it is very difficult to see why government, if it has power to undertake a losing concern, should not likewise be entitled, for the benefit of the nation at large, to undertake even greater works, which not only assist the commerce of the nation, but might in a very short period, comparatively speaking, have almost extinguished its taxation. It is now, of course, far too late for any idea of the kind. The golden opportunity presented itself for a very short period of time, and to the hands of men far too timid to grasp it, even if they could have comprehended its advantages. Finance never was, and probably never will be, a branch of Whig education, as even Joseph Hume has been compelled a thousand times piteously and with wringing of the hands to admit—and whose arithmetic could we expect them even to know, if they admitted and knew not Joseph's ? But this at least they might have done, when the progress of railroads throughout the kingdom became a matter of absolute certainty. The whole subject should have been brought under the consideration of a board, to determine what railways were most necessary throughout the kingdom, and what line would be cheapest and most advantageous to the public ; and when these points had once been ascertained, no competition whatever should have been allowed. The functions of the Board of trade were not nearly so extensive; they had no report of government engineers, and no *data* to go upon save the contradictory statements of the rival companies. Hence their decision, in almost every instance, was condemned by the parties interested, who, having a further tribunal in Parliament, where a thousand interests unknown to the Board of Trade could be appealed to, rushed into a protracted contest, at an expenditure which this year is understood to have exceeded all precedent. We have no means of ascertaining the expenses of such a line as the London and York, which was fought inch by inch through the Committees of both Houses with unexampled acrimony and perseverance. We know, however, that the expenses connected with the Great Western and the London and Birmingham bills, amounted respectively to £88,710 and £72,868, exclusive altogether of the costs incurred by the different parties who opposed these lines in Parliament. It has been stated in a former number of this Magazine—and we believe it—that the parliamentary costs incurred for the Scottish private and railway bills, during the last session alone, amounted to a million and a half.

Now, though a great part of the money thus expended is immediately returned to circulation, still it is a severe tax upon the provinces, and might very easily have been avoided by the adoption of some such plan as that which we have intimated above; and we shall presently venture to offer a few practical remarks as to the course which we think is still open to the government for checking an evil which is by no means inseparable from the system.

But, first, we are bound to state that, *as yet*, we can see no grounds for believing that the nominal amount of capital invested in the railways which have obtained the sanction of Parliament is beyond, or anything approaching to, the surplus means of the country. Foreign speculation, except in so far as regards railroads (and these are neither so safe nor so profitable an investment as at home), seems for the present entirely to have ceased. The last three years of almost unequalled prosperity have accumulated in the country a prodigious deal of capital, which is this way finding an outlet; and though it may be true that the parties who originally subscribed to these undertakings may not, in the aggregate, be possessed of capital enough to carry them successfully to an end, still there has been no want of capitalists to purchase the shares at a premium—not, as we verily believe, for a mere gambling transaction, but for the purposes of solid investment. We base our calculations very much upon the steadily maintained prices of the railways which passed in 1844, and which are now making. Now, these afford no immediate return—on the contrary, a considerable amount of calls is still due upon most of them, and the earliest will probably not be opened until the expiry of ten months from the present date. It is quite obvious that, in this kind of stock, there can be no incentive to gambling, because the chances are, that any new lines which may be started in the vicinity of them shall be rivals rather than feeders; and if capital were so scarce as in some quarters it is represented to be, it is scarce possible that these lines could have remained so firmly held. Let us take the prices of the principal of these from the Liverpool share-lists as on 27th September.

Share.	Paid.		Selling Price.		
25	10	Blackburn and Preston	19¾	to	20¼
50	15	Chester and Holyhead	20	·	20½
50	25	Lancaster and Carlisle	53½	.	54½
50	15	Leeds and Bradford	61	·	63
25	12½	East Lancashire	22	·	22½
20	9	North Wales Mineral	14¾	·	15¼
10	1	Do. New	5¼	·	5½
26	15	North British	25	·	26
50	20	South Devon	34	·	36

These lines have, in the language of the Stock Exchange, passed out of the hands of the jobbers, and most of them are now too heavy in amount for the operations of the smaller speculators. We therefore look upon their steadiness as a high proof, not only of their ultimate value, but of the general abundance of capital.

It is hardly possible as yet to draw any such deduction from the present prices of the lines which were passed in the course of last session. Upon many of these no calls have yet been made, and consequently they are still open to every kind of fluctuation. It cannot, therefore, be said that they have settled down to their true estimated value, and, in all probability, ere long some may decline to a certain degree. Still it is very remarkable, and certainly corroborative of our view, that the amazing influx of new schemes during the last few months—which, time and circumstance considered, may be fairly denominated a craze—has as yet had no effect in lowering them; more especially when we recollect, that the amount of deposit now required upon new railways is ten per cent on the whole capital, or exactly double of the ratio of the former deposits. We give these facts to the terrorists who opine that our surplus capital is ere now exhausted, and that deep inroads have been made upon the illegitimate stores of credit; and we ask them for an explanation consistent with their timorous theory.

At the same time, we would by no means scoff at the counsel of our Ahitophels. A glance at the newspapers of last month, and their interminable advertising columns, is quite enough to convince us that the thing may be overdone. True, not one out of five—nay, perhaps, not one out of fifteen—of these swarming schemes, has the chance of obtaining the sanction of Parliament for years to come; still, it is not only a pity, but a great waste and national grievance, that so large a sum as the deposits which are paid on these railways should be withdrawn—it matters not how long —from practical use, and locked up to await the explosion of each particular bubble. We do think, therefore, that it is high time for the legislature to interfere, not for any purpose of opposing the progress of railways, but either by establishing a peremptory board of supervision, or portioning out the different localities with

respect to time, on some new and compendious method.

Last session the committees, though they performed their duties with much zeal and assiduity, were hardly able to overtake the amount of business before them. It was not without much flattery and coaxing that the adroit Premier, of all men best formed for a general leader of the House of Commons, could persuade the unfortunate members that an unfaltering attendance of some six hours a-day in a sweltering and ill-ventilated room, where their ears were regaled with a constant repetition of the jargon connected with curves, gradients, and traffic-tables, was their great and primary duty to the commonwealth. Most marvellous to say, he succeeded in overcoming their stubborn will. Every morning, by times, the knight of the shire, albeit exhausted from the endurance of the over-night's debate, rose up from his neglected breakfast, and posted down to his daily cell in the Cloisters. Prometheus under the beak of the vulture could not have shown more patience than most of those unhappy gentlemen under the infliction of the lawyer's tongue; and their stoicism was the more praiseworthy, because in many instances there seemed no prospect, however remote, of the advent of a Hercules to deliver them. The only men who behaved unhandsomely on the occasion were some of the Irish members, advocates of Repeal, who, with more than national brass, grounded their declinature on the galling yoke of the Saxon, and retreated to Connemara, doubtless exulting that in this instance at least they had freed themselves from "hereditary bonds." It may be doubted, however, whether the tone of the committees was materially deteriorated by their absence. Now, we have a great regard for the members of the House of Commons collectively; and, were it on no other account save theirs, we cannot help regarding the enormous accumulation of railway bills for next session with feelings of peculiar abhorrence. Last spring every exertion of the whole combined pitchforks was required to cleanse that Augean stable: can Sir Robert Peel have the inhumanity next year to request them to buckle to a tenfold augmented task? In our humble opinion (and we know something of the matter), flesh and blood are unable to stand it. The private business of this country, if conducted on the ancient plan, must utterly swamp the consideration of public affairs, and the member of Parliament dwindle into a mere arbiter between hostile surveyors; whilst the ministry, delighted at the abstraction of both friend and foe, have the great game of politics unchecked and unquestioned to themselves. The surest way to gag a conscientious opponent, or to stop the mouth of an imprudent ally, is to get him placed upon some such committee as that before which the cases of the London and York, and Direct Northern lines were discussed. If, after three days' patient hearing of the witnesses and lawyers, he has one tangible idea floating in his head, he is either an Alcibiades or a Bavius—a heaven-born genius or the mere incarnation of a fool!

Let it be granted that the present system pursued by Parliament, more especially when its immediate prospects are considered, is an evil—and we believe there are few who will be bold enough to deny it—it still remains that we seek out a remedy. This is no easy task. The detection of an error is always a slight matter compared with its emendation, and we profess to have neither the aptitude nor the experience of a Solon. But as we are sanguine that wherever an evil exists a remedy also may be found, we shall venture to offer our own crude ideas, in the hope that some better workman, whose appetite for business has been a little allayed by the copious surfeit of last year, may elaborate them into shape, and emancipate one of the most deserving, as well as the worst used, classes of her Majesty's faithful lieges. And first, we would say this—Do not any longer degrade the honourable House of Commons, by forcing on its attention matters and details which ought to fall beneath the province of a lower tribunal: do not leave it in the power of any fool or knave—and there are many such actively employed at this time—who can persuade half a dozen of the same class with himself into gross delusion of the public, to occupy

the time, and monopolize the nobler functions of the legislature, in the consideration of some miserable scheme, which never can be carried into effect, and which is protracted beyond endurance simply for the benefit of its promoters. We do not mean that Parliament should abandon its controlling power, or even delegate it altogether. We only wish that the initiative—the question whether any particular project is likely to tend to the public benefit, and, if so, whether this is a fit and proper time to bring it forward—should be discussed elsewhere. A recommendation of the Board of Trade, which still leaves the matter open, is plainly useless and inoperative. It has been overleaped, derided, despised, and will be so again—we scarcely dare to say unjustly; for no body of five men, however intelligent, could by possibility be expected to form an accurate judgment upon such an enormous mass of materials and conflicting statements as were laid before them. And yet, preliminary inquiry there must be. The movement is far too great, and charged with too important interests, to permit its march unchecked. Of all tyrannical bodies, a railway company is the most tyrannical. It asks to be armed with powers which the common law denies to the Sovereign herself. It seeks, without your leave, to usurp your property, and will not buy it from you at your own price. It levels your house, be it grange or cottage, lays down its rails in your gardens, cuts through your policy, and fells down unmercifully the oaks which your Norman ancestor planted in the days of William Rufus. All this you must submit to, for the public benefit is paramount to your private feelings; but it would be an intolerable grievance were you called upon to submit to this, not for the public benefit, but for the mere temporary emolument of a handful of unprincipled jobbers. Therefore there must be inquiry, even though Parliament, strangled with a multitude of projects, should delegate a portion of its powers elsewhere.

And why not? It required no great acuteness of vision to see, that, even had the railway mania not risen to this singular height, some such step must ere long have been rendered imperative by the growing necessities and altered circumstances of the country. The leading feature of our age is the institution of joint-stock societies. We have taken up very lately the views which Æsop hinted at some thousands of years ago, in his quaint parabolic manner, and which Defoe, who lived a century and a half before his time, most clearly enunciated and described. We have found the way, at last, to make small capitals effect the most gigantic results, by encircling them with the magic ties of combination. No matter when it was discovered; the principle has never yet been thoroughly acted upon until now, and we know not how far it may be carried. Our fathers, for want of this principle, ruined themselves by isolated attempts —we are in no such danger, if we do not yield ourselves to the madness of extravagant daring. Put railways aside altogether, and the number of private bills which are now brought before Parliament is perfectly astounding. Twenty years ago, such an influx would have daunted the heart of the stoutest legislator; and yet, with all this remarkable increase, we have clung pertinaciously to the same machinery, and expect it to work as well as when it had not one tithe of the labour to perform.

We have always been, and we shall always continue to be, the strenuous advocates of LOCAL BOARDS, as by far the soundest, cheapest, and most natural method of administering local affairs. We can recognize no principle in the system by which a Scottish bill is entrusted to the judgment of a committee consisting of strangers, who are utterly ignorant of locality, vested interest, popular feeling, and every other point which ought to influence the consideration of such a matter. One would think, by the care which is invariably taken to exclude from the committee every man whose local knowledge can qualify him to form an opinion, that in ignorance alone is there safety from venality and prejudice—a supposition which, to say the least, conveys no compliment to the character or understanding of the British statesman. And yet this is the system which has

hitherto been most rigidly adopted. We have judges in our law courts whose impartiality is beyond all suspicion. They are placed on a high, conspicuous pinnacle in the sight of the nation, to do justice between man and man; they are fenced and fortified by the high dignity, almost sanctity, of their calling, against clamour, idle rumour, private interest, or any other element that might disturb the course of equity, and therefore their decisions are received on all sides with reverential acquiescence. Why should not the private business of the country be placed upon the same footing? Let there be three commissions issued— three permanent local boards established in England, Scotland, and Ireland, under the superintendence, if necessary, of the Board of Trade; let Parliament lay down rules for their guidance, and let every measure which at present would be launched *de plano* into the House of Commons, be first submitted to their consideration; and let their determination to reject or postpone be final, unless the legislature shall see fit, by a solemn vote, to reverse that portion of their report. In this way a multitude of loose and undigested schemes would be thrown back upon the hands of their promoters, without clogging the wheels of Parliament; and such only as bear *ex facie* to be for the public advantage, would be allowed to undergo the more searching ordeal of a committee. These boards would literally cost the country nothing, even although the constituent members of them were paid, as they ought to be for the performance of such a duty, very highly. Each company applying for a bill might be assessed to a certain amount, corresponding to the value of its stock; as it is but fair that the parties who have created the exigency, and whose avowed object is profit, should defray the attendant expense.

Supposing that the principle of these boards were admitted, it seems to us that Parliament has still to exercise a great and serious duty in laying down rules for their guidance. This is perhaps the most difficult subject connected with the railway system; and we approach it with diffidence, as it is inseparable, nay, must be based upon the two grand considerations of CAPITAL AND LABOUR. We shall endeavour to explain our meaning a little more minutely.

The reader will gather from what we have written above, that we entertain no fear that the nominal capital invested in the railways *which have already received the sanction of Parliament,* is now more than the surplus capital floating in the country which can be applied to such a purpose without injuring any portion of our staple manufactures or commerce. On the contrary, we think that it is very greatly below that mark, and therefore that it matters little, in a general point of view, by whom the stock is presently held. Sooner or later it must find its way into the hands of the capitalists, a class whose numbers are notoriously every day on the increase. Even were this not the case, and the balance otherwise, it must be recollected that the investment of that capital is not the thing of a moment. Four years, probably, may elapse before all the railways *which have obtained bills* can be completed, and during that time the calls are gradual. Unless, therefore, there shall occur some untoward and unforeseen cause, such as a continental war or a general stoppage of trade, the accumulation of capital in this country will be at least equally progressive. There is thus a future increment corresponding to the period of the completion of these public works, which may very fairly be taken into consideration, at least, as a kind of security that we have not hitherto advanced with too rash or hasty steps. But with the unchecked influx of new schemes, this security, which at best is but contingent, must disappear, and a further enormous absorption of capital, the existence of which is not satisfactorily proved, be called for. In such a state of things, it is unquestionably the duty of government to use its controlling power. The payment of ten per cent. deposit is no guarantee at all. Whilst new stocks are at a premium, a hundred pounds, in the hands of an enterprising speculator, may figure as the representative of many thousands in twenty different railway schemes. The limit of disposable capital in the country must—if all the new projects are permitted to go on —be reached, and that ere long; then comes a period of gambling whilst money is cheap and credit plentiful—a sudden contraction of currency—and a crash.

It has been found utterly impossible to ascertain the amount of capital at any time floating in Great Britain. We can, therefore, only guess from certain commercial symptoms when it is nearly exhausted. On this point the money articles in the London journals have of late contained many significant hints. The settlements on the Stock Exchange are weekly becoming more difficult, and an enormous per centage is said to be paid at present for temporary accommodation. It is understood, also, that the banks are about to raise the rate of discount; from which we infer that their deposits are being gradually withdrawn, since there is no other circumstance whatever that ought to operate a change.[*] But really it requires no calculation and no foresight to see, that the mere amount of deposits required for the new schemes must ere long lock up the whole available capital of Great Britain. Let those who think this is a bold assertion on our part, attend to the following fact. We have taken from *The Railway Record,* the amount of *new railway schemes* advertised *in a single week,* at the beginning of October. The number of the schemes is FORTY; and they comprehend the ephemera of England and Ireland only—Scotland, which, during that period, was most emulously at work, seems, by some unaccountable accident, to have been overlooked. Of the amount of capital to be invested in no less than ELEVEN of these, we have no statement. The promot-

---

[*] Since this article was sent to press, the Bank of England has raised its rates of discount one-half per cent. Our prognostication, therefore, has been verified sooner than we expected, and we are not sorry to find that great establishment thus early indicating its opinion that speculation has been pushed too far. We see no ground of alarm in the rise, but rather a security for a more healthy and moderate market.

ers apparently have no time to attend to such trifling details; and, doubtless, it will be early enough to announce the capital when they have playfully pounced upon the deposites. But there is some candour in TWENTY-NINE provisional committees, and their accumulated nominal capital proves to be—how much, think you, gifted reader, and confident dabbler in new stock? Why, merely this—TWENTY-JIVE MILLIONS EIGHT HUNDRED AND THIRTY THOUSAND POUNDS!!! Now —for we wish always to speak and write within the mark—let us calculate the eleven Harpocrates Companies and the Northern Schemes (which are more than eleven), at fourteen or fifteen additional millions; and you thus have parties engaged, *in the course of a single week*, for FORTY MILLIONS STERLING, or *about one-twentieth part of the whole national debt;* which, according to this rate of subscription, may be extinguished by our surplus capital in the short space of five months. And this is the country, where, three years ago, the manufacturer and miner were starving, Manchester in almost a state of siege, and Staley-bridge in absolute insurrection! Happy Britain, where every man has discovered the philosopher's stone!

After this, need we say anything more upon the great topic of capital? Were the nation now in its sober senses, the facts which we have stated, and for the accuracy of which we pledge ourselves, would surely be enough to awaken it to a true conception of the vortex into which it is plunging. But as every man will no doubt think—with the ordinary self-delusion of our kind—that the scheme in which he is individually embarked is an exception from the common rule; let us ask each speculator candidly to make answer, whether he has minutely examined the merits of the line which he has adopted, or whether he has thrown himself into it upon the assurances of others, and the mere expectations of a premium? If the former, let him hold. We war with no man's deliberate judgment; and that there are many projected lines in Great Britain which must ultimately be carried, and which will prove most profitable to the shareholders, is be-

yond all manner of doubt. Whether they may receive the sanction of the legislature so soon as the proprietor expects, is a very different question. But if the latter, his case is far otherwise. We have seen the prospectus of several of the most gigantic schemes now in the market, by means of which the whole length of England is to be traversed, and these have undergone no further survey than the application of a ruler to a lithographic map, and a trifling transplantation of the principal towns, so as to coincide with the direct and undeviating rail. There is hardly a sharebroker in the kingdom who is not cognisant of this most flagrant fact; and by many of them the impudent impositions have been returned with the scorn which such conduct demands. It is hardly possible to conceive that these schemes were never intended to meet the eye of Parliament; but, if not, why were they ever started? The reflection is a very serious one for those who have deposited their money.

Such projects, of course, are the exceptions, and not the rule. Still, their existence, and the support which they have unthinkingly obtained, are very lamentable symptoms of the recklessness which characterizes the present impulse. Were the tone of commercial enterprise healthy, and kept within due bounds, there would be nothing of this; neither should we hear, as we do every day, of shares which, immediately after their allocation, attain an enormous premium, and, after having fluctuated for a week or two, subside to something like their real value.

Are we then justified or not in saying, that it is the imperative duty of the legislature to look to this question of capital; that it is bound to see that the country does not pledge itself so utterly beyond its means; and that the advance of the railway system must be made slow and steady, in order to render its basis secure?

But there is another point beyond this. Supposing that all our remarks on the subject of capital were erroneous, and that our financial views were as puerile as we believe them to be strictly sound—we fall back upon an element which is more easily ascertained, and that is, LABOUR. We hold it to be a clear economical maxim, that beyond a certain point, at all events within a given time, capital, however abundant it may be, cannot *create* labour. It has passed into a sort of truism that there is nothing which money cannot accomplish —analyse it, and you will find that it is not a truism but a popular fallacy. There are many, many things which money cannot accomplish. It has no power to clear the social atmosphere from crime; it may mar the morals of a people, but it cannot make them; and still less can it usurp the stupendous functions of the Deity. It may rear labour, but it cannot by any possibility create it, after such a fashion as the crop that sprang from the sowing of the Cadmean teeth. Let us illustrate this a little.

Probably — nay, certainly — there never was a country in which labour has been so accurately balanced as in Great Britain. Our population has been for a number of years upon the increment; but the increase has been of the nature of supply, consequent and almost dependent upon 'the demand. The wages paid to the children in manufacturing districts have swelled that portion of our population to a great degree, though probably not more than is indispensable from the fluctuating nature of commerce. But, so far as we can learn from statistical tables, the number of agricultural labourers—that is, those who are strictly employed in the cultivation of the land, and who cannot be spared from that most necessary task—has been rather on the decrease. Our business, however, is neither with manufacturer nor with agriculturist, but with a different class—those, namely, who are engaged in the public works of the country. Let us take Mr. Porter's estimate, according to the census of 1831.

" The summary of the returns of 1831, respecting the occupations of males twenty years of age and upwards, throws considerable light upon the subject, by exhibiting them under several subdivisions. The males belonging to the families included in the non-agricultural and non-manufacturing classes, were given at the last census, under four distinct heads of description, viz:—

Capitalists, Bankers, Professional, and other educated men.

Labourers employed in labour, not Agricultural.

Other males, twenty years of age, except servants.

Male servants, twenty years of age.

" The whole number of males included under these heads, amounts to 1,137,270. Of *these*, 608,712 were actually employed in labour, which although, usually speaking, it was neither manufacturing nor trading, was yet necessary in the successful prosecution of some branch of trade or manufactures, *such as mining, road-making, canal-digging, inland navigation, &c.*"

Of these 600,000, now probably augmented by a tenth, how many can he spared from their several employments for the construction of the railways, and how many are at this moment so employed, with their labour mortgaged for years? This is a question which Parliament ought most certainly—if it can be done—to get answered in a satisfactory manner. It must be remarked that in this class are included the miners, who certainly cannot be withdrawn from their present work, which in fact is indispensable for the completion of the railways. If possible, their numbers must be augmented. The stored iron in the country is now exhausted, and the masters are using every diligence in their power to facilitate the supply, which still, as the advancing price of that great commodity will testify, is short of, and insufficient for the demand. From the agricultural labourers you cannot receive any material number of recruits. The land, above all things, must be tilled; and notwithstanding the trashy assertions of popular slip-slop authors and Cockney sentimentalists, who have favoured us with pictures of the Will Ferns of the kingdom, as unlike the reality as may be—the condition of those who cultivate the soil of Britain is superior to that of the peasantry in every other country of Europe. The inevitable increase of demand for labour will even better their condition, according to the operation of a law apparent to every man of common sense, but which is hopelessly concealed from the eyes of these spurious regenerators of the times. It is impossible to transform the manufacturer, even were that trade slack, into a railway labourer; the habits and constitution of the two classes being essentially different and distinct. Indeed, as the writer we have already quoted well remarks —"Experience has shown that educated men pass with difficulty, and unwillingly, from occupations to which they have been long accustomed," and nothing, consequently, is more difficult than to augment materially and suddenly the numbers of any industrial class, when an unexpected demand arises. To us, therefore, it seems perfectly clear, that even if the capital were forthcoming, there is not labour enough in the country for the simultaneous construction of a tithe of the projected schemes.

There are considerations connected with this matter which entail a great responsibility upon the government. The capitalists are, in fact, putting at its disposal the means of maintaining a great portion of the poorer population for many years to come. If this be properly attended to, emigration, which principally benefits the labourer, may be discontinued. We have now arrived at a pass when the absence of those who have already emigrated becomes a matter of regret. There is work to be had nearer than the Canadian woods or the waterless prairies of Australia—work, too, that in its results must be of incalculable benefit to the community. But the government is bound to regulate it so, that, amidst superabundance of wealth, due regard is paid to the ECONOMY OF LABOUR. It is rumoured that some railway directors, fully aware of the facts which have been stated, are meditating, in their exuberant haste for dividends, the introduction of foreign labourers. We doubt whether, under any circumstances, such a scheme is practicable; but of this we entertain no doubt, that it is as mischievous a device as ever was forged in the cabinet of Mammon! Some years ago the cuckoo cry of the political quacks was over-population. Now it seems there is a scarcity of hands, and in order to supply the want—for we have drained the Highlands—we are to have an importation from Baden or Bavaria, without even the protecting solemnity of a tariff. If this be true, it seems to us that government is bound to interpose by the most stringent measures. It is monstrous to

think, that whereas, for many years past, for mere slackness of labour, we have been encouraging emigration among the productive classes of our countrymen to a very great degree; draining, as it were, the mother country to found the colonies, and therein resorting to the last step which a paternal government, even in times of the greatest necessity, should adopt—now, when a new experiment, or social crisis—call it which you will—has arisen, when labour has again reached the point where the demand exceeds the supply, we are to admit an influx of strangers amongst us, and thereby entail upon ourselves and posterity the evils of prospective pauperism. We have been already too prone, in matters relating rather to the luxuries than the necessities of our social system, to give undue preference to the foreigner. British art has, in many branches, been thereby crippled and discouraged, and a cry, not unnatural surely, has ere now been raised against the practice. But how incomparably more dangerous it would be to inundate the country with an alien population, whose mere brute strength, without a particle of productive skill, is their only passport and certificate! This too, be it observed, is not for the purpose of establishing or furthering a branch of industry which can furnish permanent employment, but merely for carrying out a system of great change certainly, but of limited endurance. If labour required to be forced, it would certainly be more for our advantage to revise our penal institutions, and to consider seriously whether those who have committed offences against our social laws, might not be more profitably employed in the great works of the kingdom, than by transplanting them as at present to the Antipodes at a fearful expense, the diminution of which appears, in all human probability, impossible.

If, then, we are right in our premises, the two leading points which Parliament must steadily regard in forming its decisions connected with the new schemes, are the sufficiency of unfettered capital and the adequate supply of labour. Our conviction is, that neither exists to anything like the extent which would be required were the present mania allowed to run its course unchecked. But on the other hand a total stoppage of improvement might be equally dangerous; and it will therefore be necessary to steer a middle course, and to regulate the movement according to certain principles. Let us, then, first consider what lines ought *not* to be granted.

At the head of these we should place the whole bundle of rival companies to railways already completed or in progress. We are not of the number of those who stand up for exclusive commercial monopoly; but we do think that there is a tacit or implied contract between the state and the proprietors of the sanctioned lines which ought to shield the latter against rash and invidious competition. The older railways are the parents of the system; without them, it never could have been discovered what gradients were requisite, what works indispensable, what savings practicable. The expense of their construction we know to have been, in many instances, far greater than is contained in the modern estimates, and the land which they required to occupy was procured at extravagant prices. Now it does seem to us in the highest degree unfair, that the interests of these companies should be sacrificed for the sake of what is called the "direct" principle. A saving of twenty or thirty miles between Newcastle and London, is now thought to be a matter of so much importance as to justify one or more independent lines, which, despising intermediate cities and their traffic, still hold their even course as the crow flies, from point to point, and thereby shorten the transit from the south to the north of England by—it may be—the matter of an hour. We did not use to be quite so chary of our minutes: nor, though fully aware of the value of time, did we ever bestow the same regard upon the fractional portions of our existence. What the nation requires is a safe, commodious, and speedy mode of conveyance, and we defy the veriest streak-of-lightning man to say, that the present companies in operation do not afford us that to our hearts' content. It is but a very few years ago since we used to glorify ourselves in the rapidity of the mail-coach, doing its

ten miles an hour with the punctuality of clockwork. Now we have arrived at the ratio of forty within the same period, and yet we are not content. Next year, within fourteen hours we shall be transported from Edinburgh to London. That, it seems, is not enough. A company offers to transport us by a straighter line in thirteen; and for that purpose they ask leave of the legislature to construct a rival line at the expense of a few millions! Now, keeping in mind what we have said as to capital, is not this, in the present state of things, most wanton prodigality? The same "few millions"—and we rather suspect they are fewer than is commonly supposed — would open up counties hitherto untouched by the railway system—would give us communication through the heart of the Highlands, through the remoter districts of Wales, through the unvisited nooks of Ireland, and, in so doing, would minister not only to the wants of the community, but in an inconceivable degree to the social improvement of the people. Among the list of proposed schemes for next session, there are many such; and surely our government, if its functions correspond to the name, is bound, in the first instance, to give a preference to these; and—since all cannot be accomplished at once—to assist the schemes which volunteer the opening of a new district, rather than the competition of mushroom companies where the field is already occupied.

There is also a filching spirit abroad, which ought decidedly to be checked. Scarce a main line has been established from which it has not been found necessary, for the purposes of accommodation, to run several branches. Until about a year ago, it was generally understood that these adjuncts ought to be left in the hands of the original companies, who, for their own sakes, were always ready to augment their traffic by such feeders. Now it is widely different. Four or five miles of cross country is reckoned a sufficient justification for the establishment of an independent company, who, without any consultation with the proprietors of the main line, or inquiry as to their ultimate intentions, seize upon the vacant ground as a waif, and throw themselves confidently upon the public. If the matter does not end in a lease, the unfortunate public will be the losers, since it is manifestly impossible that a little Lilliput line can be cheaply worked, independent of the larger trunk. This class of schemes also should receive their speedy *quietus ;* for what would be the use of permitting the promoters to attempt the proof of an impossible case ?

England has already made a great portion of her railroads, but neither Scotland nor Ireland as yet have attained the same point. Now, in a general point of view, it will hardly be denied, that it is of far greater importance to have the country thoroughly opened up, throughout the length and breadth, than to have an accumulation of cross and intersecting railways in one particular district. We are asking no favouritism, for it has become a mere matter of choice between companies, as to which shall have the earlier preference. In point of policy, the legislature ought certainly to extend every possible favour to the Irish lines. It may be that in this railway system—for Providence works with strange agents—there lies the germ of a better understanding between us, and the dawn of a happier day for Ireland. At any rate, to its pauper population, the employment afforded by companies, where no absenteeism can exist, is a great and timely boon, and may work more social wonders than any scheme of conciliation which the statesman has as yet devised. Idleness and lack of employment are the most fertile sources of agitation ; let these be removed, and we may look, if not with confidence, at least with hope, for a cessation of the stormy evil. By all means, then, let Ireland have the precedence. She needs it more than the other countries do, and to her claims we are all disposed to yield.

But England owes Scotland something also. For a long series of years, amidst great political changes, through good and through evil report, this Magazine has been the consistent champion of our national interests ; and, whether the blow was aimed at our country by seeming friend or open foe, we have never hesitated to speak out boldly. More than twenty years ago, a measure was passed by the United Parliament which literally brought down ruin upon the Highlands of Scotland, and from the effects of which many of the districts have never recovered. Along all the western coast and throughout the islands, the manufacture of kelp was the only branch of industry within the reach of a poor and extended population, who, from their very poverty, were entitled to the most kindly regard of government. But, as it is believed, at the instigation of one member of the cabinet, himself largely connected with foreign trade, without inquiry and without warning, the market was thrown open to competition from without, barilla imported, and the staple product of the north of Scotland annihilated. To this fatal, and, we hesitate not to say, most wanton measure, we attribute the periods of distress, and the long-continued depression, which, in very many lamentable instances, have been the ruin of our ancient families, and in consequence of which the Highland glens have been depopulated. It was a cruel thing to do, under any circumstances —a wicked thing, when we remember the interest by which it was carried. There is now a great opportunity of giving us a reasonable compensation. From the introduction of the railway system, we anticipate a new era of prosperity to Scotland—a time when we shall not have to devote ourselves to the melancholy task of decreasing the population by a harsh or inhuman exile—when the crofts of the valleys shall again be tilled, and the household fires shall be lighted on the now deserted hearthstone. Therefore, in the event of a restriction, we so far claim precedence. Let the work, however, be impartially distributed throughout the kingdoms, and there can be no ground anywhere for complaint. Only let our haste be tempered with prudence, and our enthusiasm moderated down to a just coincidence with our means.

During all this torrent of speculation, what is the Currency doing ? No man seems to know. The nation has found a paper of its own quite as effective as that which is doled out by the chartered bank. The brokers are, in fact, becoming bankers, and payments of all kinds are readily made in scrip. This is an instructive fact, and may somewhat tend to disturb the triumph of the theorists who uphold the doctrine of a restrictive trade in money. We do not rely on the safety of the system, but we look upon it as a strong proof that our monetary regulations are wrong, and that there is not only a wish, but several practical ways, effectually to evade its fetters. We are not, however, going into that question, though it is by no means unconnected with our present subject. At the same time we should like to see this same article of scrip, which is fast approximating to notes, a little more protected. Has it never occurred to the mind of the Chancellor of the Exchequer, or to the Premier, who has a most searching eye, that a very profitable source of revenue to the public, and one which would hardly be grudged, might be derived from the simple expedient of requiring that *all scrip should be stamped?* There is no practical difficulty in the matter. Companies already formed, if they do not desire the benefit of a stamp—the best, and indeed at present the only security against the forger—may be called upon to pay their quota, corresponding to the number of their shares, from the fund of their Parliamentary deposit. New companies, again, might be imperatively required to issue stamps; and we confidently believe that no tax whatever would be more cheerfully assented to. Let the currency doctors do what they will, they never can drive scrip from the market. Would it not, then, be a measure of good policy to enlist it as a serviceable ally?

Whether these observations of ours may stand the test of another year's experience, is certainly matter of doubt. The period of a single month makes wild changes in the prospects of the system, and involves us not only in new calculations but in a newer phase of things. At any rate it can do no harm, in the present period of excitement, to preach a little moderation, even though our voice should be as inaudible as the chirp of a sparrow on the house-top. The speculative spirit of the age may be checked and controlled, but it cannot be put down, nor would we wish to see it pass away. All great improvement is the fruit of speculation, upon which, indeed, commerce itself is based. We have, therefore, no sympathy for that numerous class of gentlemen who profess a pious horror for every venture of the kind, who croak prophetical bankruptcies, and would disinherit their sons without scruple, if by any accident they detected them in dalliance with scrip. A worthier, but a more contracted, section of the human race does not exist. They are the genuine descendants of the Picts; and, had they lived in remoter days, would have been the first to protest against the abolition of ochre as an ornament, or the substitution of broadcloth for the untanned buffalo hide. The nation must progress, and the true Conservative policy is to lay down a proper plan for the steadiness and endurance of its march. The Roman state was once saved by the judicious dispositions of a Fabius, and, in our mind, Sir Robert Peel cannot do the public a greater service than to imitate the example of the *Cunctator.* He has the power, and, more than any living statesman, the practical ability, to grapple with such a subject in all its details. That Parliament must do something, is apparent to every reflecting man. The machinery of it cannot dispose, as heretofore, of the superabundant material. It must devise some method of regulation, and that method must be clear and decisive. A question more important can hardly be conceived, and so with the legislature we leave it.

CPSIA information can be obtained
at www.ICGtesting.com
Printed in the USA
BVHW061744240521
608000BV00004BA/833

9 781273 700866